Jess,

You are in 'ts

You are in

control of the

you get in life.

All it takes is a

decision.

[signature]

LIMITLESS

Reclaim Your Power,

Unleash Your Potential,

Transform Your Life

Kris Krohn
McLean Taylor

Limitless: Reclaim Your Power, Unleash Your Potential, Transform Your Life

Kris Krohn and McLean Taylor

Published by Limitless Press, Orem, Utah

For ordering information or special discounts for bulk purchases, please contact Limitless Press at 518 West 800 North Suite 204, Orem, UT 84057, www.LimitlessSeminar.com.

For bulk ticket discounts or to host a dedicated Limitless event, please contact Support@ LimitlessMentor.com.

Design and composition by Daniel Ruesch. www.danielruesch.net
Cover design by Andrej Semnic, a.k.a. "semnitz." andrej.semnic@gmail.com

Publisher's Cataloging-In-Publication Data
Krohn, Kris and Taylor, McLean
Limitless: Reclaim your power, unleash your potential, transform your life / Kris Krohn and McLean Taylor.—1st ed.

ISBN: 978-0-9907339-4-2
1. Self-help and personal development. 2. Self-realization. 3. Success.

Printed in the United States of America

First Edition
First printing: March 2017

You are Limitless.

It's time you knew.

CONTENTS

INTRO

PART I

Breaking Through to a Limitless Life

PART II

The Science Behind Why Belief Breakthrough
Creates Permanent, Life-Changing Results

PART III

The 9 Laws of Conscious Creation: How to Optimize, Amplify, and Accelerate Belief Breakthrough

PART IV

Manifesting Your Limitless Life

INTRODUCTION

Like most people, I met Kris Krohn at a Limitless Seminar, only I wasn't a participant as most people are when they first meet Kris. Instead, I was a performer—I had been invited to breakdance with Joshua David at Limitless. I do a lot of breakdancing, so I was used to performing at different events. But I had no idea how different my life would be because I danced that day.

We riled up the crowd a lot during our performance, and afterwards, Kris asked for my phone number, and invited me to join Joshua in teaching him some breakdancing the following Monday.

"Sure. What time?"

"6 a.m."

Yeah, right. Are they kidding me? I'm so not going. That's crazy, I thought.

That Monday, I was teaching Kris how to breakdance at 6 a.m.

I noticed he learned the breakdance moves differently than anyone I had ever taught. I used to run my own dance business, and I had never seen anyone learn the way Kris did. He would visualize things before he'd even try it. I thought he was pretty weird, but he definitely had my attention.

After we finished, Kris suggested we all walk out together.

"Tell me about yourself, McLean. Do you have any special gifts or anything? Any relationships?"

"I'm dating a girl. I went through a divorce 18 months ago." And I proceeded to tell him my story.

"Oh, you've got a great story."

When he said this, my friend Joshua and Kris exchanged this look as if they knew something I didn't. Later, I realized I was telling that story as a victim. It's called the Victim's Story.

I took ownership of that story, though. *I do have a story,* I thought. And I was proud I did. I may have been a victim, but I knew my story had taught me valuable lessons.

"I see you have a lot of drive and passion for helping the world, and I don't see you working at your company for much longer."

I thought, *Who the flip does he think he is?* But my heart disagreed; I knew there was truth to what Kris was telling me, and I knew that truth was the answer to my soul's searching.

"McLean, I see a great leader in you—someone who is going to change the world in big ways."

What does this guy want from me?

I was curious to learn what he meant, but I had to get to work that morning, so I started walking towards my $800 2001 Chevy Cavalier. I turned back and watched as Kris opened his car door VERTICALLY to get into his $140,000 BMW i8.

Who IS this guy? And why is he spending time learning to breakdance with college students?

Before I got in my car, I yelled across the parking lot at him and asked him what he does for a living. He told me he made his millions in real estate, but his real passion was changing lives and helping people step into their full potential.

That sparked my interest and I became a lot more willing to listen to what he had to say. He invited me to Limitless, and my life's trajectory took off.

At its core, Limitless is a movement—a movement grounded in belief breakthrough and the 9 Laws of Conscious Creation, expressed through the power of mentors and like-minded people living fulfilling lives. This movement is exciting and fun, but it's mostly transforming. Like all movements, Limitless aims to change the world, and it does so—one breakthrough at a time.

Belief breakthrough is literally breaking through beliefs that have held you back from your full potential and replacing them with a better "new belief" that will propel your success. It has been around for years. It's been studied by various scientists and wholeheartedly embraced by coaches, mentors, and successful people worldwide. It is central to any and all change we experience as humans, whether or not we consciously recognize it.

When Kris invited me to be a contributing author, I felt called to share my story. My life changed so significantly because of Limitless and especially because of belief breakthrough, that I wanted to show how changing your beliefs and living aligned with simple, universal truth can really be a game changer—for anyone. So I partnered with Kris to share my story.

The book is broken down simply and succinctly to provide the best information to you, while also giving you amazing resources and case studies. Specifically, it includes Kris' and my stories of how belief breakthrough, the 9 Laws of Conscious Creation, and Limitless have changed our lives drastically.

The book also includes the science behind belief breakthrough and daily practices to make belief breakthrough an integral part of your life going forward. Once you've finished this book, you'll recognize the times in your past when belief breakthrough has worked for you and be able to utilize this tool in your everyday life to create massive growth in the future.

In the back of the book, we've even included a reference of over 1,000 of the most common new beliefs to help you begin your journey to a Limitless life.

While you will find every element of the Limitless Movement contained in the pages of this book, many of which you have probably heard before, Limitless is truly something special that you must experience.

Part of the Limitless Movement is the Limitless Seminar. Put simply, Limitless is a three-day transformational event centered on educating participants on belief breakthrough, the 9 Laws of Conscious Creation, and the power of mentors. Use the tickets that come with the book and experience the energy of the Limitless Seminar.

I didn't know who I was talking to when I met Kris Krohn. I thought he was just some bro, some guy who wanted to learn how to breakdance. Now Kris is my mentor and one of my best friends. We play video games and go to the gym together every morning at 5 a.m. He has taught me belief breakthrough, coached me on personal decisions, helped me launch a successful mentoring platform, and so much more.

It's easy to say it was *Kris* who changed my life, but truly, it is a combination of all my mentors, along with the concepts taught at Limitless which have changed everything about the way I think and act, about how seriously I take myself, and how I show up everyday in both the little things and the big things.

We are all born for this kind of greatness and success. When we change what we believe, we believe we *can* change, and suddenly our lives are more focused, more fulfilled.

I know that's true; that's what happened to me. As you'll read in my story, Limitless, belief breakthrough, and the Limitless Inner Circle changed my life in numerous ways—in my finances, in my connection with others, and especially with God and my wife. I'm happier with who I am, even when I make stupid mistakes. I bounce right back and stay in my Zen when something has the potential to drag me down.

Getting tasks done and achieving results is a lot easier now. I work harder than I ever have, but when things are slow and I am relaxing, I feel good about it. Honestly, I feel good about everything, because I am living in alignment with who I am, with universal laws, and with my God.

I just love my life.

The concepts taught in this book will change your life. If you expect to finish this book the same person you were when you started it, then you are sorely mistaken. But if you want to change, and if you apply these principles in your daily life, then you *will* change.

I guarantee it.

McLean Taylor, Contributing Author
February 2017

CHAPTER 1

YOU CAN HAVE IT ALL

You are about to embark on a journey I call "limitless." In this journey, you'll discover that virtually every limitation you've perceived in your life has been created not by any external factor, but by your own beliefs.

This is a journey of exploding through your ceilings of limitations and revealing an inexhaustible well of inner resourcefulness, ingenuity, and capability that you never knew you had. It's a journey of tapping into a fathomless power to manifest anything you desire.

It's a journey of creating your life by design, rather than by default. It's a journey of manifesting the most powerful version of you and the most magnificent life you were born to achieve. It's a journey of accepting that you really can have it all—you can be healthy, enjoy incredibly fulfilling relationships, thrive financially, and expand your personal power to be who you are meant to be.

"Never underestimate the power of dreams and the influence of the human spirit. We are all the same in this notion: The potential for greatness lives within each of us."

—WILMA RUDOLPH

It doesn't take any unique natural talent. It is a skill that must be developed, but anyone can do it. It's not limited to only a select few who are somehow genetically superior. It is available to anyone willing to face themselves honestly and trust themselves unconditionally.

Limitless Accesses, Harnesses, and Unleashes Your Power

Limitless is first and foremost a mindset: a mindset of abundance, possibility, and power. It is a mindset that says, "I have within me the seeds of greatness, and it is my privilege and responsibility to cultivate those seeds and become the best person I can become." It's a mindset of believing that anything, within the bounds of natural laws, is possible for those who know and live according to those laws.

It's a mindset of believing in yourself—even and especially in the face of seemingly insurmountable challenges. It is a trust in a Higher Power who wants nothing but good things for us, and trusting that whatever opposition we experience is for our benefit.

Limitless is also a foolproof process, a methodology that anyone can apply to access and unleash his or her greatest potential. In this process, you retrain your mind to work for you rather than against you in crafting your ideal life. This strategic breakthrough process does three things:

1. Helps you identify the limiting beliefs that have been holding you back.
2. Unwinds and releases your false beliefs.
3. Instills new, empowering, limitless beliefs, which rewire your mind so you can create the life you want.

Unconditional Power, Wealth, Health, Connection, and Happiness

Another word I often use for limitless is "unconditional." To become limitless is to systematically identify and uproot all the faulty and unnecessary conditions we put on our personal power, wealth, health, connection, and happiness. These are all those "I'll be happy when…" or "If, then" thoughts we have:

- "I'll be happy when I'm making more money."
- "I will feel successful after I get that promotion."
- "My marriage would be so much better if she would stop nagging me."
- "I would love him more if he would pick up after himself."

- "I would appreciate my body more if I could lose twenty-five pounds."
- "I would be a lot more confident if I had more experience."

Limitless is about rejecting the conditions that limit our personal power, wealth, health, relationships, and happiness and choosing to be abundant, confident, and happy right now. Unconditional means that the world does not need to change. I am the only one who needs to change for my world to make sense.

Combine Belief Breakthrough with the Laws of Conscious Creation

Manifesting your ideal life is the combination of two main factors: Belief Breakthrough work and the 9 Laws of Conscious Creation. The first half of this book gives you everything you need to know about belief breakthrough. Next, I detail the laws of creation.

To illustrate how these work together, imagine a big piece of property that is littered with piles of garbage. You want to build a big, beautiful custom home on the property. But before you do so, you have to clean up all the garbage, haul it to the dump, and prepare the ground for building. Then and only then can you come in and lay a foundation, then build your home.

Belief breakthrough work is like cleaning up the garbage of limiting beliefs that clutters your mind. Next, you leverage the laws of creation to begin building the life of your dreams.

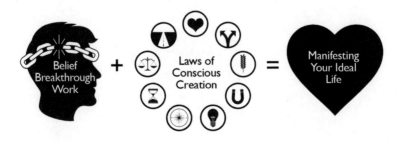

Do You Have the Courage to Live Your Limitless Life?

The limitless process is what author Jim Rohn refers to as the "magic and the mystery." The magic is that we can all have it all. The mystery is that most of us won't.

> *"Only when we are brave enough to explore the darkness will we discover the infinite power of our light."*
>
> –BRENÉ BROWN

If you feel stuck and frustrated, as I felt not that long ago, you're holding the formula you've been aching to find. If you want the magic and are willing to face the truth inside the mystery, this book is for you. Your limitless life awaits you—*if* you have the courage to uncover it…

CHAPTER 2

LIMITLESS: A MINDSET AND METHOD FOR RADICAL BREAKTHROUGH

D
eep down, we all want the same basic things: We want financial abundance to enjoy life. We want to feel healthy, energetic, and attractive. We want connected, thriving, authentic relationships. We want to feel like we're making a contribution and living our purpose every day. We want to love and to be loved. We want peace and joy to be the norm, rather than the exception.

At no point in history have all of those things been more available to most people. The average person in a developed country today has more material comforts and luxuries than kings and queens in the past. Digital technologies in the Information Age have democratized opportunity like we've never seen before. The freedom, peace, prosperity, and technology we take so much for granted leaves all of us with no excuse for not making the most of life.

Then why do so few people love their lives? Why do so many people feel unhappy in their relationships, unsatisfied in their jobs, and impotent in their purpose? Why do so many people feel so trapped and burdened? Why are true happiness and success so rare? Why, when we are presented with an overflowing buffet of everything life has to offer, do most of us eat crumbs off the floor?

"We all have the extraordinary coded within us, waiting to be released."

–JEAN HOUSTON

The short answer is that few people have cracked the code of "limitless."

Belief: The Leverage Point of All Breakthroughs

Ultimately, being limitless is about consciously choosing the results we want to manifest in our life. Most of us live by default, rather than by design. We choose the paths of least resistance. We become entitled victims who expect everything to go our way and then whine when it doesn't.

We like to believe that we have free will—that we are free agents who make conscious decisions. The stark and painful reality is that, whether or not we have free will, we don't actually exercise it. We are like actors in a play we have not written, playing the roles and reciting the lines dictated by social scripts. We are held captive by false beliefs of which we're not even aware, and which dictate our behavior.

"Everyone knows that on any given day there are energies slumbering in him which the incitement's of that day do not call forth. Compared with what we ought to be, we are only half awake. The human individual usually lives far within his limits."

–WILLIAM JAMES

Our level of agency is determined by our beliefs. The more false beliefs we have, the smaller our domain of agency. Conversely, the more our conscious beliefs align with truth, the greater our agency. But if we're not even aware of our subconscious beliefs, how can we possibly change them to expand our agency and improve our results?

If our brain is the hardware, our beliefs are the software. The programming of computer software determines its functions, capabilities, processes, and outcomes. If you want different functions and/or capabilities, you have to change the programming. Likewise, if you want to change your personal capabilities, you have to change the programming of your beliefs.

The famous quote from Ralph Waldo Emerson goes, "Sow a thought and you reap an action; sow an act and you reap a habit; sow a habit and you reap a character; sow a character and you reap a destiny." When you change the word "thought" to "belief" it brings even greater depth to the concept. Our fundamental beliefs about ourselves, others, our circumstances, and the nature of reality determine all of our actions. If I believe, for example, that I'm worthless and no one cares about me, then why in the world would I ever audition for a play, apply for a dream job, or start a business?

The leverage point of all human transformation is beliefs. When you change your beliefs, you completely alter the trajectory of your life. (I'm not talking about religious beliefs, mind you. I'm simply referring to the beliefs we create about ourselves, other people, and life that govern our behavior.)

Are There Really *No* Limits?

I'm often asked questions like: "If there really were no limits, wouldn't that mean that I could turn myself into a basketball star like LeBron James just by using the power of my mind?" "If I were really limitless, wouldn't that mean I could fly or make myself invisible?"

The reality is that there are natural laws to which we are all subject, and no amount of wishing or believing can magically make them go away. Within those laws there are limits. The law of gravity dictates that if I step off the edge of a 500-foot cliff, I'm going to fall and there will be a consequence (likely death).

No one can transcend natural laws by snapping their fingers and making something magically happen. However, in some cases other laws can be harnessed. For example, the laws of aerodynamics, which account for the forces of thrust, drag, and lift, can be harnessed to counteract the effects of gravity and lift a 750,000 pound Boeing 747 off the ground and keep it airborne for as long as it has fuel. But this doesn't mean the plane is magically making gravity disappear.

Paradoxically, natural laws create both possibilities and limitations. Think of a kite flying at the end of a string. Take away the string, and the kite plummets to the ground; it's precisely the limitation of the string that enables the kite to fly.

"Nature does not ask your permission, she has nothing to do with your wishes, and whether you like her laws or dislike them, you are bound to accept her as she is, and consequently all her conclusions."

–FYODOR DOSTOYEVSKY

To live limitlessly, therefore, doesn't mean to magically cast off all limits and become anything we want, like getting wishes from a genie in a lamp. It means working within natural laws. It means understanding and living in accordance with the proper limitations that serve us, and casting off false limitations that harm us. By living in accordance with natural laws, we unleash our full potential—the full expression of all our possibilities.

Ironically, imposing the right limits on ourselves is precisely how to expand our lives. For example, by wearing a seatbelt I increase my chances of surviving a car accident. In the name of being "limitless," I could believe a seatbelt restrains my choice and refuse to wear it. That's my choice. What I can't choose, however, are the consequences of what happens to my body when I crash with no seatbelt.

On the other hand, the belief that I'm stupid is not a helpful limit that serves me. Releasing that limit expands my possibilities.

> *"Plant seeds of happiness, hope, success, and love; it will all come back to you in abundance. This is the law of nature."*
>
> –STEVE MARABOLI

Limitless is not an illogical, pie-in-the-sky, new age fairy dust ideology. It's a rational philosophy grounded in science and wisdom. The key is to find the winning combination of embracing helpful limits and eliminating harmful ones. By limiting ourselves in all the right ways, we become liberated to express our highest potential. True limitless living, therefore, leads us to accept as many helpful limitations as we reject harmful limitations. By tying ourselves to the kite string of the natural laws of reality, we're liberated to fly.

Limitless Creates Unshakable Faith, Courage, and Confidence

> *"The important thing is this: to be able at any moment to sacrifice what we are for what we could become."*
>
> –CHARLES DU BOS

When you embrace the limitless mindset, the ultimate result is that all self-doubt and negative thinking naturally disappear from your life. You stop second-guessing yourself. You cultivate unwavering clarity, courage, and confidence. Doubt is replaced by faith. Fear is replaced by love. Envy and jealousy are replaced by gratitude. Victimhood is replaced by acceptance. Anger and anxiety are replaced by peace.

These emotions change because *you* change. You change not the nature of reality, but rather your relationship with it. You stop viewing the universe and other people as out to get you, and instead start seeing how all opposition, hardship, and conflict with other people exist for the sole purpose of serving you—of helping you learn, grow, and develop into your best self.

The universe and all natural laws exist for the sole purpose of helping you fulfill your greatest potential. The limitations of natural laws exist to release your limitless capabilities. But these capabilities are held captive by the limitations of your beliefs. Change your beliefs, and you change your destiny...

CHAPTER 3

STUCK AND FRUSTRATED: MY LIFE BEFORE LIMITLESS

I trudge through the door of our one-bedroom, 400-square-foot apartment at 9:15 p.m. I'm worn out. I've been up since 5 a.m. and it's been a long, tough day of full-time school and my full-time telemarketing job.

My wife is standing in the hall. The dim light overhead illuminates the tears streaking down her face. It's obvious she's been crying for a long time. Immediately distraught, I ask, "What's wrong, honey?"

She says, "I've been balancing the checkbook. Our bank account is completely drained. We have no money. Rent is due in two weeks and tuition is due in three weeks. Our cupboards are empty and I don't even have money to buy groceries."

I am devastated. I feel so small and helpless. I feel like I am a horrible husband and provider and that I have failed my wife.

That moment in 2002, when I was twenty-two years old, is seared into my memory forever. It was the tipping point of what had been a long string of disappointments and broken expectations. Something snapped inside me. I knew something had to change.

Like so many people, I wasn't taught the mindset of abundance growing up in my family. I have vivid memories of my parents fighting about money. My father is an immigrant from Germany and my mother has a lot of Irish blood, so to say their fights could be heated is an understatement.

When I was eight years old, while observing one of their fights about money, I felt a strong spiritual impression that I would need to take care of my parents as an adult. It came so clear and forceful that I couldn't ignore or forget it. I pondered on it a lot as I grew up. I decided I would need a career that would be able to provide for two families. As a teenager, I chose to be a doctor.

I graduated high school, then left on a two-year service mission for my church. A few months after arriving home I met my beautiful wife, Kalenn, and was immediately smitten. We courted for eight months and then were married. I told her all about my plans for becoming a doctor. I figured I would become a highly-paid specialist, though I had no idea what I would specialize in.

I enrolled in college, we rented an apartment, and my journey to wealth was officially underway. It didn't take long for reality to set in. In my first chemistry class, a science prerequisite for a career immersed in the sciences, I got a C. I wasn't slacking, either—I worked my tail off and gave it everything I had. It just didn't come easy for me.

"There is no man living who isn't capable of doing more than he thinks he can do."

–HENRY FORD

I sat down with my academic advisor and he said that if I was truly committed to becoming a doctor, I would need to retake the class and get a better grade. I signed up for the class again, and again threw my heart and soul into it. My grade did change this second time around—just not in the direction I was striving for. I got a C-! I met with my advisor again and he shot straight with me. He told me that, since I was struggling with the most elemental science classes in my first year of college, I probably wasn't going to make it as a doctor. He advised me to choose a different career.

I came home dejected that day, dreading telling the news to Kalenn. I thought she would be disappointed in me. To my surprise, she didn't really care. She believed in me. She knew I would figure it out. But I wasn't so sure. My hopes were dashed, my dream was dead.

I continued attending college, with the intention of completing a bachelor's degree while buying time to choose another major and career. While in college I worked as a telemarketer—not exactly a dream job, I can assure you.

It wasn't too long after that conversation with my advisor that I walked in on Kalenn crying as she balanced the checkbook. That was when I decided that I would have to seek my career and fortune beyond what college could provide; an extraordinary life would require something more. I looked at our finances and did some figuring. That first year of telemarketing I had made about $18,700. With the bar being set so low, and with the motivation that we were going deeper into debt each day, I set a goal to double my income over the next year.

So I set the goal and started working hard. I innovated at my telemarketing job and started improving my close rate. The previous year I had met a multi-millionaire real estate investor, who became my mentor. I learned everything I could from him. That year Kalenn and I purchased our first real estate investment, which is detailed in my book, *The Strait Path to Real Estate Wealth*. By the end of that year I had made just over $40,000. I had exceeded my goal. My belief in myself was reinforced and the feeling was incredible. I was primed for even more growth.

Again, I set the goal to double my income over the next year. For some reason I allowed my little seed of faith to feel inevitable. After 365 days of believing it was easy to double my income, it felt natural to simply maintain that pattern, since $40,000 was still below the average American income. Looking back, it seems strange because I didn't know what I know now. But I felt an almost irrational confidence and faith that my income would somehow double again.

Once again, I exceeded my goal and made more than $100,000 the next year, by getting another raise and doing more real estate investing. I continued doing this over the next two years. In 2006 I doubled my income again and made more than $200,000. That year I also I graduated from college with a degree in Marriage, Family, and Human Development. In 2007 I made about $500,000. I quit my job and "retired." I had built enough passive income that I would never have to work again. (I've never used my college degree to earn money.)

> "Most people live, whether physically, intellectually or morally, in a very restricted circle of their potential being. They make very small use of their possible consciousness, and of their soul's resources in general, much like a man who, out of his whole bodily organism, should get into a habit of using and moving only his little finger."
>
> –WILLIAM JAMES

Then, I hit my ceiling of self-imposed limitations. I became terrified. If I were to double my income again, that would mean I would make $1 million in a year, and I didn't believe that was possible for me. That was just too much. So the next year, I proved myself right: My income didn't double—in fact, it stayed exactly the same. This was a revelation to me. I realized that when I absolutely believed in my goal of doubling income, it happened. But when I no longer believed it was possible, I was right again. As Henry Ford said, "Whether you think you can or you can't, you are right. It is your thinking that makes it so."

By this time, having officially retired, I was staying at home. Being a stay-at-home dad with my wife and two-year-old daughter wasn't at all how I envisioned it would be. I love my family very much, but I felt like something was missing. I had more to contribute to society.

Six months after retiring, Kalenn and I were vacationing in Jamaica. We were walking hand-in-hand down the beach, celebrating retirement and the birth of our son, who would be arriving in three months. I will never forget her looking up at me and asking the question that would change our lives: "So what are you going to do with your life?"

I actually found the question insulting, and I was shocked that I did. I was triggered and brought back to that moment when I was financially and mentally broke, and that awful feeling of being a horrible provider. I wanted to shout, "Aren't I enough yet?! I'm twenty-six and retired! You have everything you could ever want!"

But I had completely misinterpreted her intentions through the lens of my woundedness. Kalenn was inquiring about the legacy I wanted to leave. Now that money was no longer a reason to do or not do anything, what work would I do? What footprint would I make on society?

I left our trip committed to understanding two things:

1. What was my life purpose?
2. Why was I so triggered still after so much success?

This is what led me on a compelling journey to invest in more mentors to find these answers.

I realized that if I could break through financial limitations, I could do it in other aspects of my life. So I started paying tons of money to mentors. They all did work to help me break through my limiting beliefs. They all had different systems, and I experienced varying results with them. They were all very valuable in their own right.

But I hit a point where I realized how reliant I was on my breakthrough coaches. After working for four years with one particular mentor, for example, I experienced a major trial in my business that was deeply painful. I called her anxiously to schedule an appointment. But she couldn't meet with me. In desperation, I tried doing the breakthrough work on myself. It was a bit sloppy, but it worked! I was able to step out of a place of intense pain into a place of peace and understanding. Most importantly, I stepped into a place of self-reliance, which opened up a whole new world to me.

Over the next several years I took everything I had learned from my mentors and started creating and fine-tuning my own belief breakthrough process, which for me worked better than any other methodology I had experienced before. I never wanted to get stuck again, and I now had the tools to be free.

It was like an incredibly powerful light had turned on in my soul. I was empowered to uncover any belief I had that was limiting my results in any aspect of my life, and change my beliefs to experience breakthrough after breakthrough. I overcame thousands of limitations in my marriage and family, my finances, my desire to influence for good, and my

> *"We are hoarding potentials so great that they are just about unimaginable."*
>
> –JACK SCHWARTZ

body. *Everything* shifted. After trying every other system I could find, I had discovered a foolproof, duplicable formula for breaking through limitations at will and consciously manifesting any results I desired.

The more belief breakthrough work I did, the greater the results that manifested in my life. I eclipsed my previous income ceiling. My marriage and family life have become profoundly fulfilling.

I used to consistently weigh thirty to forty pounds more than I wanted to. Over a six-month period of intense focus of breakthrough on my body

I eliminated cravings, developed confidence, restored balance in my body, developed muscle, and dropped my body fat to below 10 percent. I feel strong, look amazing, and love what I see in the mirror. My body now feels like a much more accurate reflection of how I feel inside.

I feel an intimate and immediate connection with my Higher Power and I feel divinely guided with virtually every decision I make. My family travels around the world on a regular basis. We do humanitarian work, customize our children's education, and enjoy the highest sense of freedom we ever have, balanced with taking action on how we feel called to change the world. We're in the process of building a custom luxury cabin in Sundance, Utah to be used as a special retreat for doing breakthrough work.

In short, my life has become limitlessly abundant, connected, healthy, and joyful. (And yes, I do take care of my parents; they live with Kalenn and I in our 10,000-square-foot home, which we built with an apartment for them.)

"Our deepest fear is not that we are inadequate. Our deepest fear is that we are powerful beyond measure. It is our light, not our darkness that most frightens us."

–MARIANNE WILLIAMSON

None of this has happened because I am inherently smarter, more talented, more gifted or capable than anyone else. It has happened because I have gone on an obsessive quest to uproot and eliminate every false and limiting belief that has placed a ceiling on my results. I've learned a simple, foolproof process that *anyone* can apply to experience similar breakthroughs.

In fact, as you read this book I will share with you case studies of people like you who have applied this process to catalyze dramatic improvements in their lives. I've been honored to work with these people and help them discover and unleash their own greatness. I hope I can do the same for you as you learn the belief breakthrough process and the art and science of manifesting in this book.

CHAPTER 4

THE FOUR DOMAINS
OF LIMITLESS LIVING

There are four primary domains of human potential that are determined by our beliefs. These are the domains within which we seek to break through our limits and expand our possibilities to experience greater peace, happiness, and fulfillment.

These are as follows:

1. Limitless Power

Limitless Power: Being our highest and best self in every moment.

Our personal power is our ability to consciously and courageously manifest whatever we want in life, rather than being held captive by external circumstances and events. It's our ability to change deeply embedded habits in order to change our behavior, and ultimately our results. It's our freedom to make choices, our capacity to accomplish our goals and live our dreams. On the deepest level, it is our desire and capability to live our most sacred purpose and make the mark on the world we were born to make.

> *"Within you right now is the power to do things you never dreamed possible. This power becomes available to you just as soon as you can change your beliefs."*
>
> –MAXWELL MALTZ

The less personal power we've cultivated and harnessed, the more we're subject to life taking us where it will. When fears, wounds, false beliefs, and social pressure are at the wheel, we are helpless passengers in the ride of life. But when we choose the beliefs that will govern our behavior, we take over the steering wheel and have the power to drive wherever we desire.

Our level and strength of personal power are entirely dependent on our beliefs. The more false beliefs we carry, the less power we have. Conversely, the more our beliefs are aligned with truth, the more power we have.

The Top 15 Limiting Beliefs About Personal Power

Here are the top limiting beliefs in the realm of personal power that I encounter on a daily basis in my work with people:

1. "I'm not good enough."
2. "I am worthless and unworthy."
3. "I don't deserve it."
4. "I am damaged goods."
5. "My efforts are never enough."
6. "My contribution is not recognized or appreciated."
7. "Nobody listens to me."
8. "I'm stupid."
9. "I'm afraid."
10. "I can't do it; I'm not strong/smart enough."
11. "I'm not creative."
12. "Change is too hard. I can't change myself no matter how hard I try."
13. "I don't know how."
14. "I'm helpless and powerless."
15. "I'm too busy and overwhelmed."

Cultivating our personal power is about rising from the quicksand of the victim mindset and standing on the solid ground of the victor mindset. It's about making the shift from being an "unconscious reactor" to a "conscious creator." (Interestingly, the same letters make up the words "reactor" and "creator.") It is embracing the fact that we have the power to choose our responses to whatever happens to us.

As Viktor Frankl, the psychiatrist who endured years in Nazi concentration camps, famously said, "Everything can be taken from a man but one thing: the last of the human freedoms—to choose one's attitude in any given set of circumstances, to choose one's own way." He also added, "Between stimulus and response there is a space. In that space is our power to choose our response. In our response lies our growth and our freedom."

We unleash limitless power by living as a victor. Limitless power is the ability to consciously choose and act, which expands our ability to manifest any results we desire. It gives us the capability of doing what needs to be done to fulfill our divine purpose.

Belief breakthrough work is the key to:

> *"The difference between great people and everyone else is that great people create their lives actively, while everyone else is created by their lives, passively waiting to see where life takes them next. The difference between the two is the difference between living fully and just existing."*
>
> —MICHAEL GERBER

- Conquer your greatest challenges that keep you stuck and frustrated and in victimhood.
- Stop all negative emotional triggers and reactions that make you defensive and give away your power, and take back the power you've given to other people by such reactivity.
- Develop the faith, strength, and courage to continually reach your goals and expand your possibilities.
- See your innate greatness, and unleash it to become your highest and best self and serve the world.

2. Limitless Wealth

Limitless Wealth: Having access to the resources necessary to fulfill every moment in its highest and best way.

Although most people think of wealth solely in terms of money, wealth consists of our net resources, which include people, time, effort, passion, leadership, talents, skills, etc. Limitless wealth is about expanding our resources to manifest our natural abundance.

In a limited mindset, financial prosperity is viewed as the privilege of the lucky and greedy. In a limitless mindset, abundance is understood to be the natural birthright of every child of God. We all have different talents and abilities, and those abilities do have a determining factor on our net worth. But each of us has the ability to earn as much as we desire, based on how well we align our lives with the natural laws of wealth creation.

"When you focus on being a blessing, God makes sure that you are always blessed in abundance."

–JOEL OSTEEN

The limited mind believes that money is made by coercing people or deceiving them, or by being selfish. The limitless mind understands that wealth is the product of creating value for other people; we are wealthy to the extent that we solve problems and alleviate pain for other people. *Service*, not selfishness, is the root of wealth creation.

The Top 15 Limiting Beliefs About Wealth

In my belief breakthrough work with tens of thousands of people from all over the world, here are the top fifteen limiting beliefs people have about wealth:

1. "I don't have enough money."
2. "I can't afford it."
3. "I don't deserve to be wealthy."
4. "Making money is hard for me."
5. "I can't make money living my purpose."
6. "Money is the root of all evil."
7. "Rich people are greedy and selfish."
8. "It's bad to be rich; money poisons and corrupts people."
9. "Poverty keeps me humble."
10. "I don't handle money well."
11. "More money, more problems."
12. "Money doesn't matter."
13. "People will treat me differently if I become wealthy."
14. "Money can't buy happiness."
15. "You can't have good relationships and money."

Who do you think has these beliefs more: people who lack financial wealth, or people who have it? Exactly.

Money is just pieces of paper that are value neutral. (People say money doesn't grow on trees, but that's exactly where it grows—it's just paper!) It has no intrinsic value itself. The only value it has is what people place on it. It can do nothing but what people do with it. Money can only be what you believe and want it to be. If you believe it's evil, it will manifest evil results in your life. If you believe it's good, it will manifest good results in your life; money magnifies our beliefs.

"The world is full of abundance and opportunity, but far too many people come to the fountain of life with a sieve instead of a tank car, a teaspoon instead of a steam shovel. They expect little and as a result they get little."

—BEN SWEETLAND

Money is just a resource, and one of many resources. Do you have dreams? What will it take to achieve them? Resources. If you want your dreams to come true, you must create the necessary resources for them to manifest. If you want to take your family to Disneyland, money is one of the resources you'll need. If you want to go on a cruise with your wife, you'll need money. If you want to start an orphanage, or create a community center for inner-city youth, or publish a book or a million other possible dreams, you need money. You can have your dreams or you can have your false beliefs, but you can't have both.

One of the things I love about money is that you can't fake it; either you have it or you don't. Money, therefore, can be a great indicator of your current belief system. Some people are always drowning in debt and feel like they never have enough money. Others just break even, and few ever get ahead in any meaningful way. The most important factor that determines your financial health is your beliefs.

To clarify, keep in mind that money is just one of many resources. Our greatest resource is people. Small dreams take few people to achieve, big dreams take many people. The best way to expand our wealth is to increase our relationships and attract the people into our lives who can help us fulfill our dreams.

"Acknowledging the good that you already have in your life is the foundation for all abundance."

—ECKHART TOLLE

Spiritual teacher Arnold Patent said, "We don't create abundance. Abundance is always present. We create limitations."

Abundance is our natural state. All we have to do is remove our limitations—our beliefs about wealth—to reveal the wealth we've had access to all along. Becoming limitless through belief breakthrough allows you to:

- Eliminate debt and all money stress.
- Make better financial decisions based not on fear or greed, but in alignment with your highest and best self.
- Consistently expand all your resources, including your financial wealth, to create the life of your dreams.
- Leverage your wealth to make a greater difference in the world and leave a legacy.

3. Limitless Health

Limitless Health: Having the physical health, energy, and ability to fulfill every moment in its highest and best way.

The less healthy we are, the more limits we have on what we can accomplish and enjoy.

If you're struggling with weight, physical ailments, chronic pain, disease, your energy level, or any physical health problem at all, the problem is likely not physical at all, but rather mental. Our beliefs guide our biology. You can try a lot of different things, as I have, but the only permanent solution is to identify and uproot the beliefs in your mind that are holding your body hostage. The only way to discern your body's natural limits from your self-imposed limits is to evaluate your beliefs.

"Diseases of the soul are more dangerous and more numerous than those of the body."

—CICERO

I struggled with my body fat for years. I tried every diet imaginable. Some of them worked for a while, but I always yo-yoed back. I spent a decade of working hard in the gym. It wasn't until I discovered belief breakthrough work that I was able to make any permanent progress. (Yes, I am claiming that this book is the ultimate solution to permanent weight loss.)

After years of zero progress, my body was completely transformed within a matter of months. In my case, my physical results were being dictated by my childhood belief that I wasn't loved. And when I didn't feel loved, I would turn to sweet food to numb the emotional pain.

Physical health challenges are tangible manifestations of intangible false beliefs, which promote poor health. We create what we believe. If we believe we are worthless and that nobody wants us, then we will manifest results that will make that belief come true. Our limiting beliefs produce an identity crisis that we feed with unhealthy patterns and addictions. Obesity from overeating can be one form of that.

"The greatest wealth is health."

—VIRGIL

The Top 15 Limiting Beliefs About Health

Here are the top limiting beliefs about health that I've uncovered in my work with people:

1. "I don't know how to take care of my body."
2. "My body doesn't show results fast enough."
3. "I need food as a reward."
4. "It's too hard to live a healthy lifestyle."
5. "Losing weight is hard."
6. "Diets don't work for me."
7. "Working out is hard."
8. "My body doesn't respond to exercise."
9. "I'm doomed to poor health because of my genes."
10. "My genes make me fat, and there's nothing I can do about it."
11. "I don't have time to exercise."
12. "My body is weak."
13. "My body can't do that."
14. "I'm too tired to take care of my body."
15. "I'm getting old; nothing I do will make my body feel and look better."

Interestingly, the false beliefs that manifest health problems usually don't have to do with our physical bodies themselves, but rather come from deeper traumas. For example, people who were mistreated or shamed as children often gain weight as a protective shield as adults.

Belief breakthrough work gives us the power to:

- Eliminate disease, ailments, and chronic health problems.
- Create more energy.
- Shed our "fat suit" and step into our ideal bodies.
- Gain mastery over our body and mind.

4. Limitless Connection

Limitless Connection: Having unconditional love for ourselves and others to fulfill every moment in its highest and best way.

Connection refers to our relationships with our spouses, our children, our families, our friends, ourselves, with God, and every person on the planet. Relationships can be the source of our greatest joy in life—and the source of our greatest pain. And the number one factor that determines the health, strength, and joy of our relationships is our beliefs.

I had an experience one time with my seven-year-old son, Kaiser. It was in the morning and Kalenn and I were trying to get the kids off to school. But Kaiser just wouldn't listen to me. I was getting really frustrated. I hit a tipping point and started being angry and forceful. As expected, a lot of drama and tears ensued. Realizing what I had done, I did my best to apologize and patch things up. But as the kids left for school, the tension and pain were still palpable.

I immediately sat down and started searching for the belief that had triggered my emotions and actions with Kaiser. What I discovered was that I had the belief, "People must listen to me." When that belief was violated by Kaiser ignoring me, I snapped. I considered whether keeping this belief was worthwhile to my relationships, and the answer was no. I changed that belief to several new beliefs: "I honor the agency of others."

"Sometimes people listen to me and sometimes they don't and I'm okay either way." "I listen to me." I'm far more patient with my children and other people as a result.

What hinders connection in relationships is placing conditions on ourselves and each other. These conditions emerge in the form of judgment, blame, and shame, such as:

- "My wife needs to do a better job of cleaning."
- "My husband needs to be more ambitious."
- "My son is lazy."
- "My father is such a jerk."
- "My friend is selfish."
- "I'm such an idiot."
- "I could love myself if I didn't keep screwing up."

What we're really saying when we judge, blame, and shame is that we can't love an individual fully *unless* he or she behaves just how we want him or her to behave. By releasing limiting conditions, we're enabled to let our natural unconditional love flow. As we do so, barriers between us and other people dissolve and people are attracted to us. And the way we release our conditions on and judgments of other people is to identify and eliminate the core, underlying beliefs that create them in the first place.

> *"When you stop expecting people to be perfect, you can like them for who they are."*
>
> –DONALD MILLER

Furthermore, we can do this without exposing ourselves to being hurt by people with ulterior motives. We can love and respect everyone, while using appropriate boundaries to honor ourselves and keep ourselves safe.

The Top 15 Limiting Beliefs About Connection

Here are the top limiting beliefs about connection that I've encountered:

1. "I'm not worthy of being loved."
2. "I don't trust myself and/or other people."
3. "I am not wanted or needed."

4. "No one loves me or cares about me."
5. "No one values what I have to offer."
6. "No one respects me."
7. "No one understands me."
8. "I am alone."
9. "Love hurts.
10. "I'm afraid of commitment."
11. "I'm not safe to be who I really am in relationships."
12. "I attract dysfunctional relationships."
13. "Other people hurt me. The only way to avoid getting hurt is to avoid close relationships."
14. "I offend people."
15. "I hate myself."

In this book, I'll teach you how to change and replace all these limiting beliefs with new, empowering beliefs that give you the connection you crave. Belief breakthrough holds the keys to:

- Love yourself unconditionally, stop self-criticism and shame in their tracks, and feel at home and at peace within yourself.
- Eliminate conflict in your marriage and family and create peaceful, happy, and deeply fulfilling family relationships.
- Find the love, acceptance, and belonging you've been craving.
- Gain the strength to open yourself to vulnerability in relationships, thus creating greater intimacy.

Living as Your Highest and Best Self

Imagine that you possessed in every moment: 1) the courage, strength and fortitude to be your highest, best, most authentic self, 2) all the necessary financial resources you need, 3) the physical health to show up fully, and 4) the unconditional love to see people and serve them as their highest and best selves whether they showed up that way or not.

What would your life be like? How much joy and fulfillment would you feel? This internal fulfillment transcends any amount of external rewards we can experience: money, praise, recognition, validation, etc.

Becoming limitless is the process of expanding our power, wealth, health, and connection, and facing each moment at our highest and best in each of these domains. As we do so, the peace, joy, and fulfillment that have always seemed to elude us become our natural state of being.

PART I

Breaking Through
to a Limitless Life

Why do we get stuck in life? Why do we hit ceilings of limitations and, no matter how hard we try, no matter how many personal development seminars we attend, we can never seem to break through them?

And why do we feel such an innate sense of power and potential underneath all our limitations? As poet Gregory Orr put it, "If we're not supposed to dance, why all this music?" Is there really more to us—an untapped, unlimited capacity that could be unleashed if only we knew how? Or are we just deceiving ourselves into believing that we have more to offer?

No. You're not just deceiving yourself. You *do* have more to offer. You do have amazing gifts, power, and potential that, if unleashed, would astound you and would reveal a whole new world of possibility.

The question is, *how* can you unleash them? And how can you do it in a systematic, predictable way, versus just hoping for breakthroughs that come sporadically and unreliably?

CHAPTER 5

THE ROOT SOURCE OF OUR SELF-IMPOSED LIMITATIONS

As a child, Amber loved gymnastics. Her parents enrolled her in gymnastics classes and she loved every minute of them. At home she was constantly doing cartwheels and other tricks and performing her routines. Her favorite thing to do was the uneven bars, and she would always practice at the park.

When she was eight years old she decided she wanted to be a gymnast when she grew up. Gushing with excitement, she went to tell her parents about her newly-created dream. She thought they would be as excited as she was. It didn't quite turn out that way. As soon as she told them, her dad said, "You won't be able to be a gymnast because you'll be too tall. You can grow up to play in the WNBA." (Her father was a huge sports fan and loved basketball. Since Amber was always taller than her friends, he had high hopes that she would take on his interests.)

Fighting back tears, Amber smiled and said, "Okay," and walked away completely dejected. She dropped out of gymnastics soon after. Her dream was crushed and she put it on a shelf. At that moment, she decided that what she wanted didn't matter. She had to make sure everyone else was happy except for herself. She adopted as a guiding belief, "I cannot speak up for myself and assert what I want."

This one belief has had a profound impact on Amber's life. She has made countless decisions that she didn't want because she tried to make everyone else happy first. As a teenager, she started dating a guy who wanted her to drink with him. She had no interest, but she did it because she was afraid he would leave her. She hated drinking every time she did it. This was a common theme throughout her dating life. She said, "I thought I had to be someone else for guys to like me. If they would move away, I would try to figure out what they would want from me, and I would change who I was to give them what I thought they wanted. I had to prove that I had worth, and I had to have that external validation from the men in my life."

At the time of writing this, Amber is twenty-seven years old and going through a divorce. She had married her husband because her family and friends loved him and kept telling her that she'd be crazy not to marry him. But she didn't love him. When she expressed her hesitancy to get married, people told her things like, "You're overthinking it. You're not getting any younger." She had many opportunities to break it off but, afraid of hurting him and disappointing other people, she caved to the pressure and accepted his proposal. She did her best to make herself fall in love for over four years, but it just didn't work.

"The greatest barrier to someone achieving their potential is their denial of it."

–SIMON TRAVAGLIA

Thankfully, through limitless breakthrough work, Amber is coming home to her authentic self. She's making decisions based on what is true to herself, not what other people want. She says she's never felt more free and happy. She's also taking her dream off the shelf and getting back into gymnastics. And the crazy thing is that she only turned out to be 5'4". Although her father's prediction was wrong, she allowed it to determine the course of her life.

Amber's story perfectly illustrates how we develop our limitations. As children, we all experience traumas. From these emotionally charged traumas we create beliefs—about ourselves, our self-worth, our capabilities, our place in and value to the world. These traumas can be singular major experiences, or the accumulation of relatively minor, though influential, experiences (e.g. a parent who doesn't abuse you forcefully, but repeatedly and subtly shames you and sends you the message that you're not measuring up to his or her expectations).

Furthermore, the traumas that shape our beliefs don't even have to be real. What creates our beliefs isn't what happens to us, but how we *interpret* our experiences. It doesn't matter whether our traumas are real or perceived; the mind doesn't distinguish between the two. In other words, we can experience something as damaging to ourselves when, in fact, the damage is all in our heads.

As children, we are great observers, but poor interpreters. Imagine a six-year-old boy who goes to his father and asks him to play with him. His father brushes him off and says he doesn't have time. This could easily be interpreted by the boy as, "I'm not important." But being a child, what he can't see is that his father is under a lot of pressure on a major project at work. The boy's interpretation is not true, and yet it creates his beliefs about himself as if it were true.

The beliefs we accumulate from our wounds in our childhood determines our paradigms, all our possibilities, all our limitations. Our behavior and results as adults are determined by our perceptions and interpretations as children. Our beliefs dictate our destiny!

The sad part of this is that as children, our brains haven't fully developed yet. Think of the vast array of life-determining choices we make before we've even developed the complete ability to think rationally. Abstract thought doesn't develop until mid-adolescence. We have very little emotional intelligence to make sense of life when we make the most important choices that will determine our life's results. This produces adults with major blind spots who can't see why they're struggling in life. Without extensive belief breakthrough work, most of us *never* see our blind spots.

When Delwin was growing up, every year his family would mark how tall each person was on the door frame of their laundry room to track how much they had grown throughout the year. He always wanted to be as tall as his dad and his brothers, and year after year he would get closer.

One year he and his younger brother went to get measured. Delwin went first and his mark was just a few inches below his dad and older brothers. His younger brother went next and measured taller than Delwin, and very close to the height of their father. Delwin was stunned and couldn't believe that his brother had outgrown him. He felt utterly disappointed.

He remembers thinking at that moment, "I am the runt of the family and will never be as tall as I want to be. I will always fall short." He adopted the belief, "I am not good enough and no matter how hard I try I will always fall short and be small."

As an adult, this belief came true. He constantly acted small and insignificant around others. No matter how hard he worked and tried hard to climb the corporate ladder, he would continually fall short, which was reflected in his paycheck. His friends had big dreams and experienced big results that to him seemed easy to obtain, while his dreams were small and any big goals seemed out of reach. He fell into debt and remained in debt for years because he couldn't bring himself to think bigger than his income.

Anthony was eleven years old when his family (his parents and five siblings) went out to breakfast one morning. As they were all looking at the menu, his older brother asked their dad if he could order steak and eggs. After a moment of consideration, their dad agreed. Anthony thought steak and eggs sounded pretty good too, so he asked if he could order some as well. His dad said he didn't have enough money for both of them to have steak and eggs, and since his brother had asked first, he could have them but Anthony couldn't.

From this experience, Anthony decided, "I'm not as important as others. Other people always get to go ahead of me." The belief that arose and determined his life results was, "I can never have what I want." As an adult he's a hard worker and very service-oriented. But, as he admits, his service is not truly altruistic; it's a product of his false belief, which makes him put other people and their needs and desires above his own. His own needs and desires are always his last priority. As a result, he often doesn't get his needs met and feels neglected and frustrated.

Tari's dad was in the Air Force, so her family moved a lot as she was growing up. Every time they moved she lost personal possessions that were important to her. As a result, as an adult she became a self-admitted hoarder.

She clings tightly to things. She keeps them with the "intent of doing something wonderful with them," as she puts it, but they usually just get put in storage and are never used. She's always had storage units full of stuff, and every time she and her husband have moved they've dragged it all with them. Her husband complains often about all her "junk" and tells her he's never moving it again. She recently was throwing out old magazines when the thought came to her that she was throwing away her dreams (since she has such an emotional attachment to things). This was a big realization for her that revealed why she clings to material possessions so tightly, even when she didn't use them.

The point is this: By the time we've reached adulthood, we've already made all the foundational choices that will determine our results. Our fate has been assigned by the beliefs we've incorporated. Our results are locked in. By the age of twenty, we already know how successful you're going to be by age fifty or sixty, and you're not going to surprise us. The results we experience as adults are entirely predicated upon the beliefs we embrace as children. We continue finding abundant evidence to support our limiting beliefs, thus burying us deeper and deeper into the same results.

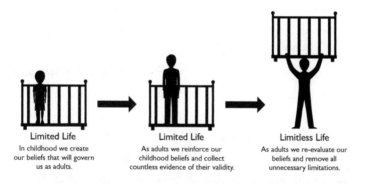

Limited Life	Limited Life	Limitless Life
In childhood we create our beliefs that will govern us as adults.	As adults we reinforce our childhood beliefs and collect countless evidence of their validity.	As adults we re-evaluate our beliefs and remove all unnecessary limitations.

If you adopted the belief as a child that you're not worthy of financial abundance, as an adult you'll always struggle financially.

If you adopted the belief as a child that you're unlovable, you'll never find true love as an adult, or if you do, you'll sabotage it. If you chose to believe that you're unattractive, you will do whatever it takes to make that belief come true. You'll make yourself as unattractive as possible and never attract someone who finds you beautiful inside and out.

If you chose to believe that no one values you, you won't be able to market yourself, either in the job market or as an entrepreneur. You'll always have a ceiling on what you can become and accomplish and the amount of money you can make.

Your entire life—your behavior, your relationships, your levels of success and fulfillment—was measured, staked, and claimed by your childhood choices through experiences of trauma, which determined your beliefs. And most of these beliefs do not serve you—in fact they cripple you.

"The difference between what we do and what we are capable of doing would suffice to solve most of the world's problem."

–MAHATMA GANDHI

We make so many limited choices in childhood, and we continue supporting these choices as adults. Even worse, we continue creating more limiting beliefs in adulthood from the patterns we learned in childhood. Our wounded inner child is really at the helm of most of our decisions, causing us to continue making ridiculous and limiting choices throughout our lives.

Take a moment and sit with this. How does it feel to consider that you are trapped inside a cell of limiting beliefs, which were created subconsciously at an age when you didn't even understand what you were doing, or what the long-term ramifications would be? How does it feel to entertain the idea that you are a prisoner of past interpretations, which were completely distorted and misguided?

I'm guessing you feel a bit like Neo in the movie *The Matrix*, when he was told that his entire life was a lie—that everything he thought was real was just an illusion inside his mind. You find it unacceptable. You want to reject it. You want to believe that you have free will, that you control your destiny. You, like all human beings, have an innate yearning for freedom. We all balk at the suggestion that our freedom is an illusion.

The painful truth is that we are all far less free than we imagine ourselves to be. The reason for this is that our most influential beliefs are deeply embedded in our subconscious mind, so we're not even aware of them. They are like gravity, which we can't see or touch, but we can see the results and physical manifestations of them. No one escapes this. In fact, I believe it is part of a divine plan to give us the opportunity to rise out of our self-imposed limitations.

The challenge with these subconscious beliefs is that, once we make a choice and take on a belief, we have a default setting of never revisiting the choice. Unless we make a great conscious and consistent effort to unearth and change our beliefs, they are basically set in stone—not because they can't be changed, but because we typically don't analyze them once they're made.

Our inner child gets stuck when our traumas remain unresolved. Our inner child is healed and we become at peace when we revisit and resolve the choices from our childhood that are limiting us as adults. By healing the inner child, we return to a more authentic, natural, peaceful, and contented state.

The Proof is in Your Results

If you're resisting the assertion that you're a prisoner of your beliefs, I won't ask you to believe that. What I will ask you to consider is whether or not you are living your ideal life. Are your relationships as connected and fulfilling as you want them to be? Is your career everything you dreamed it would be? Is it bringing out the best in you and making you feel valued, important, and fulfilled? Are you earning as much money as you would like? Are your health and physical condition where you want them to be? Do you live with unstoppable courage and confidence? Do you feel like you draw from a limitless source of strength and power to accomplish anything you set your mind to?

If you answer "no" to any of these questions, you can rest assured that subconscious beliefs are blocking your progress.

We Can Break Free

Thankfully, we *can* change our beliefs to break through our ceilings of limitations. We are *not* condemned to be constrained by our false beliefs forever. We can go back and identify the choices we made and the beliefs we made as children. We can become more self-aware of the beliefs that are guiding our behavior and results. We can re-navigate our past, reconsider our misguided interpretations and poor choices we made as children, and make new choices and adopt new beliefs that serve us better.

We can learn to expand our consciousness and therefore our agency—and to do it on a predictable basis, so that we're constantly expanding our possibilities.

Remember Delwin, who as a child adopted the belief, "I'll always fall short," which caused him to act small and insignificant as an adult? After belief breakthrough work, which first helped him identify his limiting belief, he changed his belief to, "I am significant. I play big. I dream big and fulfill many miracles. I live beyond my potential."

It wasn't too long after this shift in his beliefs at a Limitless event that Delwin quit his job as a graphic designer and started his own mentoring business. He has replaced his income and has produced more in one month than any other month of his life.

He says, "Incredible shifts have happened since choosing into this new belief. I have shown up big around other people, being more warm, kind and assertive. I set higher goals and have bigger dreams. Miracles are more frequent and abundant. I exercise more and stand taller knowing that I am a unique individual with purpose and power. I am an awesome provider for my wife and kids. I am the master of my finances and I control the flow of money. I present on stage with more power and confidence. I bring more value to those around me because I am willing to play big and I expect the same from those whom I mentor.

"Most importantly, I feel like I have control of my life. I'm able to choose what I want to spend my time doing. I have much more freedom and power."

Anthony, who as a child chose the belief, "I can never have what I want," has always felt neglected and hasn't known how to get what he wants. After changing his belief to, "I am important and resourceful! A way is always provided to accomplish all of my desires!", his life has completely transformed. He says, "I feel so much more grounded, peaceful, and powerful. I am able to step up for myself and create what I want. In situations where in the past I would have held back, I now am comfortable putting myself out there. It's actually been shocking to me how assertive I can be in public settings now.

"The biggest transformation for me is in my relationship with my wife and family. Before belief breakthrough work, I had a tendency to withdraw and even stonewall when my needs weren't getting met. It caused conflict in our marriage and kept me from getting what I wanted. Now, I'm much more confident in expressing myself and asserting my desires. I can talk openly and honestly with my wife. It's made a huge difference in our relationship and the peace in our home."

Tari, who became a hoarder as an adult because of her childhood experiences of moving around a lot, used belief breakthrough work to release her attachments to stuff. Interestingly, she started losing weight rapidly in conjunction with her belief breakthrough work. She said both her stuff and her weight had provided a sense of comfort to her, but were actually very limiting. Now, the stuff and the weight are both leaving her life as she changes her beliefs.

"You've heard of people calling in sick. You may have even called in sick a few times yourself. But have you ever thought about calling in well? It'd go like this: You'd get the boss on the line and say, 'Listen, I've been sick ever since I started working here, but today I'm well and I won't be in anymore.' Call in well."

—TOM ROBBINS

She says, "I feel happier, lighter, more free. I have made several runs to my local thrift store to drop off truckloads of stuff. Every time, I have driven away happy.

"Releasing myself from the commitment to my stuff has also freed me to live my true purpose. I'm stepping into my purpose as a healer and helping other people experience the same breakthroughs I have. I have a lot more confidence now. I stand tall and I'm much more balanced because I'm more aligned with my purpose rather than being distracted by all the stuff."

Belief breakthrough work is about uncovering and revisiting all our limiting beliefs to question their continued validity. Most of our limiting beliefs have hit their expiration date and need a serious upgrade. For example, a woman who has been raped may adopt the belief, "Men are not safe." That may serve her during her healing journey, but eventually that belief will need to be changed if she ever wants a thriving marriage.

Belief breakthrough is about consciously choosing empowering beliefs that bring out the best in us and serve us in creating a joyful, fulfilled life.

This process is all part of a divine design. Life is so perfect! The experience of creating limiting beliefs as children, then rediscovering our power and potential as adults, is exactly what we were born for. Although few people ever fully escape the limitations we take on as children and youth, every one of us has divine potential. We are equal in our intrinsic worth.

"As people question what they are believing, they begin to live a fearlessness that they never believed possible."

–BYRON KATIE

The great test in life is whether we can identify and overcome our limitations to manifest our full potential. You were born for this, and I know with all my heart that you can do it. And the limitless breakthrough system you're about to learn is the greatest tool for doing so.

CHAPTER 6

BELIEF BREAKTHROUGH WORK: THE LEVERAGE POINT OF LIMITLESS LIVING

When Alex was in kindergarten, he saw the alphabet on the wall. He knew the alphabet well, having it learned it from the song. But he thought the last stanza said "y n z" instead of "y **and** z." He innocently asked, "Why do you only have one n in alphabet? There's supposed to be two: one before m and one before z."

All the kids in his class laughed at him and the teacher corrected him. In that moment he felt like hiding. He just wanted to fit in and to have friends. From this experience he created the belief, "I am dumb. I feel like I am on the outside looking in." He decided that he was different than other people, and that it was safer to hide his true self.

As he grew up, he often didn't speak up for himself. His belief cost him friends and opportunities and made him deny his gifts, causing him to play small to fit in. It also cost him countless thousands of dollars of income.

Through belief breakthrough work, Alex went back into his past, uncovered his false belief, and then changed it to, "I am supported and my insights bring joy. I am here to share my gifts and encourage others to do the same. I learn from my mistakes and grow with each one."

Since doing so, Alex reports, "I have been able to speak my mind more fully. I have also been more confident in the ways that I reach out to connect to others. I am more willing to help others see the truth in them and have been able to attract more people to my business. The biggest change has come in my own mindset. I have been able to spend less time worrying about what other people think and spend more time being effective."

Change Your Core Beliefs to Change Your Life

As we learn from his story, the essential process of belief breakthrough work is to 1) uncover the false and limiting beliefs we created from our interpretations of experiences as children, and 2) consciously change them into new, empowering beliefs that serve us better. There's more to it, as you'll learn in the next chapter, but that's the essence.

> *"He who cannot change the very fabric of his thought will never be able to change reality, and will never, therefore, make any progress."*
>
> –ANWAR SADAT

Remember that as a child your reasoning abilities weren't fully developed. You made critical choices without understanding what you were even doing, or what the long-term consequences would be. As an adult, you're more conscious. Your brain is more developed now. You can look back at your childhood experiences through wiser, more mature eyes. You can see things you didn't see as a child. You can reinterpret the events in your past that have crippled you thus far in your life, such that they can now begin to serve you and make you better. *You can transform your darkest hours into your greatest triumphs.*

This process is your chance to have a do-over. You get to go back to those major traumas and see them as stepping stones, rather than stumbling blocks. And as you do so, your life in the present is radically transformed. This is the power of choice on steroids!

The reality is this: Your current beliefs, and the choices that emerge from them, can only give you more of what you've already been getting. If you've struggled with excess weight or poor health up to this point in your life, nothing will change significantly until you change your original beliefs. If you struggle with money, without a drastic upgrade in your core, subconscious beliefs, you'll *always* struggle with money. If you and your spouse constantly fight, no trick or technique will get you out of that pattern other than examining and changing the core beliefs causing the conflict.

To put it more bluntly, without significant change, overweight people actually get more overweight. Depressed people become progressively more depressed. We are always either progressing or degenerating—there is no middle ground. The more steeped we stay in our false beliefs and the older we get, the more we reinforce our limiting beliefs. We continually find more and more proof that our beliefs are reality. There is a heavy price to pay for not doing breakthrough work!

If you want something new to manifest in your life—whether it be more money, a stronger marriage, better health, or more personal power—then you have to change something inside you first. And that something is your core beliefs, which up until this point have been completely subconscious.

"Whether you think you can or you think you can't, you're right. It's your thinking that makes it so."

–THOMAS FORD

Break Out of Your "Limit Zone" and into the "Limitless Zone"

From our childhood beliefs we all create a "zone of limitations." This zone tells us how much love, acceptance, abundance, joy, and power we are worthy of and have the capability of manifesting. All of your current results in every area of your life fall inside your zone of limitations. Breaking out of this limit zone requires deep inner work, not superficial strategies.

If you believe that you're not worthy of abundance, you can learn everything there is to know about finance, investing, and business and you still won't be able to increase your income in any meaningful way. If you believe you're unattractive and unwanted, and this belief creates excess weight in your body, no diet or exercise plan in the world can keep the weight off.

The only way to break out of your limit zone and create new possibilities is to go deep inside yourself to 1) uncover the core beliefs governing your choices and results, and 2) consciously change them.

False Beliefs are Created by Strong Emotions

In order to create a permanent belief, two elements are required: 1) a significant, memorable experience, and 2) strong emotions. Beliefs are created from our interpretations of our experiences. Strong emotions drive the beliefs deep in our subconscious mind. Logic is a powerful tool but emotions are the fuel that breathe life into every belief and action. In the case of false beliefs, we feel strong *negative* emotions and interpret our experiences in negative ways. This is why our worldview is formed by our traumas—whether real or perceived.

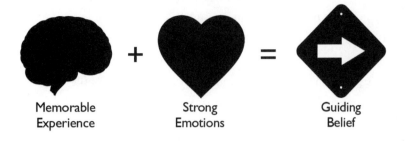

| Memorable
Experience | Strong
Emotions | Guiding
Belief |

There are three levels of human memory: working memory, declarative memory, and procedural memory. Working memory is active memory. It's what you're thinking right now. It is electrical and temporary. Declarative memory is stored memory, or all the things you can remember. Declarative, or long-term, memory is chemical rather than electrical, which means it is much more permanent than working memory. Procedural memory is muscular memory, such as how you know how to tie your shoes or brush your teeth.

Science tells us that our long-term declarative memories are formed by a combination of salience and repetition. In cognitive neuroscience, salience is defined by how well an object, person, or experience stands out relative to others. "Saliency detection" is how we learn to focus our limited perceptual and cognitive resources on the most pertinent data. And, as we've learned, the things that strike us as most salient are the things that we perceive to threaten our physical or social survival.

Experiences with a high degree of salience (or trauma) require only a repetition of one to be embedded in our long-term memory. To drive this home, can you remember exactly where you were the moment you heard about the Twin Towers being hit by hijacked airplanes on September 11, 2001? See what I mean? That one-time event had a high degree of salience, so you'll remember it forever.

Essentially, strong negative emotions provide the salience factor that drives our interpretations of experiences into chemical declarative memory, where it influences us for the rest of our lives.

New Beliefs Need an Emotional Anchor

Limiting beliefs are created by the combination of 1) an interpretation of an experience and 2) strong negative emotions. The choices that really stick with us throughout our lives are those where we've anchored a belief to a powerful emotion. Therefore, if we want to upgrade our limiting beliefs to limitless beliefs, we need to 1) reinterpret our experiences in more empowering ways to create new beliefs, and 2) anchor the new beliefs in positive emotion. We have to detach from the old emotion and attach to a new emotion. Living a limitless life is intentionally creating experiences that include strong positive emotions that we anchor to our most empowering beliefs.

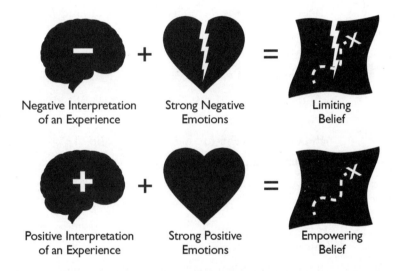

Negative Interpretation of an Experience + Strong Negative Emotions = Limiting Belief

Positive Interpretation of an Experience + Strong Positive Emotions = Empowering Belief

This is one of the reasons why our Limitless breakthrough events are so powerful and life-changing for people—they create a supportive environment where positive emotions can be generated, harnessed, and channeled to anchor new beliefs. I will show you how to do this in your everyday life. However, nothing beats the power of a live event to anchor new beliefs. (Check the back of this book for details on our next event and two free tickets.)

In the next chapter, I'll reveal the step-by-step system for changing your beliefs. For now, I just want you to understand the reasoning behind the process.

We can't change the past, but we *can* change our interpretations of the past, and the decisions we made about ourselves and our experience. We can't change what happened to us, but we *can* change our perception of what happened to us.

It's never too late to reevaluate old choices that aren't working for us. In fact, I find that the moment someone learns about belief breakthrough work, whether they are in their twenties or their eighties, they have a powerful awakening of how limitless they really are.

Why Change Our Limiting Beliefs?

"You are in charge of how you react to the people and events in your life. You can either give negativity power over your life or you can choose happiness instead. Take control and choose to focus on what is important in your life. Those who cannot live fully often become destroyers of life."

—ANAIS NIN

Before I reveal the formula to eliminate limiting beliefs, it's important to have a compelling "why." The opportunity cost of a limiting belief is missing out on amazing memories with people, generating more income, creating a healthier body, and more. But there is more than just what you are missing out on.

Repeated thoughts are a form of worship. If you worship a false belief long enough, it produces emotional pain and suffering that needs to be treated. We feed these identity crises with addictions to escape the pain, such as sugar, TV, sleeping, workaholism, pornography, drugs, alcohol, negative self-talk, shopping—the list is endless.

If you make a list of your go-to addictions, which you use to mask your emotional pain, and evaluate the financial, time, and emotional cost on a daily basis, you may be astounded to find how much time and energy you spend coping with your limitations. Yes, you are missing out on what your potential will produce. But you are also experiencing life in each moment at a fraction of your possible happiness and fulfillment.

Belief breakthrough is the systematic way to change our interpretations and beliefs in order to upgrade our lives. The complete system is revealed in the next chapter.

CHAPTER 7

THE BELIEF BREAKTHROUGH PROCESS

The work I've done with mentors set me on a quest to create a uniform and universal process that could be used not only on myself, but for anyone else as well. I believe the system you'll learn in this chapter to be the definitive and most powerful belief breakthrough system. I spent years creating and fine-tuning it. This process has been tried and tested not only in my own life, but also in the lives of thousands of people through private mentoring, my live events, and the work of certified belief breakthrough coaches.

This process can be used any time you wish. However, I've found that it is most helpful to go through it when I feel emotionally triggered (upset, angry, fearful, etc., when someone says or does something to touch on my deepest wounds). Emotional triggers are evidence of deeply rooted experiences out of which we formed our core beliefs.

The 9 Steps of Belief Breakthrough

- Step 1: Ground
- Step 2: Identify a Limiting Belief
- Step 3: Explore Your Memories
- Step 4: Identify the Deeper Limiting Belief
- Step 5: Examine the Cost of the Limiting Belief
- Step 6: Give Yourself Permission to Shift
- Step 7: Create a New Belief
- Step 8: Rewrite Your Story
- Step 9: Anchor Your New Belief

The purpose of grounding is to transcend the normal chatter of our minds to access a deeper, more intuitive wisdom. It's a simple process of deep breathing to get into a meditative state.

Close your eyes and breathe through your nose. Breathe in as deeply as you possibly can, filling your lungs. When your lungs are completely full, hold it for a brief moment, then slowly release all the air out of your lungs. Do this for five or six repetitions. As you inhale, breathe in light with the oxygen, and as you exhale, breathe out stress and anxiety.

Clear your mind of logic and ideas, and simply detach from thoughts; this is not a mental or logical process. Over time and with practice, grounding can become your natural state. This sets the stage for the next steps.

Step 2: Identify a Limiting Belief

Once you feel solidly and effortlessly grounded, ask yourself this question: "What is the number one limiting belief coming up for me?"

Then listen for the intuitive answer—not the answer that comes from your head, but the one that comes from your heart. Trust that whatever comes up for you is exactly what you need to work on in this moment. Write down your answer.

If you're dealing with specific issues or triggers, you can alter this question accordingly. For example, suppose you're really struggling financially and you want to understand why. You can ask yourself, "What is the number one limiting belief causing me to struggle financially?" Or if you get triggered by your spouse a lot, you could ask, "What is the number one limiting belief that is creating conflict in my marriage?" Or suppose you're in the middle of a work meeting and someone cuts you off as you're speaking, and you get triggered. Get grounded and ask, "What is the number one limiting belief that caused me to get triggered by being interrupted?"

We're used to running away from our triggers because we don't want to deal with the emotions. But you'll find that your triggers are the very thing you want to move toward. And the sooner after they occur that you do the breakthrough work on them, the better. Your triggers and negative emotions are like an "x" that marks the spot of where the real gold of breakthrough work is found.

Step 3: Explore Your Memories

Once you've identified your top limiting belief, ask yourself, "What is the first memory that comes up when I think this thought?"

Take your time with this. Be patient. Do your best to connect with the first memory that comes up. This may not be the earliest memory you have about this belief, and it may not be from childhood. Trust that whatever memory that arises is the perfect place to focus your breakthrough work.

The more specific and detailed the memory, the easier and more effective it is to change the belief. How old are you? What's happening? Go through the experience as if it is happening right now for the first time. Let it out. Feel it as deeply as you can.

If you're persistent, you'll find that you can always get to a memory. It's easy to mistrust obscure thoughts that arise from the mist of memory— but remember that mistrust is at the heart of every limiting belief. Push past your mistrust of your memories and trust what comes up—especially if it doesn't make sense or seem relevant.

Understand that you may have hundreds of supportive memories strengthening the original memory of the limiting belief. All of them are important. Don't get stuck trying to find the first moment that created the original belief. Trust your memories as you explore them.

Step 4: Identify the Deeper Limiting Belief

Think of the memory and sit with it. Breathe it in. Allow yourself to remember and feel the feelings. Keep in mind author Colin Tipping's advice, "If you can't feel it, you can't heal it."

As you sit with the memory, ask yourself this question: "What did I decide about myself when I experienced this?" In Step 2 you identified an initial belief. But what comes from this step is actually the deeper limiting belief that needs to be explored. This is the most pertinent belief that will create relief from the negative emotion. Write down your answer in as much detail as possible.

Step 5: Examine the Cost of the Limiting Belief

Ask yourself how this belief is showing up in your life and affecting your results today. Explore how it impacts all aspects of your life, including finances, physical health, relationships, and personal power. Explore the impact the belief has made on the past, in the present, and what the foreseen cost will be in the future if the belief continues unchanged.

"We do not need magic to transform our world. We carry all of the power we need inside ourselves already."

–J.K. ROWLING

Try to be concrete and specific by identifying experiences that reveal this belief in action. For example, instead of being vague like, "It has caused a lot of conflict in my marriage," identify a specific conflict you had with your spouse that you know was evidence of this belief.

Here are a few guidelines to really explore the story surrounding your false belief:

- Put words to the emotions this belief brings up.
- What am I feeling right now as I sit with this belief?
- Is this a pattern for me?
- How often do these feelings come up for me?
- What is my coping mechanism when I feel this way?

Step 6: Give Yourself Permission to Shift

Sometimes we have a hard time shifting our beliefs because we're not sure if we actually can. Giving yourself permission to shift means to consciously embrace the truth that you really can shift your beliefs and make a change.

I find it useful to get permission from myself before moving onto changing the belief. You can do so by asking yourself any of the following questions:

- Is this belief actually true?
- Do you want this belief to be true?
- Are you ready to let go of this sabotaging belief?
- Are you ready to make a different choice?

Step 7: Create a New Belief

We can't change the past, but we can change the decisions we made based on our interpretations of past events. In painful experiences, we often learn the wrong lessons. Our original beliefs are by default set to exist indefinitely. This belief breakthrough process allows us to revisit past choices and beliefs, and consider if they are still serving us—or if they ever did.

Once you've identified your false belief from a past decision, create a new, empowering belief that will serve you best, to replace the old limiting belief. For example, if your old belief was, "I don't manage money well," your new belief could be, "I am wise and disciplined in managing my money. I create abundance." If your old belief was, "I push people away," the new belief could be, "I effortlessly attract into my life people who love and support me."

There are three rules to help you create the most effective new belief statements:

1. Present: State your new belief in present tense. Don't use words like "will," "can," "might," or "want." Also, state your new belief in first person.
2. Positive: State what you want instead of what you don't want.
3. Powerful: Find a statement that really resonates with you personally.

For example:

- "I attract all the wealth into my life that I need to fulfill my divine purpose."
- "I easily release excess weight."
- "I am worthy of love."

Write down your new belief. (If you struggle with creating or wording new beliefs, see the examples in the New Beliefs Reference Guide in the Appendix at the back of this book.)

Initially, this new belief may feel more like an illusion than reality. But keep in mind that your subconscious mind can't distinguish between illusion and reality. Accept your new belief and it will become true in your mind.

Whether our beliefs are true or false, limited or limitless, we are going to be right either way. Our minds will make us right. The words we use are our own self-fulfilling prophecies. Use new words to create new results.

Step 8: Rewrite Your Story

Conjure the original memory from which you created your false belief. Now imagine yourself in this moment choosing into your new, empowering belief instead of the old, limiting belief. In essence, rewrite the story at the point of origin. Imagine reinterpreting the experience in a way that serves you better. (Remember: We can't change the past, but we can change our interpretations of the traumatic experiences, from which emerged our limiting beliefs.)

How does this feel? Open your heart to really feel the emotions of choosing into the new belief. Sit with those emotions and soak them in.

SOLICIT THE HELP OF SOMEONE YOU TRUST

Who do you know in your life whom you implicitly trust to support and assist you in overcoming this belief? This could be anyone: a friend from childhood, a current friend, a parent, a spouse, a child, an aunt or uncle, a favorite teacher, a mentor, you as your highest self, or deity. Mentally ask this person to guide and support you in the process of rewriting your story.

Even though you are now empowered with a new belief, it can be difficult to trust an idea that may not yet feel true. When you do the wrong thing long enough, it can begin to feel like the right thing. Enlisting a trusted person to help you makes it easier to believe the new belief.

In your mind, go right to the moment in the memory you conjured where you are choosing into the belief that is limiting your current results. Imagine that your trusted advisor is standing right beside you in this moment, experiencing it with you. You are about to make a decision to adopt a false belief that is going to cripple you for the rest of your life.

What would he or she say to you in this moment? What words of support, encouragement, love, wisdom, and power would he or she offer to help you heal the pain of this experience and rewrite your story?

Write down your answer in as much detail as possible. Imagine it coming straight from your trusted advisor, giving you exactly what you need to hear to be empowered, rather than crippled by this experience.

Step 9: Claim the New Belief in the Present

Remember: Dominant negative beliefs are formed when emotional anchoring experiences are combined with limiting beliefs about ourselves. To counteract this, it's not enough to just create a new belief—we also have to combine the new belief with powerful emotions. You will feel emotion as you uncover your false beliefs and the memories around them and finally address the unresolved negative emotions from the past. There are also methods for heightening your positive emotions as you receive the validation of a new belief.

Your goal in this step is to shift the energy and emotion anchored to the memory to a strong, positive emotion. To this end, state your new belief out loud with confidence, conviction, and power. Say it repeatedly. Allow yourself to deeply internalize it. Reclaim your power by claiming and owning your new belief!

COMMIT TO THE NEW BELIEF

You have just found a new belief that will serve you better. Now, even more important is that you commit to do the work to own this new belief, so that it can override the old belief and begin serving you.

You may not have a lot of evidence yet that this belief is true. You will begin creating this evidence as you choose with faith to believe this new thought. Are you willing to dedicate the time, emotion and energy to reciting this belief with power every day? Are you willing to commit to do the work on this new belief? What can you do to immediately begin putting this new belief into action?

Write down your answers and commit to reviewing them regularly until you are living them consistently.

> *"We are all functioning at a small fraction of our capacity to live fully in its total meaning of loving, caring, creating and adventuring. Consequently, the actualizing of our potential can become the most exciting adventure of our lifetime."*
>
> –HERBERT OTTO

ADDITIONAL TOOLS

Here are a few more tools you can use to claim your new belief and really anchor it in your mind:

Find evidence to support the new belief. In the past, you interpreted every experience as evidence of your false belief. Now you get to shift your perspective and reinterpret your experiences as evidence of your new belief. Write down three specific ways in which this belief has already manifested as true in your life. Then answer these questions:

- What do you think the results of this new belief will be?
- Who would you be without your old, limiting story?
- Who could you become if you were to anchor this new belief?
- How docs that feel?

Hold onto those feelings to anchor the new belief.

If you're not sure if simply stating your new belief out loud is enough or that the new belief is really "taking," then take this a step further, as you desire. Shout it as loud as you can. Stand up on a chair and proclaim it for all the world to hear. Do whatever you have to do to deeply feel the new belief and to really believe it. You can get creative with this. Put your new belief into a song and sing it loud and proud. Dance while you're singing it. Celebrate the creation of your new belief. Laughter, joy, gratitude, and fun are all good anchors. Nothing is off limits here. The bigger and more ridiculous the celebration the better! It may feel silly—but can it be any sillier than how you've allowed your false belief to impact your life for decades?

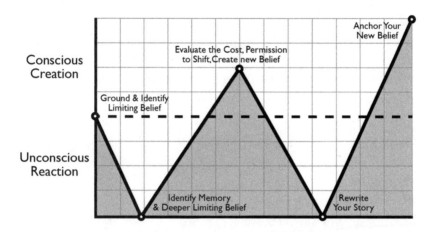

Examples of the Belief Breakthrough Process

Below are three examples of this process in action from my clients. These are taken from worksheets they have completed during live Limitless events. These are shared with their permission, and I have not edited anything in them.

EXAMPLE 1: *Holly*

What is the number one limiting belief coming up for you?
That I Am Weak... Others are taking advantage of me and loved ones in ways that involve authority figures. Bullies, because they

lost sight of what it meant to care for someone, because someone didn't take care of them in a positive unconditional loving way.

What is the first memory that comes up for you when you think the thought, "I am weak"?

My Adoptive Mother Who took advantage of us physically, mentally, emotionally, sexually. She was a teacher at an Elementary School. Both my brother and I felt we had no one to turn to at school or police, etc. Because Both ways had been taken away from us because of her. Because of our birth father as well.

What did you decide about yourself at that moment?

Two things... 1) That I had to be the one to figure it out. 2) I don't know what to do. Because of these two things it showed up that it was my fault, and that I am weak, and because I am weak that makes me worthless, because of that I don't matter.

How is this belief affecting your results today?

Even up to recently, Financially, Legally, Emotionally, Mentally. Physically. It has been costing me, my life in these ways.

What new belief would support you more?

That I am strong, and that I am always worth it. I am always enough. I always try my best and that is what matters. I matter.

Whom would you trust to give you this advice?

My Heavenly Mother & My Birth Mother.

Let's go right to the moment where you are choosing into your limiting belief. What would they say to you?

They are telling me... How strong you are to have not given up where many have, how beautiful you are, and how much we love you. We are so proud of you for how fast you rise up even when you fall, remember this is only a piece of why Heavenly Father

& our Savior chose you to do what needs to be done. You love everyone, no matter what. Now let others love you & know that you are incredible. There is always an abundance of angels that surround you. Because we all love you so much.

How did you feel after the breakthrough, and what results have shifted in your life since taking this on?
I was able to stand up for myself. By looking to intuition I knew what I needed to say. Even when I was dealing with a really hard moment.

EXAMPLE 2: *Trenton*

What is the number one limiting belief coming up for you?
I am not accepted into circles of influence.

What is the first memory that comes up for you when you think the thought, "I am not accepted into circles of influence"?
When I was in elementary school, I had some friends that one day as we were hanging out together, all suddenly took off running from me. I began to run after them and was unable to catch them.

What did you decide about yourself at that moment?
People don't want to be with me. I am not accepted and influential people run away from me.

How is this belief affecting your results today?
Everyone I meet that has influence, I sabotage the relationship mostly with my energy of, "I don't belong in this circle!" It has cost me millions of dollars because I have missed out on promotions, and personal business opportunities I have not taken because I didn't feel like I belonged. I was unable to lift my circle of influence to people who would lift me.

What new belief would support you more?

I am influential! I guide people! I change lives! I am compassionate! I extend love to all! I change the world wherever I am called! I am a hero! I am heard! People seek me! I have the answers!

Whom would you trust to give you this advice?

Anthony, another friend that was not part of this experience who has always been a good friend.

Let's go right to the moment where you are choosing into your limiting belief. What would he say to you?

He thanked me for being me and for being a friend. He told me how influential I have been in his life and that I would be an influence in other's lives. He invited me to play on the jungle gym when he saw that I was about to make a decision that would affect my life. He told me that he was my friend no matter what.

How did you feel after the breakthrough, and what results have shifted in your life since taking this on?

I have recognized that I fit in with influential groups and people. I have seen mentors come into my life and leaders who have involved me in processes and have had meaningful conversations with me. I am supported and accepted! It will help my business and life tremendously!

EXAMPLE 3: *Josh*

What is the number one limiting belief coming up for you?

I'm not meant to be great.

What is the first memory that comes up for you when you think the thought, "I'm not meant to be great"?

I was 9 and my parents decided to pull me out of school.

What did you decide about yourself at that moment?

If I'm not smart enough for school, how could I possibly hope to achieve anything special?

How is this belief affecting your results today?

There's always this lingering doubt that it isn't going to work out. Any time I start something new or exciting, I have this though that it isn't going to last because I'm not meant for greatness.

What new belief would support you more?

Greatness is my purpose.

Whom would you trust to give you this advice?

My Dad.

Let's go right to the moment where you are choosing into your limiting belief. What would he say to you?

Don't let this define who you chose to become. We pulled you out of school because it wasn't the highest and best way for you to receive your education. You're destined for so much better than school can teach you.

How did you feel after the breakthrough, and what results have shifted in your life since taking this on?

I feel so much more hopeful. My attitude has changed from "this will never last" to "I'm so grateful I get to experience this, and I'm going to make the most of it whether it's brief or eternal." I'm much more inclined to try and to take massive leaps of faith, because the fear it won't last is now gone.

CHAPTER 8

MAKING BELIEF BREAKTHROUGH
A DAILY HABIT

Belief breakthrough work can be helpful when you do it just a few times. But where it becomes really powerful is when you make it a daily habit. I encourage you to go on a proactive "search-and-destroy" mission to uncover and change every single limiting belief you have. You will be amazed by how many limiting beliefs you uncover in yourself as you commit to doing the work consistently.

Here are the steps and tools you need to do it:

1. Use the Belief Breakthrough Script

Now that you've learned the full process, you can use the following condensed script to process limiting beliefs. The purpose of this script is to use it for daily, quick use. Every time you get emotionally triggered, every time you feel fear or anxiety, every time you get into any conflict, use this script to identify the limiting beliefs causing the emotions or conflict and process them on the spot.

BELIEF BREAKTHROUGH SCRIPT

Step 1: Ground

Use deep breathing with your eyes closed to get into a meditative state. The purpose of grounding is to separate from your thoughts and connect to intuition. Clear your mind of all thoughts and prepare to receive answers.

Step 2: Identify a Limiting Belief

Ask yourself, "What is the number one limiting belief coming up for me?" Listen for the intuitive answer. Trust that whatever comes up is exactly what you need to work on in this moment, especially if it doesn't seem to make sense.

Step 3: Explore Your Memories

Ask yourself, "What is the first memory that comes up when I think this thought?" Trust that whatever memory arises is the perfect place to focus your breakthrough work.

Step 4: Identify the Deeper Limiting Belief

Ask yourself, "What did I decide about myself when I experienced this?" What comes from this is the deeper belief than you found in Step 2 and is the one you really need to work with.

Step 5: Examine the Cost of the Limiting Belief

Ask yourself, "What is the cost of believing this thought?" Examine how this belief is showing up in your life. How has it affected your results in the past and present? How will it affect you in the future if you don't change it? Consider how it impacts other aspects of your life, including finances, physical health, relationships, and personal power.

Step 6: Give Yourself Permission to Shift

Consciously choose to shift your beliefs and make a change.

Step 7: Create a New Belief

Make the choice to change your old limiting belief to a new, empowering belief that will serve you better. State the new belief in first person and in the present tense.

Step 8: Rewrite Your Story

Go back to this memory from which you created your false belief. Imagine reinterpreting the experience in a way that serves you better and that is more aligned with the truth of the new belief.

Step 9: Claim Your New Belief

Shift the energy and emotion anchored to the memory to a strong positive emotion. State your new belief out loud with confidence, conviction, and power. Say it repeatedly. Declare it in a way that feels most authentic to you. Commit to living this new belief, and find evidence to support it.

2. Build Your "Belief Manifesto" and Recite It Daily

As you embark on your "search-and-destroy" mission, one of the most powerful techniques is to keep a journal of all the false beliefs you uncover, and the new beliefs you change them to. Add to your list every day.

Your list of new beliefs becomes your life "manifesto," a statement of empowerment. State all your new beliefs out loud every day. Recite them with conviction and feeling. You can even record yourself reading them, with your favorite inspirational music in the background. Listen and celebrate. Imagine the beliefs as if they are in full force in your life.

For example, your belief journal could look something like this:

OLD BELIEFS	NEW BELIEFS
I never have enough money.	I always have as much money as I need to fulfill my purpose in any moment.
I don't deserve to be wealthy.	Financial abundance is my birthright—I deserve to be wealthy!
Making money is hard for me.	Making money is easy for me.
I need food as a reward.	I need food to give me health, energy, and vitality.
Losing weight is hard.	Losing weight is easy.
I don't know how to take care of my body.	I honor my body and take good care of it.
I'm not worthy of being loved.	I am worthy of being loved.
I am not wanted or needed.	I am wanted, needed, and valued.
No one values what I have to offer.	Many people value what I have to offer.
I am worthless and unworthy.	I am worthy and priceless!
I'm not good enough.	I am good enough.
I don't deserve it.	I deserve it.

Imagine the power of reciting all these new beliefs with power and conviction every day for thirty to sixty days. What could change in your life?

3. Use the "New Beliefs Reference Guide" to Uncover and Replace Limiting Beliefs

There's a simple, yet extremely effective tool I use with every attendee of my events to help them make a daily commitment to change their beliefs. I give them a Limitless wristband, which has a black side and a red side. The idea is to start out each day with the wristband showing the black side. Your daily challenge is to uncover and change at least one false belief. As you do so, you flip the wristband to display the red side. This is a visual reminder that you are daily breaking through your limitations, rewriting your story, and reclaiming your power.

To help you with this, I've included as an Appendix at the back of the book a "New Beliefs Reference Guide." In this guide you'll find the most common limiting beliefs I've encountered in working with thousands of people, along with sample replacement beliefs for each of them. Simply reading through the list can be a powerful way for you to identify and replace the beliefs you see showing up in your life. You can use this as an ongoing reference tool in your daily belief breakthrough work.

Have fun with this! The more false beliefs you change and the faster you do it, the faster your life will change and the more quickly you will see tangible results. I've proved that this works in my own life. And the thousands of people I've worked with are living proof that not only is this possible, but it's guaranteed—*if* you do the work. You have nothing to lose—except your limitations.

4. Start with the Top Sixty Limiting Beliefs

In Chapter 4 I gave you the top fifteen limiting beliefs in each of the four domains of limitless living. Here they are again, but with corresponding new beliefs. This is a helpful reference tool to see examples of what new, empowering beliefs look like. Note that I'm not imposing these specific new beliefs on you, but simply giving you examples to help you create your own that resonate with you.

Top 15 Limiting Beliefs About Wealth

OLD BELIEFS	NEW BELIEFS
I don't have enough money.	I have more than enough money for my needs and wants.
I can't afford it.	I am an expert at allocating my resources.
I don't deserve to be wealthy.	My birthright is wealth, health, freedom, abundance, prosperity, and joy.
Making money is hard for me.	Making money is easy for me.
I can't make money living my purpose.	I am prosperous as I serve others with my purpose.
Money is the root of all evil.	Money is a beautiful resource to bless the world.
Rich people are greedy and selfish.	Money magnifies my desire to take care of my family and do incredible good in the world.
It's bad to be rich; money poisons and corrupts people.	I am wealthy, grounded, and good.
Poverty keeps me humble.	I humbly attract and access the resources I need.
I don't handle money well.	I am responsible with money.
More money, more problems.	Money offers solutions.
Money doesn't matter.	Money is a useful resource.
People will treat me differently if I become wealthy.	I treat all people with love and respect.
Money can't buy happiness.	I am happy, content and peaceful with the resources in my life.
You can't have good relationships and money.	I grow my wealth and my meaningful relationships.

Top 15 Limiting Beliefs About Health

OLD BELIEFS	NEW BELIEFS
I don't know how to take care of my body.	I intuitively care for my body.
My body doesn't show results fast enough.	My body progresses perfectly.
I need food as a reward.	I reward myself with improving and increasing health.
It's too hard to live a healthy lifestyle.	It's easy to live a healthy lifestyle.
Losing weight is hard.	I easily release excess weight. I step courageously into my healthy body.
Diets don't work for me.	I make the best food choices to fuel my healthy life.
Working out is hard.	I get fit doing what I love.
My body doesn't respond to exercise.	I love exercise. My body loves to exercise.
I'm doomed to poor health because of my genes.	I create a legacy of health.
My genes make me fat, and there's nothing I can do about it.	I am whole. Health is my birthright.
I don't have time to exercise.	I love creating time to exercise.
My body is weak.	I am strong.
My body can't do that.	I can do anything.
I'm too tired to take care of my body.	I am energized as I care for my body.
I'm getting old; nothing I do will make my body feel and look better.	I look and feel amazing.

Top 15 Limiting Beliefs About Connection

OLD BELIEFS	NEW BELIEFS
I hate myself.	I love myself.
I'm not worthy of being loved.	I receive all the love I choose.
I don't trust myself and/or other people.	I trust myself and my intuition. I use my intuition to make good choices.
I am not wanted or needed.	I want me. I need me.
No one loves me or cares about me.	I love me. I care about me.
No one values what I have to offer.	I value what I have to offer.
No one respects me.	I respect myself.
No one understands me.	I understand me.
I am alone.	I am supported. I am surrounded by love.
Love hurts.	Love heals.
I'm afraid of commitment.	I am committed to what is important to me.
I'm not safe to be who I really am in relationships.	I embrace my authentic self. I love being me. I accept me.
I attract dysfunctional relationships.	I bring love and unity to all my relationships.
Other people hurt me. The only way to avoid getting hurt is to avoid close relationships.	I embrace others. People are free to choose how they feel about me and I love them either way.
I offend people.	I speak my truth and accept the responses of others.

Top 15 Limiting Beliefs About Personal Power

OLD BELIEFS	NEW BELIEFS
I am worthless and unworthy.	I am worthy.
I'm not good enough.	I am more than enough.
I don't deserve it.	I accept myself. I am enough.
I am damaged goods.	I am whole. I am complete.
My efforts are never enough.	My efforts are always enough.
My contribution is not recognized or appreciated.	I recognize, appreciate, and validate me.
Nobody listens to me.	I hear me.
I'm stupid.	I am smart.
I'm afraid.	I am confident.
I can't do it; I'm not strong/smart enough.	I can do anything. I am strong. I am enough.
I'm not creative.	I am a creator. I am creative.
Change is too hard. I can't change myself no matter how hard I try.	Change is easy. I love and embrace change.
I don't know how.	I have access to the knowledge I need.
I'm helpless and powerless.	I have all the support I need. I am empowered by my abilities.
I'm too busy and overwhelmed.	My life is balanced and feels amazing.

How Daily Belief Breakthrough
Can Change Your Life

Here are just a few testimonials (unedited) of people sharing the impact daily belief breakthrough has on their lives:

Mariah H.

"Daily, consistent belief breakthrough over a very short period of time has allowed me to release 30 Limiting Beliefs of excess weight, let go of paralyzing perfectionism and embrace deep healing surrounding real childhood trauma. I am more peaceful, fulfilled, and confident as I continue to do this work."

John W.

"With Belief Breakthrough, I don't have an area in my life that has not improved. Relationships, family, health, wealth, personal power, and I found my message and passion. I have helped others do the same. I am in business working for myself empowering people with the tools to heal from PTSD and get their life in order through Belief Breakthrough."

Jacqueline S.

"As a Belief Breakthrough Coach, I have seen people overcome things that in my nightmares I would never come across. They have experienced real life terrors, and yet the breakthrough process brings them peace, joy, and reconciliation that can only come from internal work. I have seen this have lasting affects, especially when they continue doing the work."

Matthew P.

"As a Father, I used to be quick to frustration. The truth is, I wasn't that excited about being a Dad in the first place and I felt guilty for feeling that way. It's taken effort over the past year plus, and lots and lots of breakthrough, but I rarely feel tempted to resent my parental responsibilities anymore, in fact, they more often feel like privileges! Also, my wife compliments me about how I've changed—that I'm more quick to calm and to seeking understanding when children behave inappropriately. As I continue to find my triggers and break through the limiting beliefs that cause them, I feel more calm, confident, and true as a Husband, Father, and Man."

Kiera T.

"As I have been focused on daily Belief Breakthrough, Miracles have occurred in my life. The most impactful is my ability to step out of fear and into Faith! I believed I lived by faith when I was living by fear! I have heard the term, Faith not Fear, pretty much my entire life but never really understood it. Ok, maybe I understood it like a 3 year old understands the alphabet. I could recite it and knew it was important but had no idea how it actually worked so it could benefit me. BB has opened my eyes, heart, and mind to understand how to step into faith and even the next level which is actually being able to know how to choose it, and experience peace!

"I lived most of my teenage and all of my adult life in fear. I tried to live by faith but was lacking the tools to actually do so. I was that paranoid mother that wouldn't let my children out of my sight. If I didn't KNOW where they were at all times and know they were safe I would panic. There were times when if my husband wouldn't answer the phone when I called I would go straight to 'what if he is dead'! Even to the point of checking dispatch to see if there had been an accident! Pushing my kids, husband and family away! Which is exactly what I was afraid of, loosing them. One in particular, is my oldest daughter, who for the past 6 years has been distant. She didn't come around much and we had a lot of distance between us. Over the last couple of months we have slowly become closer and closer. My relationships with her is amazing, I have my daughter back!

"Daily, I look at my fears, doubts, insecurities, and the lies I believed, bringing the hidden things into the light where I can see them and consciously choose faith and truth. I'm stepping out of my smallness and into my greatness and it no longer scares me. It excites me!"

> *"Power is the faculty or capacity to act, the strength and potency to accomplish something. It is the vital energy to make choices and decisions. It also includes the capacity to overcome deeply embedded habits and to cultivate higher, more effective ones."*
>
> –STEPHEN R. COVEY

The more belief breakthrough work you do and the more consistently you do it, the more your life will change. In my experience in my own life and in helping thousands of others, we each need to conquer at least hundreds of limiting beliefs to see dramatic change manifest in our life. You don't have to do this overnight. Small, incremental steps each day adds up over time to dramatic improvements. If you want to speed up the fulfillment of your dreams and goals, speed up the rate at which you do belief breakthrough work.

PART II

The Science Behind
Why Belief Breakthrough
Creates Permanent,
Life-Changing Results

ACCORDING TO HARVARD PROFESSOR GERALD ZALTMAN, 95 percent of our thoughts, emotions, and learning occur without our conscious awareness. Most cognitive neuroscientists concur. NeuroFocus founder Dr. A.K. Pradeep estimates it at 99.999 percent.

Dan Ariely, professor of psychology and behavioral economics at Duke University and author of *Predictably Irrational: The Hidden Forces that Shape our Decisions*, concludes from years of empirical research that, "...we are pawns in a game whose forces we largely fail to comprehend."

David Eagleman, neuroscientist at Baylor College of Medicine and author of *Incognito: The Secret Lives of the Brain*, adds that, "...consciousness is the smallest player in the operations of the brain. Our brains run mostly on autopilot, and the conscious mind has little access to the giant and mysterious factory that runs below it."

In this section, we'll shed light on this "giant and mysterious factory" and learn the science of how we create our limitations. As we turn the light on to illuminate our subconscious mind, we're empowered to become more conscious. And as we do so, we become more free and powerful.

CHAPTER 9

HOW OUR BRAIN WORKS
TO LIMIT OURSELVES

O ur brain is wired for limitation. That's the bad news. The good news is that, by understanding how our brain works, we can harness and leverage it to work in our favor rather than against us.

Bruce H. Lipton, PhD, is an internationally-recognized stem cell biologist, a well-respected pioneer in the cutting-edge field of "epigenetics" (the study of how our genes can be changed by environmental factors and the power of thought) and the bestselling author of *The Biology of Belief: Unleashing the Power of Consciousness, Matter, and Miracles.* According to Dr. Lipton, the subconscious takes in 20 million bits of information per second (conservatively). In contrast, the conscious mind takes in 2,000 bits per second and can process a maximum 40 bits of information in the same time.

In other words, our subconscious mind perceives and processes incomprehensibly more than we are consciously aware of. We have the ability to consciously interpret very little of everything we're taking in. (Have you ever seen the online video where researchers ask you to count how many times people pass a basketball, and then afterwards reveal the crazy and incredibly obvious thing you missed as you focused on counting? If not, check it out, and other similar examples, here: http://www. theinvisiblegorilla.com/videos.html. Trust me, if you question the assertion that our conscious brain only registers a small percentage of what our senses actually perceive, these videos will make you a believer.)

In light of this, here's the critical question: *What does our brain tend to focus on?* If we can only make sense of very little of what we're perceiving, what will we actually see?

What we see is based on shortcuts the brain routinely takes, which evolved largely in response to threats to our survival. As science writer David Disalvo writes in his book, *What Makes Your Brain Happy and Why You Should Do the Opposite*, "Years of neuroscience have led to the current understanding of the brain as a prediction machine—an amazingly complex organ that processes information to determine what's coming next. Specifically, the brain specializes in pattern detection and recognition, anticipation of threats, and narrative (storytelling). The brain lives on a preferred diet of stability, certainty, and consistency and perceives unpredictability, uncertainty, and instability as threats to its survival—which is, in effect, our survival."

Psychologist Dr. Rick Hanson adds that our brain has developed in response to threats to create a pervasive "negativity bias" that makes us prone to feeling threatened. Our early ancestors faced serious and daily threats of being eaten, stomped, poisoned, etc. As a result, our brains are constantly on the lookout for bad news and hyper-sensitive to apparent threats. We zero in on bad news and fixate on it with tunnel vision. Good news, on the other hand, is essentially ignored. "In effect," Rick says, "the brain is like Velcro for negative experiences but Teflon for positive ones."

He further explains,

Basically, in evolution, there are two kinds of mistakes: (1) You think there is a tiger in the bushes but there isn't one, and (2) You

"The consummate truth of life is that we alter our destiny by altering our thoughts. The mind is our most crucial resource, our crowning asset, our ultimate arena of battle."

–DENNIS DEATON

think the coast is clear, no tiger in the bushes, but there really is one about to pounce.

These mistakes have very different consequences. The first one will make you anxious, but the second one will kill you. That's why Mother Nature wants you to make the first mistake a thousand times over in order to avoid making the second mistake even once.

This hard-wired tendency toward fear affects individuals, groups (from couples to multinational corporations), and nations. It makes them overestimate threats, underestimate opportunities, and underestimate resources.[1]

We also learn from Charles Duhigg's book, *The Power of Habit: Why We Do What We Do in Life and Business*, that "the brain is constantly looking for ways to save effort. Left to its own devices, the brain will try to make almost any routine into a habit, because habits allow our minds to ramp down more often. This effort-saving instinct is a huge advantage…An efficient brain…allows us to stop thinking constantly about basic behaviors, such as walking and choosing what to eat, so we can devote mental energy to inventing spears, irrigations systems, and eventually, airplanes and video games."

Here's what all of this means: We get wounded, and then create false beliefs in a misguided attempt to protect ourselves from further wounding. False beliefs are essentially a conditioned shortcut to keep us safe. So what we tend to focus on, as we're taking in 20 million bits of information per second, are the things that we perceive to either 1) pose a threat, or 2) offer a reward. And these perceptions are all seen through the lens of our false beliefs.

"If the doors of perception were cleansed everything would appear to man as it is: infinite."

—WILLIAM BLAKE

As we subconsciously sift through mountains of data, our false beliefs determine what we see and focus on, and how we interpret our experiences. This is why we can't even see breakthrough opportunities, even when they are right in front of us and plain as day! Our brains will literally not allow us to see things outside of the parameters we have set with our false beliefs.

Consider this belief: "If I stand out from the crowd, people will make fun of me." That belief gets filed away and creates a shortcut to save you energy and time when you encounter situations that appear to threaten you with humiliation. And it does actually work to keep you safe from such a threat.

The question is, what is the cost of such protection? What opportunities does it prevent you from taking advantage of? What learning and growth does it stifle? Furthermore, does humiliation really even hurt us? And can we choose whether or not to feel humiliated?

"The reward for conformity is that everyone likes you except yourself."

–RITA MAE BROWN

Again, we create all these false belief shortcuts subconsciously as children, without being aware of what we're doing and the long-term effects they will have on our future choices. Then, as adults, we have no idea that this programming even exists. This is exactly what our brain is wired to do. That wiring may have served us well to save us from tigers in the bushes in the past. But in our modern world, where environmental threats are minimal, that wiring works against us.

Our Brain Makes Our Beliefs True

As I've said, whether our traumas are real or perceived doesn't matter; the mind processes perceived traumas in the same way it processes real ones. Experimental and clinical psychologists have proven repeatedly that our nervous system can't tell the difference between an actual experience and an imagined experience. In other words, our brain makes our beliefs "true," even though they are not Truth.

"The mind is its own place, and in itself can make a heaven of hell, and a hell of heaven."

–JOHN MILTON

In one study, volunteers were asked to play a simple sequence of piano notes each day for five consecutive days. Their brains were scanned each day in the region connected to the finger muscles. Another set of volunteers were asked to imagine playing the notes instead, also having their brains scanned each day. Consider the results:

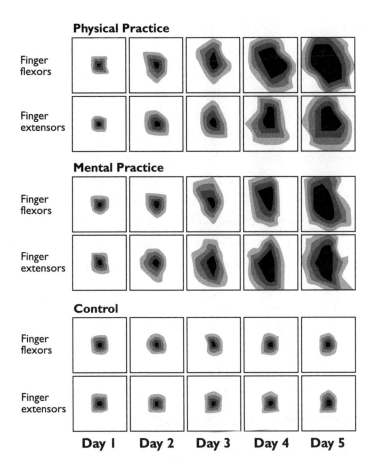

Physical Practice

Finger flexors

Finger extensors

Mental Practice

Finger flexors

Finger extensors

Control

Finger flexors

Finger extensors

Day 1   Day 2   Day 3   Day 4   Day 5

The top two rows in the image show the changes in the brain in those who played the notes. The middle two rows show the changes in those who only imagined playing the notes. Compare this with the bottom two rows showing the brain regions of the control group, who didn't play nor imagine playing the piano. Incredibly, the changes in the brain in those who imaged playing piano are the same as in those who actually played piano.[2]

A 2013 study from the Karolinska Institutet in Sweden further showed how imagination can alter mind-brain function. Christopher Berger, a doctoral student at the Department of Neuroscience and lead author of the study, said, "We often think about the things we imagine and the things we perceive as being clearly dissociable. However, what this study shows is that our imagination of a sound or a shape changes how we perceive the world around us in the same way actually hearing that sound or seeing that shape does. Specifically, we found that what we imagine hearing can change what we actually see, and what we imagine seeing can change what we actually hear."

Another researcher in the project, Professor Henrik Ehrsson, reported that, "This is the first set of experiments to definitively establish that the sensory signals generated by one's imagination are strong enough to change one's real-world perception of a different sensory modality."[3]

"We act, or fail to act, not because of the will, as is so commonly believed, but because of imagination. A human being always acts and feels and performs in accordance with what he imagines to be true about himself and his environment."

–MAXWELL MALTZ

We can choose to view and interpret the world and our experiences optimistically or pessimistically, and depending on our lens, we alter our perceptions of reality. Author Christopher Bergland wrote of the study that, "Mental imagery and visualization can alter how we perceive the world around us. To a large extent, your mind can create reality at a neuronal level. By choosing to look on the bright side and see the proverbial glass as perpetually half-full the world around you will seem more hopeful and full of possibility."[4]

As far as your brain is concerned, what you imagine to be happening is actually happening. In other words, *whatever you choose to believe, you get to be right—your brain literally makes it so!* Whatever you interpret manifests not only in your beliefs and your paradigm, but on a physical level in your nervous system and stress responses. As Bruce Lipton puts it in his book, *The Biology of Belief,* "…science recognizes that the fate and behavior of an organism is directly linked to its perception of the environment. In simple terms, the character of our life is based upon how we perceive it."

We See What We Want to See

Once our beliefs are created and embedded in our subconscious mind, we find evidence to support them, and we filter out evidence that contradicts them. Our world only makes sense if we're right, and our brain will do anything and everything to make our beliefs right. If I believe that I'm a fat person and there's nothing I can do about it, then all of the evidence I see in my life will confirm this belief. Subconsciously, I will eat in ways that create fat. My lifestyle will prevent me from losing fat. Unless I change my belief, it is literally impossible for me to lose weight and keep it off—*my brain will not let me.*

This is true because of a psychological phenomenon called cognitive dissonance, a term created in 1956 by social psychologist Leon Festinger. Wikipedia defines cognitive dissonance as:

> a discomfort caused by holding conflicting cognitions (e.g., ideas, beliefs, values, emotional reactions) simultaneously. In a state of dissonance, people may feel surprise, dread, guilt, anger, or embarrassment. The theory proposes that people have a motivational drive to reduce dissonance by altering existing cognitions, adding new ones to create a consistent belief system, or alternatively by reducing the importance of any one of the dissonant elements.[5]

Put simply, it is a psychological mechanism that drives us toward internal consistency between our beliefs and behaviors. Festinger coined the term after observing the reactions of a UFO cult when their prophecy that the world would end on December 21, 1954 failed to materialize. Rather than conforming their beliefs to reality, they simply changed their beliefs: Their founder proclaimed that they had spread so much light that God had decided to save the world from destruction.

"It is a paradoxical quality of human nature that we tend to downgrade ourselves while upgrading others who possess no more—and often less—talent for attaining lofty goals."

–MELVIN POWERS

You and I may not believe in UFOs, but we do mental tricks that are equally as crazy on a daily basis. We perceive everything that happens to us through the lens of our pre-existing beliefs. If anything seems to conflict with our beliefs, we simply alter the data to fit into them—or we ignore it entirely. We cannot live with cognitive dissonance, so we perform mental acrobatics to be consistent so that our world makes sense.

When Blake was in the fourth grade, he was placed in a group for kids who were more academically advanced than their class members. His mother told him, "Just remember, you're no better than anyone else." From that point on, whenever he thought about playing harder or aspiring higher, he heard her voice and backed off. He never gave his full effort because of the belief he adopted: "I can't play full out at 100 percent." Underlying that was the belief that extra effort and achieving excellence were somehow wrong.

As an adult, in a subconscious effort to prove these beliefs as true, he settled in every aspect of his life and learned to be content with mediocrity. He approached relationships as temporary; he enjoyed people's company until they grew tired of him and then he started over. He allowed his body to deteriorate into poor health, which resulted in depression, diabetes, and low energy. He never pushed for a better career or income. His spirituality suffered because he failed to give any effort.

When Wendy was nine years old, she lived with her biological father and step mom. In their blended family there were twelve kids living in a tiny house. One time she was in an argument with her younger sister. Her sister Kathy, who was six years older than Wendy, came to intervene. The argument escalated and her younger sister started telling Kathy stories of things Wendy had done to her. When Wendy tried to explain and defend herself, Kathy slapped her across the face, grabbed her by the jaw, and screamed at her to shut up.

Hurt and infuriated, she tried to say more but Kathy's mind was made up. Kathy then grabbed her hair and threw her into her room. She had to stay there until her parents got home from work. When they did, Kathy played the sweet girl and told them it was all Wendy's fault. Wendy said as little as possible and apologized. Her parents sent her to her room for the rest of the evening without dinner, and she cried herself to sleep.

Wendy created the belief, "I can't say what I want or how I feel because what I say upsets people." She decided that she wasn't worth listening to, that she doesn't matter, and that she makes people mad when she talks.

As an adult, Wendy has subconsciously worked hard to make these beliefs true. She told me, "I say what I think people want to hear, and that doesn't work because it's not coming from my heart. My words sound fake and rehearsed and a lot of times really intense to force my words to be heard. Sometimes I ask for things that I don't really want. This has caused a lot of confusion and frustration in my relationships. This has especially cost me a secure and stable relationship with my husband because I don't open up to him the way I want to. I don't know how to express my true feelings and I hold back what's in my heart."

The only way for Blake and Wendy to change their results is to change their beliefs. The same is true for all of us. Our brains will literally not allow us to perform above the level of our beliefs, because we can't bear to live with inconsistency. Unfortunately, in order to maintain consistency, most of us don't change our beliefs—rather, we conform our lives and results to fit into the tight box of our beliefs.

"As a single footstep will not make a path on the earth, so a single thought will not make a pathway in the mind. To make a deep physical path, we walk again and again. To make a deep mental path, we must think over and over the kind of thoughts we wish to dominate our lives."

–HENRY DAVID THOREAU

The joyful, fulfilled life we really want is right in front of our faces, but we fail to see it because we perceive only limited options through our limited beliefs. Belief breakthrough allows us to expand our consciousness to see more hope, love, joy, and possibility in the information that we consciously process. More precisely, we can train our brain to seek out a reality that will best serve us. What if we could retrain our brain to only see the opportunities that enable our best self to manifest?

When we view information through a negative lens, we gravitate toward limiting beliefs when we experience cognitive dissonance. The opposite is also true. Belief breakthrough allows us to intentionally step into cognitive dissonance by consciously stepping into a positive thought. Conscious positive thoughts outweigh the negative.

The brain is a great servant but a horrible master. If we're running our lives on autopilot, with little or no understanding of what's going on "under the hood," then our brain is the master. It steers us to where our false beliefs lead. Ultimately, this results in self-destructive behavior, unfulfilling relationships, financial struggles, an inability to achieve goals, poor self-esteem, and a million other undesired results.

The only way we can take control of the steering wheel is to become consciously aware of the false beliefs we created as children, and then reprogram them into truer, more empowering beliefs.

Because of modern science we know how our beliefs create pathways in our brains that we habitually use. Imagine walking through the grass of the savannah. As you walk, you stomp down the grass. Eventually, by taking the same route every day, you create clear trails. But some of the paths put you close to dangerous cliffs and animals. Conscious belief breakthrough work is like using a bulldozer to carve out a new trail that is safe and designed to free us to live our limitless life.

CHAPTER 10

WHY WE CLING TIGHTLY TO OUR FALSE BELIEFS AND LIMITATIONS

As children we choose to adopt hundreds, even thousands of beliefs. In our underdeveloped state, these choices are often irrational, erroneous, and ridiculous. We create deeply embedded, sweeping beliefs at the slightest provocation based on events that happen in one moment.

These beliefs stick with us and continually damage us throughout our lives, but we're not even aware of them. It's like hiring a first-time, drunken sailor to chart a navigational course around the world, and then stubbornly adhering to that course even when it proves to be dangerously wrong and our ship crashes into rocks. Even worse, as rocky and dangerous as the journey is, we never think to question the map we were given.

Or, it's like having a board of directors in our mind who run our decision-making process. Our board is filled with members who represent our most powerful memories, which created limiting beliefs. This means that we have a bunch of discontent, angry, and sad inner children calling the shots for us as adults!

For example, imagine a little girl who tries out for a school play and wins a part. But during the performance, she completely forgets her lines and feels humiliated. She adopts the belief, "I can't perform in front of others." But just because she had one embarrassing experience doesn't actually mean that she can't perform for others. All that happened was that she forgot her lines. And yet she made a huge decision that impacts how she shows up for the rest of her life based on one event.

When Mariah was nine years old, she was sexually abused by an adult whom she loved very much, and whom she thought had her best interests at heart. From that devastating trauma, she developed the belief, "I can't trust."

"If you are pained by external things, it is not that they disturb you, but your own judgment of them. And it is in your power to wipe out that judgment now."

–MARCUS AURELIUS

As an adult, she's now realizing how much this decision made from one experience has cost her. She explains, "I haven't ever fully trusted myself to move forward in my life. I keep a part of all my relationships closed off. I don't allow myself to be fully vulnerable, which creates disconnection. I look for outside approval. I'm not fully able to validate myself because I feel like I can't trust myself. The irony is that I can't trust others fully either so I am never able to feel validated or safe to move forward. I question when I should trust. I walk away when there is opportunity for growth. I play small. I run away and hide. I allow fear of manipulation to make my choices."

As a teenager, Timothy showed interest in girls, but felt that the interest wasn't reciprocated. From these experiences he created the belief, "I am unattractive," and decided he wasn't worth loving.

Soon after that, he discovered pornography. Because of his core belief about himself, his habit of viewing pornography developed into an addiction, which plagued him for more than twenty years. He said, "It destroyed my wife's self-confidence and damaged and nearly ended our marriage several times. It took time from my life that I will never get back."

How Our False Beliefs Serve Us—and Limit Us

As the stories above illustrate, we create our false beliefs in a misguided attempt to protect ourselves from pain, distress, embarrassment, humiliation, fear, etc.

The little girl who forgets her lines creates the belief, "I can't perform in front of others," because this belief will prevent her from ever performing again, thus sparing her the potential humiliation. As an adult, she may indeed avoid some humiliating moments by living according to this belief. But sadly, she will also miss out on the best opportunities that will stretch her to her full potential. By running away from embarrassment, she also runs away from fulfillment and lives a safe, though mediocre and limited life.

Mariah created her belief, "I can't trust," to protect herself from being hurt like that again. She closed herself off and hid her truest, most precious self from the world. Ironically, in this attempt to protect herself, she also prevented what she wanted the most: to be seen and truly loved.

Timothy created his belief, "I am unattractive," to prevent him from feeling rejected by women; in feeling unattractive, he wouldn't put himself out there or make himself vulnerable for women.

All of our false beliefs serve a purpose: to protect us. And the truth is, they can actually work. They do create a protective shell, a defensive barrier around our hearts and our most authentic selves. They can save us some pain and distress.

But in the process, they also prevent us from experiencing the highest levels of joy and fulfillment. They stifle our potential. They may keep us safe (as we perceive), but by doing so they also keep us small. So in truth, the "safety" we create from false beliefs is a prison cell we build around ourselves. By keeping people out and preventing them from hurting us, we also keep ourselves locked inside. By protecting ourselves from the pain we don't want, we shut out the love, joy, and abundance that we want the most. Limiting beliefs often serve us for a specific period of time—but not if they have a default setting of staying indefinitely and never getting reviewed.

> *"Most of what you fear does not even exist. Much of what you love is closer than you realize."*
>
> —STEVE D'ANNUNZIO

Our limitations as adults were created by the false beliefs we chose as children. As adults, we accept and even cling to our limitations because they keep us "safe" and "protected." This is why belief breakthrough work requires a willingness to change. Until people are willing to change, they fight fiercely for their limitations. They can give you every logical reason why they believe what they do. They give excuse after excuse after excuse to explain why they're not living the life they want. They do anything and everything but allow themselves to open up to the risk of being hurt again.

This is completely understandable and I have deep compassion for it. I say this not as a criticism, but simply to help you understand what goes on in your own mind so that you can break from your conditioned patterns. As author Elizabeth Gilbert wrote, "Argue for your limitations and you get to keep them."

When the consequences of living small, hidden, and protected become too painful, you'll open yourself to risk, hope, and possibility. As poet Elizabeth Appell wrote, "And the day came when the risk to remain closed in a bud became more painful that the risk it took to blossom."

Take Responsibility to Transcend Victimhood

In victim mode we blame other people for why our life isn't better. Is there someone you can think of to blame for your life? If so, you may be stuck in victimhood. This is not a judgment, but simply a tool to recognize an area where you may be stuck.

Staying in victim mode justifies our poor behavior and poor results. It means we don't have to own that we are the creators of our story. To experience powerful change, combine compassion with responsibility.

Notice carefully how you feel when I use the word "responsibility." How do you feel about that word? Most people feel blame, shame, and pain towards that word. We cringe at hearing, "It's your responsibility" because what we really hear is, "It's your fault."

"The moment you take responsibility for everything in your life is the moment you can change anything in your life."

–HAL ELROD

I invite you to change your orientation around responsibility. Taking responsibility is about empowering ourselves to change things in our life. Until we accept responsibility, we have no power to change anything because we have no power over our circumstances. If we didn't cause something, then we can't fix it.

When you break the word down, all it means is response ability—the ability to respond. Responsibility is your ability to choose your actions and reactions. It is your ability to choose how you spend your time and energy. It is your ability to create different outcomes. It's not about being blamed for your life. It's about waking up from the slumber of irresponsibility and saying, "I have the ability to change anything I want." It's an empowering word, not a blaming or shameful word.

Responsibility, when properly understood, is one of the most exciting, powerful, and joyful principles we have to create our ideal lives. The people who take the least responsibility for their circumstances and results have the least power and ability to improve them. Likewise, those who take the most responsibility have the greatest power and ability to improve their circumstances and results.

We often interact with other people and experience something that triggers us. Maybe we don't like how they treat us, or they make a decision we disagree with. Whatever the circumstance, ultimate responsibility means recognizing that the person with the reaction is the one with the problem. But the person with the problem also has the solution.

True responsibility is taking accountability for your thoughts, emotions, and triggers. If an interaction with someone produces a problem within you, then the first step is seeing that it's *your* problem, not theirs, and letting go of your belief that *they* need to change in order for you to feel resolved. You can only change yourself. Resolve the limiting belief in yourself, and then regardless of whether the other person changes, you get the benefit of returning to peace and empowerment.

"The best years of your life are the ones in which you decide your problems are your own. You do not blame them on your mother, the ecology, or the president. You realize that you control your own destiny."

—ALBERT ELLIS

Accept the unalterable reality that you and only you are responsible for the results you're getting. You are the common denominator in any circumstances that don't go your way. It's not your parents, it's not the people who have wounded you throughout your life, it's not your boss, it's not your spouse—it's you. You can't change anything that has happened to you, but you can change how you respond.

The beliefs you've created as defense mechanisms in response to wounds don't serve you. They limit you. Yes, you've been hurt. Yes, you've suffered. And you can grieve all those wounds and hold them in compassion, while also taking responsibility for your life.

CHAPTER 11

HOW TO UNCOVER FALSE BELIEFS DEEPLY EMBEDDED IN YOUR SUBCONSCIOUS MIND

I learned a principle of psychology called the "Johari Window" from one of my mentors, a super successful businessman who sold one of his companies for nine figures. The concept was created by psychologists Joe Luft and Harrington Ingham in 1955 (the term came from combining their first names). It's a simple and useful tool for illustrating and improving self-awareness, and creating mutual understanding between individuals within a group.

Johari's Window says there are certain things we are aware of and certain things we're not aware of or don't consciously realize. Similarly, there are certain things others are aware of and certain things that others do not know. The choices we make and how we interact with others depend on our level of self-awareness, as well as how much others know us.

The concept is illustrated in the following chart:

THE JOHARI WINDOW MODEL

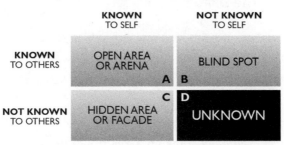

Our greatest levels of success and happiness in life come from quadrant A—the things we're self-aware of and the things other people know about us. If a person is a good listener and knows she is, and others also know that about her, then others will have more faith in her ability. Our interpersonal relationships thrive in this area.

Quadrant B refers to the things other people know about us but we don't understand about ourselves—in other words, our blind spots. If they are positive, they are useless to us. If they're negative, they damage our credibility and relationships.

The things in quadrant C—our secrets we hide from others—tend to make us uncomfortable. If we're hiding positive things, it's because we're afraid of shining our light and therefore, these things do us no good. Our negative things are our fears and bad habits, which reduce our trustworthiness.

Our greatest area of potential growth lies in quadrant D. These are the things hidden in the dark that neither we nor others see. Our deeply rooted fears and deeply buried talents lie in this quadrant. They are sometimes exposed when we face major challenges, but they usually remain hidden. As I learned from my mentor, this quadrant is also the most dangerous to us. We don't know what we don't know, and this is the information that can hurt us the most. And most of us will never know that we don't know.

What we learn from the Johari Window is that the more aspects of ourselves that we can move into the open quadrant A, the happier and more successful we can become, both within ourselves and in our relationships.

How to See in the Dark

The question is, how can we bring our hidden fears and undiscovered talents into the light? How can we uncover the false beliefs that govern all of our choices and behavior—especially since they are buried so deeply in our subconscious mind?

The answer is revealed in an old Southern proverb: "Whatever is down in your well will eventually come up in your bucket." What this means is that you don't even need to know the point of origin of any false belief—all you need to see is how it's manifesting in the present. It's certainly helpful to uncover those original memories to reprogram at the source. But even if you can't remember the memories themselves, you can still find evidence of the false beliefs.

Your "bucket water" is manifest in a number of ways, including the following:

Your Circumstances and Results

Our external life is a reflection of our internal beliefs. If we don't like something in our life, the place to start is to examine our root beliefs that are causing our results. Our roots become our fruits—in other words, our beliefs become our results.

Before awakening through belief breakthrough work, we believe that some life circumstances are bigger than us—that there's nothing we can do about them. When we awaken to limitless, we understand that we are greater than any circumstance life has to offer.

Your Emotional Triggers

Another place to look for evidence of false beliefs is our emotional triggers. When we feel upset or angry by the actions of other people, we tend to blame them. But our anger is triggered by something inside of us, not what they did.

The following emotions are clear indicators that we hold a false belief:

- Fear
- A feeling of being victimized
- A sense of being imprisoned, inhibited, restricted, trapped, controlled
- Helplessness, powerlessness
- Defensiveness
- Frustration, stress

- Confusion, a feeling of directionlessness, dissatisfaction
- A sense of defeat or disempowerment
- A sense of being disheartened or unmotivated
- Anger
- Guilt, shame
- Jealousy, envy, resentfulness
- Depression, despair, misery
- Uncertainty about choices and desires, indecision
- Addiction
- Cynicism, pessimism
- A feeling of inferiority
- A feeling of being rejected, unloved
- Embarrassment

These emotions, rather than being things to avoid, can be wonderful teachers for us. When they arise, we want to move towards them and explore why we're feeling this way. As I explain in my previous book, *The Conscious Creator*,

> There is a powerful way to handle negative emotions that arise from the actions of others. That is to first recognize the people to whom you've given your power—anyone who pushes your buttons or frustrates, upsets, or offends you in any way.
>
> Then accept those people as your teachers. Understand that the buttons they've pushed are *your* buttons. You, not the other person, are the one who is upset. Ask yourself what higher law you have to learn.
>
> More often than not, when we're hurt by what other people say about us, it's because there's some truth in their words...

Your Criticisms of Others

In psychology there's a common term called "projection." Projection means to see in other people things we don't like about ourselves. For example, a person who is a habitual liar may constantly accuse other people of being untrustworthy. As Carl Jung said, "Everything that irritates us about others can lead us to an understanding of ourselves."

We constantly project our beliefs onto others. Our negative judgments about ourselves and others are the best evidence we can find for the need for belief breakthrough work.

Use Your Intuition to Identify False Beliefs

Intuition is a deep inner knowingness that doesn't require analytical reasoning. Intuition is the bridge between our unconscious and conscious parts of our mind. Intuition is a source of deeper wisdom than we can find through analytic thought, because it's accessing our subconscious—things that can't even be seen by our conscious mind. Intuition also involves accessing our higher self and a greater divine wisdom, with all the knowledge we need to make the highest and best choice in any given moment. When you know how to tap into your intuition at will, you can *always* identify false beliefs.

"The important thing is this: to be able at any moment to sacrifice what we are for what we could become."

−CHARLES DUBOIS

It's a simple matter of learning how to shut off your thoughts and tune into something deeper than the mind. It's feeling for answers in your heart, rather than thinking for answers in your head. I'll teach you how to do this in Chapter 17.

Doing the Work

Belief breakthrough works only to the extent that we can actually uncover and see our false beliefs. This can be a difficult task, given that our false beliefs reside in our subconscious mind. By paying attention to the "water" that comes out of our "well," using intuition, staying consistent with the work, and engaging with mentors, we shed light on our subconscious mind to reveal the root sources of our struggles and limitations.

I've given you the nine steps of the belief breakthrough process. I've shown you the science of why it matters. But all of this knowledge is worthless if you don't actually do the work! Most people just read through books and, even if they gain value from them, they rarely apply the knowledge practically to their life. I implore you to not do this with this book.

I urge you to do more than read this book, but also to actually apply it. Do the work of belief breakthrough. Use the belief breakthrough script on a daily basis. Never rest content with the knowledge that a single false belief is still lodged in your mind and limiting your results. Don't stop doing the work until you've completely purged your mind of all limiting beliefs—which means *never* stop doing the work.

Don't be a passive reader. Be an active participant in making your life as magnificent as you are underneath your layers of limiting beliefs.

PART III

The 9 Laws of
Conscious Creation:
How to Optimize, Amplify,
and Accelerate
Belief Breakthrough

TO "MANIFEST" MEANS to turn your thoughts that are in alignment with the laws of nature and your purpose into physical reality. As powerful as belief breakthrough work is, it's not the complete package of what you need to manifest your ideal life.

Belief breakthrough works in conjunction with the 9 Laws of Conscious Creation. Belief breakthrough is the methodology by which we purge negativity and purify our minds and emotions. The more belief breakthrough work we do, the more powerfully we can apply the Laws of Conscious Creation to dramatically boost our results.

The Laws of Conscious Creation are the context in which we apply belief breakthrough. The laws are the engine; belief breakthrough is the fuel.

THE NINE LAWS ARE AS FOLLOWS:

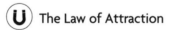 The Law of Attraction

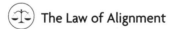 The Law of Alignment

 The Law of Choice and Accountability

(⧗) The Law of Gestation

(⚔) The Law of Faith

(🌾) The Law of the Harvest

(✳) The Law of Purpose

(💡) The Law of Intuition

(♥) The Law of Connection

Belief breakthrough work is all about the Law of Alignment, which is one of the hardest laws to apply at its deepest and purest levels. Its importance cannot be overestimated. The belief breakthrough process is the "how to" of this law. Now you're going to learn the remaining laws and how all of them fit together to manifest the life you want. Once you understand the nine laws, I'll reveal a formula for leveraging them to manifest breakthrough results in your life.

CHAPTER 12

THE LAW OF ATTRACTION

Like attracts like. We attract into our lives the people, things, situations, and experiences that match our deepest beliefs and thoughts. We attract what we think about most. Our dominant and persistent thoughts eventually manifest as physical reality.

All sages and wise men and women through the ages have taught us the power of our thoughts.

In Proverbs, Solomon taught, "As [a man] thinketh in his heart, so is he." The Buddha said simply, "What you think, you become."

James Allen says it more poetically in his classic, *As a Man Thinketh*:

> Man is made or unmade by himself; in the armory of thought he forges the weapons by which he destroys himself; he also fashions the tools with which he builds for himself heavenly mansions of joy and strength and peace. By the right choice and true application of thought, man ascends to his Divine Perfection; by the abuse and wrong application of thought, he descends below the level of the beast. Between these two extremes are all the grades of character, and man is their maker and master.

"The human brain emits frequencies, which when focused, are picked up by other human brains and passed through the ether to affect other physical matter."

–THOMAS EDISON

Thoughts are not inert or impotent abstractions. Thoughts are things, and they manifest in our external world. Our thoughts are far more powerful than most of us understand. All our success—or lack thereof—is predicated on the quality of our thoughts. As Emerson wrote, "Great men are those who see that thoughts rule the world."

In his popular book, *Think and Grow Rich*, Napoleon Hill taught that "our brains become magnetized with the dominating thoughts which we hold in our minds, and by means with which no man is familiar, these 'magnets' attract to us the forces, the people, the circumstances of life which harmonize with the nature of our dominating thoughts."

Norman Vincent Peale added in *The Power of Positive Thinking*, "The person who sends out positive thoughts activates the world around him positively and draws back to himself positive results." In other words, what we focus on grows.

The Law of Attraction can either work to our benefit or to our detriment. A lifetime of negative thinking will manifest negative results. Likewise, the more positive our thinking, the more positive our results. Successful thinking catalyzes successful actions. *Nothing is more important than choosing the thoughts we entertain and cultivate.*

"Our lives seem so muddled because we keep walking into scenes in which we, along with the people around us, have no clear idea what we want."

–DONALD MILLER

The Law of Attraction fails to have power for most people because they're not clear on what they want. They focus more on what they *don't* want than on what they do want. Ask people what they want and they'll usually start detailing everything they don't want: "I'm sick of living paycheck to paycheck." "I'm tired of my loveless marriage." "I hate my job." And because this is what they focus on most, they continue receiving exactly what they say they don't want. As James Allen wrote, "You are today where your thoughts have brought you; you will be tomorrow where your thoughts take you."

Unfortunately, most people are largely unconscious of their thoughts. Their minds run on autopilot. They're careless about what they allow to enter their minds. They passively watch TV and movies, listen to music, surf the Internet, and hang out with negative people—without understanding the impact all of these things have on their lives. In this unconscious state, people are essentially powerless to change their reality. They're sleepwalking through life. They're captives of the media and of circumstances. Furthermore, all of these actions program them to continue getting more of what they don't want.

To change our lives, we have to start not on our physical reality, but on our intangible thoughts. For as Albert Einstein said, "The world we have created is a product of our thinking; it cannot be changed without changing our thinking."

How the Law of Attraction and Belief Breakthrough Work Together

Our core beliefs from childhood *are* our most dominant, persistent thoughts. In fact, they are so dominant that they have been embedded into our subconscious mind, where they influence us on a daily and even momentary basis, whether we realize it or not. All of our life's results are based these core beliefs.

Using the Law of Attraction with belief breakthrough work helps us to change our dominant, persistent thoughts by changing our beliefs. The more powerful our core beliefs are, the more powerful our daily thoughts become, and the more we're able to attract into our lives.

Case Study: Amanda M. Heals Chronic Illness

Amanda tried to use the Law of Attraction to heal a chronic illness. When nothing happened, she concluded that it didn't really work. But she was missing critical information, which she discovered at a Limitless event in September 2016. Here is her story in her own words:

"I was sexually abused by several men from the age of two until twenty. I was a happy, shining, energetic child. I wanted attention and I wanted to be involved. My mother said people were enamored by me.

"Unfortunately, something about me seemed to attract the wrong kind of attention. Because of the abuse, I adopted the belief, 'I attract evil when I am in my brilliance.' I felt like I had to become unattractive. To do that, I developed a mystery chronic illness at the age of eight. I experienced debilitating migraines where I couldn't even see. My vision would go black.

Sometimes I would lose my hearing, and everything would sound like I was standing under a waterfall. These episodes could be triggered by anything: a vacuum, trash compactor, a light switch being turned on. They would last for two or three days.

"By the age of ten I could hardly stand on my own. I couldn't attend my eleventh birthday party. I stayed in a back room and could hear that people had arrived and were talking and having fun. But I was in too much pain to come out. I went to several doctors and took a lot of tests and none of them could figure out what was wrong with me.

"I lived like this for about twenty years before discovering the Law of Attraction. When I learned it, I was excited. I really believed it would work. So I started focusing on the thought, 'I don't want to be sick.' I ran this through my head all the time. But when nothing happened and my pain remained the same, I felt dejected. I thought either the law didn't work or I was doing it wrong.

"Several years later my daughter was born. Her pregnancy triggered many more deep symptoms for me. I became so sick I was bedridden. I couldn't even take care of myself and didn't have the energy to bathe regularly.

"I became really bitter. I thought, 'I've had my turn being sick. Why does this keep coming back?' I was barely surviving as a wife and mother. I basically gave up. I had a pulse but I wasn't really living.

"A friend gave me tickets to a Limitless event. At the event we talked about the Law of Attraction and how we attract what we focus on the most. What I hadn't realized before was that I had been focusing on what I *didn't* want, not what I actually wanted. I kept saying, 'I don't want it, I don't want it, I don't want it.' I didn't realize I was really cementing it inside myself. Of course I kept getting more of it!

"I further realized that I had put on a 'sick suit.' I had been using my illness as a protection against my deep childhood wounds from the abuse. It was my way to check out. I had been to years of counseling but this was my first realization of what I had been doing.

> *"To create power is like a magnet, this is true because this creative power operates like a magnet. Give it a strong clear picture of what you want and this creative power starts to work magnetizing conditions about you—attracting to you things, resources, opportunities, circumstances and even the people you need, to help bring to pass in your outer life what you have pictured."*
>
> –CLAUDE M. BRISTOL

"Along with my belief that I attract evil in my brilliance, I also uncovered a belief that I'm powerless. I changed both of those beliefs when I realized that I get to choose. I have power over my experience. I had been passively waiting for the Law of Attraction to just bring something to me, but I could make it happen for myself.

"I made the decision at the event that I was done with being sick and miserable. I chose to release my beliefs and symptoms and to become healthy. I woke up the next morning pain-free and energetic for the first time in as long as I can remember. Since then I've used a lot of visualization. As a child I had a super active imagination, but I lost it as I aged. I brought that back and began imagining myself healthy and free. I envisioned dancing, being strong, and stepping into my power.

"It's all manifesting so much faster than I ever thought possible. It's been like a switching on a light. I feel like me again. I've had minor symptoms since then, but they no longer control my life and I'm able to work through them and relieve them. The Law of Attraction really works! All I had to do was choose differently."

TAKE ACTION AND APPLY THE LAW OF ATTRACTION
Write down the top three things you want to attract in the areas of health, wealth, connection and power:
HEALTH
1
2
3

WEALTH
1
2
3

CONNECTION
1
2
3

POWER
1
2
3
Write or print out your list and post it in conspicuous places throughout your house where you'll see it every day.

CHAPTER 13

THE LAW OF ALIGNMENT

Everything we think, say, and do must be in alignment with what we want to manifest. When our beliefs and actions are out of alignment with truth, it creates pain and problems in our lives. The more closely our beliefs are aligned with truth, the greater power we have to manifest our creations.

We can't manifest what we want when our beliefs are misaligned with our desires. A person can say he wants to be a millionaire, but if deep down he believes he's not worthy of having money, it's never going to happen. Our beliefs must be pure, whole, and undefiled by contradictory beliefs and desires. We must be single-minded in order to gather the power we need to accomplish our goals and realize our vision.

> *"Live as if you were living already for the second time and as if you had acted the first time as wrongly as you are about to act now."*
>
> —VIKTOR FRANKL

Furthermore, our beliefs must be aligned with truth. We tend to assume our beliefs are truth, but this isn't necessarily the case—in fact, very often it's not. Truth is independent of belief. It is absolute, objective reality regardless of what we believe about it. Believing the earth is flat doesn't make it so, for example.

We lack power to the extent that our beliefs are false. The more aligned our beliefs are with truth, the greater power we have to manifest a positive, purposeful reality. False beliefs hamper our creative power and lead to poor and mixed results.

We're all limited by false beliefs in one way or another. Through the Law of Alignment, we have the consciousness and tools to overcome them.

In *Think and Grow Rich*, Napoleon Hill teaches that our brain is both a transmitter and receiver of energy. He says the subconscious mind is the "sending station," which broadcasts thought, and the creative imagination is the "receiving set," through which the energies of thought are picked up. Holding conflicting beliefs makes us transmit mixed signals, which can even stop transmission entirely. Conflicting thoughts essentially cancel each other out and obstruct the Law of Attraction.

Interestingly, although few people are truly aligned in their beliefs and desires, we have a natural instinct to be aligned. That instinct is cognitive dissonance, or the discomfort we feel when we hold conflicting beliefs, desires, or behaviors, which I detailed in Chapter 9. Essentially, cognitive dissonance is an awareness of misalignment.

Sadly, however, we tend to handle our cognitive dissonance and align ourselves in counterproductive ways. For example, suppose a person is torn by the desire to smoke and the fact that smoking is unhealthy. To eliminate the cognitive dissonance, he would have to align one with the other. In other words, either he'd have to stop smoking, or he'd have to convince himself that he can beat the odds or that smoking will be worth the cost. Most of us choose the latter.

Instead of leveraging cognitive dissonance to our advantage, we use it to justify misaligned behavior and self-deception instead. We fiercely defend our false beliefs because we can't bear the thought of being wrong. We can't stand not being consistent, so we'll do anything necessary to be consistent, even if it means deceiving ourselves and rejecting truth. We become very selective about our perceptions and see what we want to see in order to keep our false beliefs. Once we accept a false belief, all evidence points to that belief being true.

In this self-deceived state, we don't want to take responsibility for our own emotions, behavior, choices, and results. We play the victim card and blame other people and circumstances for our failures. We thus remain disempowered and unable to get what we truly want.

Misaligned people have given their power away through victimhood, blame, or negativity, or through simply not having a clear vision. No one can actually take our power from us. We simply relinquish our power and then point to people and circumstances as the reasons why we've done so. But in reality, our power is waiting for us to take back anytime we want it.

Think of a car that's out of alignment. If you take your hands off the steering wheel, it's going to veer off the road. You may have your GPS set to a particular destination, but if you let your misaligned car have its way, you'll never get there. You have to take control of the steering wheel. Even better, you can get to the root of the problem by taking your car in to the shop and getting it aligned so it's easier to steer. Being misaligned in our beliefs is like driving a misaligned car with our hands off the steering wheel. It's no wonder we can't arrive at our desired destination!

> *"We have been taught to believe that negative equals realistic and positive equals unrealistic."*
>
> –SUSAN JEFFERS

The real challenge with this law is that most of our misaligned desires and contradictory beliefs originate in our subconscious mind. So most people aren't even aware of their existence, let alone aware of how to conquer them.

Getting into alignment all comes down to one thing: engaging in regular belief breakthrough work.

How the Law of Alignment and Belief Breakthrough Work Together

The Law of Alignment helps us bring our hidden, subconscious beliefs into the light because of the principle of cognitive dissonance. As we become more conscious about what we want, and then focus our conscious thoughts on our goals and dreams, any beliefs that contradict them are brought to the surface.

For example, suppose you want to increase your income from $60,000/year to $150,000, but subconsciously, you don't believe you're worthy of it. Your goal and your belief can't co-exist—either you have to change your goal to align with what you believe you're worthy of, or you have to change your belief to enable your dream to come true. As you leverage the Law of Attraction, that subconscious belief of unworthiness will be brought to the surface, and you'll be able to purge and replace it through belief breakthrough work. This is the Law of Alignment in action.

Case Study: Amanda S. Quits Smoking

Amanda had a breakthrough experience when she attended her first Limitless event, in which she had a breakthrough experience. This is her story, in her own words:

"I started smoking at age fourteen. I'm thirty-five now, and I can't tell you how many times I've tried to quit smoking. I've tried medication, hypnosis, fake cigarettes, you name it. My husband and I almost got divorced because he hates the smell. To mask the smell on my clothes, I would smoke in a robe, which I would carry with me everywhere. I even had cancer a few years ago and I smoked right through it. Every time I tried to quit something would bring me back to cigarettes.

"It's frustrating to me because I feel like such a hypocrite. I'm in a network marketing organization that promotes health products, and here I am smoking. I've also been in personal development for over fifteen years. I've studied with many mentors. I knew I needed to change, but I just didn't know how to do it.

"A friend of mine told me about Limitless and I agreed to go. However, I went with a very skeptical mind. I thought, 'What's he going to tell me that I haven't already heard?'

"I slowly opened up, however, as I could tell that there was something different here. Kris made a statement that you can change anything if you are in alignment with your beliefs. It got me thinking that just maybe this could be the way out of smoking for me. Wouldn't it be cool if I could actually quit for the last time?

"Kris took me through the belief breakthrough process. The number one limiting belief that came up for me was, 'No matter what I do, I can't quit smoking.' Next, he asked me to think of the first memory that came up when I had that thought. I remembered being caught smoking by my mother when I was fourteen or fifteen. She got really mad and grounded me. I thought it was strange because she smoked. The hypocrisy made me really angry.

"I realized that in that moment I made the decision that I make bad choices because I make them. Meaning, I own my choices. They're mine to make, so I'm okay with them. That decision didn't serve me well. I got into a lot of things I shouldn't have growing up.

"I changed my belief to, 'I choose to make good choices.' A couple weeks later, I wrote in my journal, 'I am a nonsmoker. I am putting it out there and making it real and believing it.'

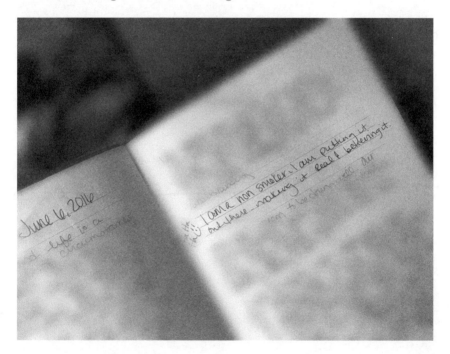

"I was halfway joking, but I could really see the possibility. A couple weeks after that I got down to my last cigarette. I didn't buy another pack, and I haven't since.

"It's the strangest thing to me that I can't explain. I went from smoking at least a pack and a half a day to quitting cold turkey. I have no emotional connection to cigarettes. I've had no cravings or withdrawals. I even bought some e-cigarettes and carried them around like a crutch. I haven't needed them at all.

"It's also catalyzing major changes in every aspect of my life. I started going to the gym and hired a personal trainer. I've lost weight. And my husband loves that I no longer stink like cigarette smoke!

"Most importantly, I've stopped being a hypocrite. The Law of Alignment has really come true for me. Once you make a decision and it aligns with who you are and what you believe, your whole world will change. It's like when you throw a stone into a pond—you never know what the ripples will do when they hit the shore."

TAKE ACTION AND APPLY THE LAW OF ALIGNMENT

Commit to going through the belief breakthrough script every day for thirty days and witness your life transform.

CHAPTER 14

THE LAW OF CHOICE AND ACCOUNTABILITY

We are solely responsible for the results in our lives. Regardless of outside influences or circumstances, we can always choose what we think and what we do, and we are accountable for the results that we create because of it. While we cannot always control what happens to us, we can choose how we perceive it and how we respond. The more accountability we take for our reality, the greater power we have to change it.

Our perception of reality is a choice, not a condition. Our experience in life is our creation, whether we realize it or not. If we want something to change in our lives, we have to take accountability for it instead of blaming other people or circumstances.

This law gets us out of victim mode, where we're stuck and powerless. We're held hostage by negativity. We whine that life won't cooperate with our idea of fairness. We're in a constant argument with reality, believing that things should be different than they are.

"Men are often capable of greater things than they perform. They are sent into the world with bills of credit, and seldom draw to their full extent."

—SIR HUGH WALPOLE

We are creating life every moment. Life isn't happening to us—we are responsible for our life. We are the authors of our story. We can author our story either consciously or unconsciously. Unconscious creation—allowing our subconscious negative beliefs to determine our results—leads to mediocrity and misery. Conscious Creation, on the other hand, leads to a fulfilling life. Conscious Creators create their world just the way they want it to be. And until we accept that we are responsible for everything we create, we will lack the power to create our ideal life.

The law doesn't mean that we have the power to choose everything that happens to us. In fact, most of what happens to us is completely out of our control. We can't control the weather, the economy, or natural disasters. We can't control whether or not other people drink and drive and crash into us on the freeway. We can't control whether or not we get a terminal disease.

This law isn't about transcending reality—it's about accepting reality as it is, and choosing our *response* to reality. We can choose to be angry by events, circumstances, and the choices of other people, or we can choose to see the gift in them and learn from them. We have the undeniable power to choose to interpret events and circumstances with empowerment rather than victimhood.

"If you haven't the strength to impose your own terms upon life, you must accept the terms it offers you."

–T.S. ELIOT

Victimhood is a choice, not a condition. Victimhood limits our Conscious Creation and gives our power away. If we've been wronged by another person—no matter how severe the offense—and if we hold tightly to the hurt and offense, we've ironically given our power to that individual. Fear is also a choice, not an inevitable condition. Yes, fear comes naturally to human beings. But that doesn't mean we have to be enslaved by it.

We make decisions based on our perceptions. And if our perceptions are flawed and disempowering, how can we ever make wise decisions that lead to true success, wealth, and security? And how can we ever refine our perceptions if we never analyze them consciously?

As Viktor Frankl so poignantly taught in *Man's Search for Meaning*, there is a space between stimulus and response. We don't have to be captive to automated responses. Unconscious people waste their lives whining that their failures are not their fault. They'd rather absolve themselves of guilt and live a life of mediocrity than take responsibility and live a life of greatness. But to be a Conscious Creator means to live and choose from that space between stimulus and response, between events and reaction.

How the Law of Choice and Accountability and Belief Breakthrough Work Together

There's a common tendency to blame other people or circumstances for the limiting beliefs we've accepted. "I can't trust men because of how my father treated me." "I'll never be healthy because my mother got me addicted to sugar and processed foods." "I can't make more money because of what I was taught by my parents."

But until we accept that *we* have created our beliefs based on our interpretations of events, we will never have the willingness or ability to change them. Changing any belief is predicated upon the fact that we are the creators of our beliefs. What people have done to us is their responsibility; the beliefs we've created about what they did to us is *ours*. We can't change something for which we don't take ownership and accountability. Taking accountability for our beliefs is the first step to changing them.

If we haven't yet taken accountability for our beliefs, doing belief breakthrough is one of the best ways to do so. Implicit in belief breakthrough is the assumption that we are the creators of our beliefs; otherwise, we would have no power to change them.

Case Study: Michelle Gets Released from Prison

Michelle is a member of our Limitless "tribe" with a heart-wrenching and amazing story. This is her experience with the Law of Choice and Accountability in her own words:

"In 2006 I was twenty-three years old. I was married with two sons, twenty-two-month-old James and six-month-old Hunter. Up until that point I had done everything 'right.' Life had been easy and happy. I believed that because of how good I had lived, I deserved certain blessings. In my mind, life should work out according to my blissful expectations.

"All that was shattered when my oldest son James fell out of a second-story window and was gravely injured. After he fell, it took him about five hours to die. In that time I pleaded with God for a miracle. In fact, I felt entitled to one because of my 'good' life. But it didn't happen.

"I was beyond devastated. When he died, I died with him and my bed was my casket. I fell into a deep, dark depression and spent the next five years mostly in bed with the covers over my head. I hid from the world. I was racked with anger, resentment, bitterness, and hatred toward God, myself, and everyone who couldn't take the pain away. I felt like I was in an emotional prison. I was like a black hole, a vacuum for light. No light could escape because I was so inward focused.

"After five years of that, I couldn't take any more. I wanted to commit suicide. I told God I was done. More precisely, I told Him that I was either done, or I needed to learn how to live again. A glimmer of light peeked through my darkness. I would visualize a ladder and climbing one step at a time out of that black hole.

"I made a promise to God, myself, and the world that I was going to figure out how to be happy again, and I wouldn't stop until it happened. And I wouldn't settle for anything less than complete joy.

"The first thing I tried was to have fun every day. But after about two weeks of that I realized that I could be completely miserable while having 'fun.' It didn't provide true joy and it wasn't sustainable.

"Then, God taught me that to be happy I must find a way to make somebody else happy. I was praying for release from my prison one day and God said, 'Go find somebody to serve.' I walked out of my bedroom and into my living room. I looked out the window and saw that my neighbors had tall weeds in their front lawn. So I grabbed my lawnmower and pushed it over to their house. They didn't speak English. They looked at me like I was nuts and I said, 'Please just let me mow your lawn.' I did it and to this day they don't know how much I needed that opportunity.

"I also created a little pass-along card that said, 'You've been a victim of a random act of kindness. Pass it on!' I would use it in really simple ways. I'd buy people ice cream cones at McDonald's and give them a card, or pay for someone's dessert at a restaurant and have the waiter give them the card.

"The second principle I learned was gratitude. It sounds cliché but my goal became to find something to be grateful for every day. I started a gratitude journal and would write down everything. I realized I needed to train my brain to think and feel a different way. It wasn't something that was going to just magically happen. I needed to be the one to choose something different and to implement new actions.

"Another thing I did was to look at myself in the mirror every time I started crying. I would smile and make funny faces at myself until it made me laugh. I still do it to this day because it's so therapeutic for me.

"Everything was going great. I wasn't 100 percent, but I had improved dramatically. Then, I was hired to be a destination wedding photographer in Yorkshire in London. I was so excited! I felt like God had been slamming doors for me for so long, and finally one had been opened for me.

"I made my preparations and flew across the ocean. When I arrived in the U.K., an agent asked for my paperwork. I gave him what I had and he said it wasn't right and that they would need to detain me and ask me some questions. I was detained for seven hours at the airport. They took my picture and fingerprints. They finally came back and said they had determined that I was not an 'authentic visitor' and they were sending me back to the U.S. Yet another door being slammed in my face, I thought.

"We are all faced with a series of great opportunities brilliantly disguised as impossible situations."

–CHARLES R. SWINDOLL

"They told me they were going to take me to a facility. I was thinking it would be a lousy hotel. But when a prison vehicle showed up, I realized I would be held in a jail. They escorted me to a cell, with bars on the windows and a small cot, and the door slammed shut. I was left alone.

"I broke down. I told God, 'I'm done. I refuse to find the silver lining in this. When is it my turn to get a silver platter?' But I also said something else: 'If you need me to keep learning, I will.' That simple thought broke down all my defenses. In that moment I chose to put my life into God's hands and said, 'Whatever you need me to learn and do, I will choose it. I will submit to whatever you need me to go through.'

"It created such a freedom to realize that I'm not in control of my life but I can trust in God and trust that He knows what's best for me. I had fought against every source of opposition I had experienced, and in submission I found freedom from bondage.

"As I submitted I felt God say to me, 'Now I can work with you.' I realized that even though I was literally locked up I had all the freedom in the world to learn from the experience and choose how I was going to react. My jail experience was the greatest silver lining of all.

"I tell people now that adversity is God's university. Our tribulations are just our education, and our trials are just our tests. God is our mentor. My son died from an accident, but it was not an accident that he died. I did receive a miracle—but it wasn't for him to live, but for me to live through his death."

TAKE ACTION AND APPLY THE LAW OF CHOICE AND ACCOUNTABILITY
Ground and ask this question: What are the top five things in my life for which I have not taken responsibility? Write down your answers:
1
2
3
4
5
After you make the list, correct your past choices and beliefs and shift into alignment by taking appropriate action.

CHAPTER 15

THE LAW OF GESTATION

There is a natural gestation period for all acts of creation—the bigger the goal, the longer the gestation period. Just like seeds that take time to grow before they yield fruit, our dreams and goals must be nurtured and cared for over time until they are manifested into reality. Patience and perseverance allow for dreams to become reality.

All acts of creation manifest in their own time. When something doesn't manifest on our schedule, it means we have a false expectation and we're out of alignment with truth. In that case, either the creation itself needs more time or we haven't become who we need to become in order to be worthy of the creation.

The gestational period applies both to the creation itself as well as to the creator. For the creation to manifest, the creator must become equal to the creation.

The gestation period serves two purposes. First, it gives us time to take the practical steps required to achieve the vision. And second, it proves that we'll pay the price. Anything worth truly manifesting is worth trading time and effort to achieve.

If your dream is worth achieving, then you need the staying power to stick with it regardless of time or obstacles. Most people fail at great ideas because they want it all to happen now. They're not willing to pay the proper price for their dream. With the right expectation, you can stick to the effort required to gestate and birth your creation.

The gestation period for mice is twenty days. A human baby takes nine months. For elephants, it takes twenty-two months. This is a simple way to visualize the truth that the bigger your goal, the longer the required gestational period.

Many people get discouraged when they create an expectation of when something should manifest, and it doesn't manifest on their expected time schedule. The truth is that we're not that great at guessing accurately the required gestational period for acts of creation. Others see the long, hard road ahead of them. They have a sense of how much time it will take. So instead of nourishing their vision with small, consistent actions, they freeze up and that vision dies in the womb.

What would happen if an expecting mother were to somehow take a break from making her baby for a day? The fetus could be harmed, or even die. Similarly, we kill our dreams when we take a break from gestating by investing in counterproductive thoughts, believing in counter-evidence, or doubt the viability of our creation.

This is an unfolding process. You just take action today, without knowing how it will develop exactly. One step leads to another. Doors open up that you didn't even see before. You follow your bliss and meet people, form new relationships. These open even more doors. Small, consistent actions in the right direction are the key. You have to trust the process, and you have to persevere.

You have no way of knowing the gestation period of your creation until you get there. You get to learn to become present and take your creation one day at a time. It's arrogant to think we can take everyone else's free will and all other circumstances into account and create an accurate expectation for something we have never done. Creation and living limitless is all about stepping into results and creations you have never manifested. You get to master being present, patient and at peace to create space for your creation to manifest.

There are ways to quicken the gestation period—for example, the purer your beliefs, the shorter the gestation period. The more consistent you are with your belief breakthrough and alignment work, the less you impede the gestation period, and the more you allow things to manifest on the perfect timetable. Remember that the gestation period is about creating yourself as much as it is about manifesting your vision into physical reality.

Suppose you want to become a millionaire, but you have thirty false beliefs preventing you from doing so. Changing one of those false beliefs will not manifest a million dollars overnight. In this case, during the gestational period you will need to change every false belief that prevents you from achieving your goal. Perhaps these beliefs include, "Money is the root of all evil," or, "Rich people are unethical," and so on.

Christ spoke of having the faith of a mustard seed. A mustard seed, if planted today, does not bear fruit tomorrow. It first manifests as a tiny sprout. That sprout grows into a bigger plant with its first leaf and so forth. The mustard seed

"Genius is eternal patience."

–MICHELANGELO

has faith that it will unfold as it was meant to, all in its own time, and you must have the same faith in your vision and yourself.

As you work toward your purpose and uproot your false beliefs, you'll start seeing evidence that something is happening, but at first you will not see fruit. You must continue the journey. Improvement does not always manifest in immediate achievement. The seeds of success you plant today must be cultivated and nourished over time. Achievement is often made up of months, years, even decades of trying and failing and manifesting small results one at a time, until eventually your greatest creations grow to fruition and bear fruit.

One critical key to applying the Law of Gestation is to learn the right lessons along the journey. As we set out to achieve any goal, we either achieve the goal or we don't. But even if we don't achieve the goal, with the right mindset we can learn valuable lessons and, in effect, still be successful as a result. If we learn the right lessons, we gain wisdom that can help us the next time we set out to achieve something.

Consider the diagram on the following page, which I refer to as the "Results and Lessons of Success" quadrant:

	RESULT ACHIEVED	RESULT UNACHIEVED
LEARNED LESSON	**SUCCESS** Lessons & Results	**SUCCESS** Lessons
UNLEARNED LESSON	**SUCCESS** Results	**VICTIM STORY**

In quadrant one, the upper left, you get your desired result and you learn valuable lessons. This is a success by any measure.

In quadrant two, the lower left, you achieve your result but you don't learn any new lessons. This is still a success.

In quadrant three, the upper right, you don't achieve the desired result but you still learned the right lessons from the experience. This is still a success!

The problem comes in quadrant four, where we neither get our result nor learn the right lesson from the experience. In this quadrant, we become a victim of our failed attempt. We blame ourselves, others, or both. We see nothing redeeming about our experience. You interpret your failure as evidence that if you try, you will fail.

Whatever you do, do not get stuck in that quadrant! It's too easy to be in one of the other quadrants and to choose success by either achieving your desired result, learning valuable lessons, or both.

How the Law of Gestation and Belief Breakthrough Work Together

Applying the Law of Gestation takes patience. Belief breakthrough is one of the most effective ways to cultivate the patience necessary to manifest great things.

As our dreams and goals are in the process of manifesting, it can be very tempting and easy to interpret events in negative ways. "The deal fell through; it must not be meant to be." "He won't even take my call. I'll never be able to make that connection." "My business failed. I'm doomed to fail."

But as challenging events arise, we can use belief breakthrough work to find the lessons and create beliefs that continue building our faith and patience through the gestation period. "The deal fell through; when it happens, it will be even better than it was structured." "He won't even take my call. What an excellent chance to build my perseverance!" "My business failed. Look at all the lessons I learned in the process! I'm so much closer to success now."

Managing and improving our beliefs through the gestation period keeps us motivated and on track.

Case Study: Heilala Goes to Japan

I first met Heilala at a Limitless event. She had a major life goal that, deep down, she didn't think would ever be possible. But it happened much sooner and in a way she never would have expected. Here is here story in her own words:

"I saw my first anime movie in 2009, and I fell in love. That, and my love for sushi gave me a bit of an obsession with Japan. Ever since then I have wanted to visit Japan. In fact, I would move to Japan if I could.

"Several years later my husband attended a Conscious Creator event with Kris Krohn. After that event he and I sat down and started talking about our goals and writing them down. Going to Japan was at the top of my list. I even went and got my passport to get the ball rolling. I did some research on flights and other details, and for a family of five it was just too expensive. It didn't look like it was going to happen, at least not any time soon. So I pushed it to the side. I had it on my vision board, but I didn't actively work on it because it just seemed so far away.

"In September of 2015 my husband and I were at a retreat with a friend who goes to Japan every year. We talked a long time with him about it. As we were talking I kept hearing a voice in the back of my head saying, 'It's never going to happen. It would take a huge miracle.' After that conversation I felt deflated and kind of gave up on the idea.

"But then in October I attended the Limitless seminar. I had some major breakthroughs and something ignited within me. I wrote down my list of goals again, this time believing they would be possible. Again, Japan was at the top of my list. But I still didn't know how I was going to make it happen. I started doing belief breakthrough every day. I zeroed in specifically on beliefs that would prevent me from achieving my dream of visiting Japan. I felt like I was not worthy of receiving my dream, so I worked hard to change that belief in myself.

"I attended the next Limitless event in November. This time, I brought my friend who regularly visits Japan with me. During the event he told me he was looking for someone to go with him in the spring and asked if I'd be interested. He teaches hula dancing in Japan and, since I am a Polynesian dance instructor, he wanted me to come and help him teach. Of course, I was ecstatic and eager to go. We discussed flight and hotel costs. It was a lot cheaper than if I were to go with my family, but still a bit much for me.

"I kind of left it hanging. I was afraid that if I pursued it too hard, the opportunity would disappear. A couple months later, in January of 2016, I sat down one day and wrote down all my goals along with a detailed plan for how to achieve each of them. I set a goal to visit Japan that year. The very next day my friend randomly called me. He told me that if I could go, he would pay for everything. Furthermore, he would pay me $1,000 for helping him teach dance lessons.

"I discussed it with my husband and he told me to go. Everything aligned just perfectly. We went in April and spent a week there. Everything was paid for and they treated us like royalty. We ate at all the best restaurants. It was everything I had dreamed of and more. It was one of the best, most memorable experiences of my life. What's more, it's looking like I will be able to do the same trip every year.

"This was a lesson in timing for me. For the many years that I had my goal, things would keep coming up to get me engaged in the goal again, and then nothing would happen. The timing had to be just right.

"And what enabled the timing was belief breakthrough work. Had the opportunity arose before I learned that, I would not have been able to go—not because I was any different, but because I had to give myself time to work on my beliefs. He had multiple opportunities to invite me but didn't until the time was right. I needed to prepare myself, and when I did, the timing fell into place just perfectly."

TAKE ACTION AND APPLY THE LAW OF GESTATION
1. Journal about a time you set out to accomplish something and did. In hindsight, what meaningful lessons did you learn about yourself that enabled you to succeed?
2. Now think of a goal from the past that you set but didn't achieve and felt a sense of failure about it.
• Make a list of any false beliefs you have reinforced from not achieving your goal.
• Make a corresponding list of new beliefs that will help you.
• What meaningful lessons are you learning in your attempts to achieve the goal?
• What new beliefs do you get to instill about gestation, patience and perseverance to create the necessary space to achieve your goal?

CHAPTER 16

THE LAW OF FAITH

Faith is the foundation to all actions leading to creation. Without faith we have no power to act. As Conscious Creators, we work with complete faith to manifest our desires. We act on that faith with courage, without requiring evidence from our past.

Conscious Creators work with complete faith that they can manifest their desires, and they act on that faith with courage, despite having little or no evidence from their past accomplishments. In fact, they have the ability to move forward with confidence in spite of any counter-evidence.

Conscious Creators understand that they have the power to manifest anything in which they have complete faith. Note that faith can work either for or against us. People who believe they're fat and put faith in that belief will develop conscious and unconscious behaviors that will surely manifest fatness. Whatever you put your faith in can manifest. Therefore, Conscious Creators are vigilant about what they choose to put their faith in.

This law gives power to the Law of Attraction. It's about more than just thinking about your goals. *It's believing with unwavering faith that you will achieve them, long before you achieve them.*

Everything a Conscious Creator manifests was not there beforehand. Conscious Creators know that all new, improved, or expanded creations will be manifestations that previously never existed. They have faith in their truth—that it will manifest without any evidence, other than the fact that they have manifested intentionally before. Conscious Creators know they can manifest anything they choose to believe.

Unconscious creators operate from the perspective of "I'll believe it when I see it." Conscious Creators operate from the opposite perspective: "I'll see it when I believe it."

Many people struggle with this law. It sounds crazy and even scary. "You want me to imagine making $200,000 a year when the most I've ever made is $60,000?" "You want me to imagine speaking on stage when I'm terrified of public speaking?" Nothing new has ever been created unless someone first believed it was a reality even before it was created.

The idea of going through life hoping that something will become true but without actually *believing* that it will keeps you stuck in the Catch-22. To create new results, you have to believe in something you've never accomplished. You have to live with it in your mind as if it has already been fully manifested. You have to feel the full range of emotions as if your goal is already reality. This is the process of bringing the ethereal into material.

When you upgrade your belief system, you'll have no prior evidence to back it up. You must act in courage and accept with complete faith that this new statement is your new truth. This creates a paradox in the mind because you have to hold space for a creation in your mind even though it does not yet exist in reality. Most people will not allow themselves to hold space for any paradox intentionally. A masterful Conscious Creator has the faith to easily hold space for the paradox of what they desire until it manifests.

In the following graph you can measure what kind of space must be held for a paradox, based on whether your creation manifests quickly, slowly, or erratically. The white area in the graph represents the evidence and results that show your progress. The grey area represents the difference from your present reality to where you want to be—the area where we need faith in order to see our desire manifested.

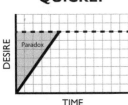

MANIFESTING QUICKLY

DESIRE / TIME

Paradox

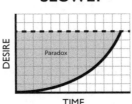

MANIFESTING SLOWLY

DESIRE / TIME

Paradox

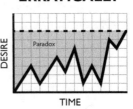

MANIFESTING ERRATICALLY

DESIRE / TIME

Paradox

Ultimately, you are taking the future you are creating and bringing it into the present. Your goal is to hold space for the paradox as your goal or dream moves from the ethereal to the material—whether your creation is large or small, or will take a small amount of time or decades. Holding faith in the creation is like using machines to manually pump lifeblood into your creation until it is viable to breathe and live on its own.

Everything you want to create in your life isn't there yet. You're going to create new beliefs that are going to feel like a lie, because you have no prior evidence of their being manifested in your life. The secret is that you must move forward in faith, despite the lack of evidence. You must move forward believing with courage that it is your new truth—and taking action on the new belief, despite the fact that it hasn't been your belief before now.

Living the Law of Faith requires commitment. Conscious Creators look at an acorn and see a forest, then act with diligence to make that forest come to pass. They commit time, energy, money, and other resources to projects, without any external guarantee that those projects will pay off. Their faith manifests their vision.

Speaking of vision, that's the fundamental discipline of this law: consistently visualizing your desired outcome. High-performing athletes use this technique all the time. I recently had an opportunity to visit Kenya. High up in the mountains of Africa where the air is thin, overlooking Kenya's Great Rift Valley is a village referred to as the "Village of Champions." Some of the best runners in the world have come from this town.

"A committed person paints a picture of a possible future and then works to bring that picture to life. They see it before it happens. They believe it before it's true. And they take action."

–ROY H. WILLIAMS

I got to race a 5K against seventy of their fastest runners. The fastest I have run a mile on a treadmill was 4:50. But in the heat of the sun and in that elevation, I got worked. Within the first fifteen seconds I felt like a pack of cheetahs had blown by me. Within the first minute they were all completely out of sight. I came in dead last.

After the race I met Asbel Kiprop, who has won three world championships in the 1500-meter race and who was at the village at the time. I asked him and his friends about their training. They train three times a day. But Asbel told me that the mental training is just as important, if not more so, than the physical. Along with their physical training, they also have a regimen of imagining how fast they are, imagining their time, and seeing themselves winning.

The human imagination is more powerful than I think any of us realize. Tapping into it even to a small degree will revolutionize your life. If you rely on your five senses alone, you'll do only what you've seen done before. You'll never take the leap into uncharted territory. The key is having absolute, doubtless faith.

This is one major reason why unconscious creators can never manifest what they want: They don't actually have faith that they can get what they want. The frequency of desire they transmit with their thoughts is canceled out by their frequency of disbelief.

So make the choice! Choose to either believe in what you want that has not shown up yet, or choose to believe in what currently is. Your choice will determine your future.

How the Law of Faith and Belief Breakthrough Work Together

Nothing kills faith more than false and limiting beliefs. For your faith to be unwavering, your beliefs must be pure. The more aligned with truth your beliefs are, the greater faith you will have.

There's a mutually-supportive relationship between our faith and our beliefs. The stronger the faith we cultivate, the more our beliefs are elevated and purified. And the more we elevate and purify our beliefs, the more our faith naturally increases.

Case Study: Julie Finishes Her Painting

Julie had a vision of a painting. But she didn't know how to do it. She used the Law of Faith and it all unfolded in a miraculous way over thirteen years. Here is her story in her own words:

"I've been painting since before I was two years old. I have been blessed to attend over eight years of art school and receive instruction from some of the best. I am a well-trained artist, yet there are many techniques. I will always be learning.

"I was listening to the Bible one day and I heard the part in Luke chapter 22 when Christ was in the Garden of Gethsemane and he fell on his face and prayed and an angel and strengthened him. I saw a painting in my mind of this scene and got excited about it. I could see it so clearly.

"I had no idea what I was getting myself into. There are many techniques in art. I was anxious to see the finish of this piece, so I prayed to know what method of painting to use. I didn't get an answer, so I went to an art museum to check out painting methods.

"While I was there, I met a friend who is also an artist. He told me he had a feeling he needed to teach me a specific method of painting called 'Verdaccio.' He told me about it, and I went to the library and found a book about it. I had never used this technique.

"I went home and took a nap. I dreamed I was painting in this technique. After my nap I was awake for a while then felt sleepy. Again, I dreamt of that technique. In the middle of the night I woke up looked at a painting on my wall and thought, 'Oh, that's Verdaccio.' Then I went back to sleep and the rest of the night again dreamt of this technique. By morning I had a pretty good understanding of this method of painting, having dreamt about it three times.

"As I worked on painting the face of Christ one morning, I became frustrated with my inability to paint what I could clearly see in my mind. It was 5:00 a.m. I knelt down and prayed for help.

"I became sleepy and had another dream. In the conclusion of the dream I had a significant moment. I was standing on the catwalk above a very tall velvet red theatre curtain and a voice told me to climb down it and then I would be where I wanted to be. I emphatically replied, 'I can't; I will die!'

"The words I heard in response were imprinted into my soul: 'Don't you get it? If I tell you you can do it, you can.' I grabbed onto the curtain and to my surprise the curtain wrapped itself around me as if it was alive. Wrapped in the safety of the curtain, I slid down to my freedom. 'Don't you get it? If I tell you you can do it, you can.' That voice has never left me since, and it has sustained me in my journey.

"I continued studying the painting technique and working on my painting over the course of many years. First it was the book. Then it was the video instruction. Then a dear friend who took from the master of this technique taught me for free for two years.

"One day a woman came into the art store where I worked. She had a ticket to attend a very expensive two-day workshop taught by the master who teaches this technique, not just all over the United States, but also in Italy where he grew up and first learned it. It was the very same technique I had been studying. She said, 'Would anybody like a free ticket?' I took the ticket and was able to study under this master and learn things I could not receive from other sources.

The process of learning this technique was about seven years from start to finish. It is Leonardo DaVinci's technique learned from studying the notes he wrote upside down, backwards, and in Italian. It's the same technique he used to paint the Mona Lisa.

"From the very beginning I knew exactly what the painting looked like. I visualized it constantly throughout the process. There were times when I couldn't see specific details, but they would be revealed to me as I kept at it. For example, I knew what the nose should look like but I did not have access to a model with the right structure. So I sculpted models, I looked at magazines and sculptures still not being able to create the right lighting. After prayer, miraculously I was lead to a man who had the perfect nose, during a store fire drill where I had to sit outside momentarily. I looked up at the custodian and his nose was perfect. Gathering all my courage I ask him to be the model for the nose. He agreed and told me he was use to modeling for his mother.

"I can't begin to tell you how many little miracles happened along the way. It took me thirteen years to finish this painting. What kept me going was the image I had in my mind of the finished painting, and that voice telling me, 'Don't you get it? If I tell you you can do it, you can.' When I was finished I fell on my face and cried. With the constant help of heaven, it was more profound than I had envisioned it. And so were the lessons I learned from its creation.

"This painting would not have materialized had I stopped. I titled the painting 'Commitment,' which speaks both literally to what Christ did for us, but also symbolically in what it means for us. You step into a journey and you have to finish it. That is where the beauty and the miracles come in. You trust that God will send angels to help you. You can do anything when you know heaven is behind you. There are always angels with you during your darkest moments, and it's usually people you know.

"If you don't have that vision of what you want to achieve, you can't do it until you can see it. You have to have that vision. If you can't see it, you have to spend some time sitting and meditating until you can see it. Once you see a picture in your mind, it's easy to paint. If you don't know how to do something, you just figure it out. You just take action and things fall into place. You keep moving forward and you'll be led to each next step along the way."

TAKE ACTION AND APPLY THE LAW OF FAITH

Decide on a goal that is important to you that you have not achieved yet. Make sure your goal is important enough to you that you would train any amount of time to achieve it.

Ground and visualize yourself as if your goal has been attained. Visualize until it feels real enough that you feel the emotions that accompany its completion.

Now that you have experienced the success in your mind, make the decision that your goal has already manifested.

As you live as if your goal has already been attained, continue visiting this visualization so that it is real in your mind while taking action and moving forward despite any evidence in your reality that it is not so. Live this level of commitment until your goal manifests.

Write down your goal here:

LIMITLESS

CHAPTER 17

THE LAW OF THE HARVEST

Our life is like a garden. We reap what we sow. Every word we speak, every thought we think, and every choice we make is a seed for creating our future. All results in our lives are the fruits that grow from our beliefs and the choices we make because of those beliefs. We can alter our results by altering the beliefs that bear them.

With the decline of local agriculture and the small family farm, vital knowledge has been lost in our culture. Specifically, we've forgotten the Law of the Harvest—that the harvest we experience in life is the direct result of the seeds we have planted.

We live in an age of shortcuts, quick fixes, and convenience. We want what we want and we want it now. We have very little concept of planting now to harvest later. Farmers know there's a natural rhythm to life, that nature is predictable, and that you can't cheat her.

Removed from nature as we are, we've forgotten these truths. We spend forty years of our lives cultivating the seeds of false beliefs about money, and then expect our money problems to be fixed with lucky breaks and lottery tickets. We procrastinate studying during school, then cram for the exams. We fill our bodies with processed junk, then expect pills to cure our diabetes, heart disease, and cancer. We indulge in selfishness and lust and are then surprised when our

"Did you ever consider how ridiculous it would be to try to cram on a farm—to forget to plant in the spring, play all summer and then cram in the fall to bring in the harvest? The farm is a natural system. The price must be paid and the process followed. You always reap what you sow; there is no shortcut."

–STEPHEN R. COVEY

marriages suffer. We rarely spend time with our children, and then try to buy their love at Christmastime.

Quick fixes may seem to work for a short time, but long-term they always fail. As Dr. Sidney Bremer observed in his book, *Spirit of Apollo*,

> Nature is evenly balanced. We cannot disturb her equilibrium, for we know that the law of Cause and Effect is the unerring and inexorable law of nature; but we do fail to find our own equilibrium as nations and as individuals, because we have not yet learned that the same law works as inexorably in human life and in society as in nature—that what we sow, we must inevitably reap.

If we want to change our results and boost our harvest, we have to tune out of advertising messages and pop culture and tune into nature. The fruit we harvest is the result of the seeds we have planted and the roots we have developed. When we are frustrated with our harvest (or lack thereof), we must consider our seeds and roots.

The quality and abundance of our fruit can never exceed the depth and maturity of our roots. Are your roots deep and mature enough? Are they giving your "tree" enough nutrients?

All seeds have in their DNA a set timeline for fruition. Therefore, faith, hope, persistence, and patience are our greatest allies in our quest for abundance.

In nature, all organisms bear fruit after their own kind. Plant an apple seed, and an apple tree grows. Plant a corn seed, and a corn plant grows. Likewise, human beings bear fruit after their own kind. Our fruit is the circumstances and results of our current life. The circumstances of our life now are the results of the seeds we have planted and roots we have developed in the past. The question isn't whether or not we're bearing fruit. The question is whether or not it's the fruit we want.

In Buddhism, the Law of the Harvest is referred to as karma. Karma is defined as "the universal law of cause and effect; the volition behind each action, which produces favorable or unfavorable results in the future." In his book *A Path with Heart*, Buddhist teacher Jack Kornfield explains,

Karma means that nothing arises by itself. Every experience is conditioned by that which precedes it…

To understand how to work with the karmic patterns in our life, we must see that karma has two distinct aspects—that which is the result of our past and that karma which our present responses are creating for our future. We receive the results of past action; this we cannot change. But as we respond in the present, we also create new karma. We sow the karmic seeds for new results.

How the Law of the Harvest and Belief Breakthrough Work Together

The most powerful way to change our future results is to change our beliefs. Our beliefs *are* the seeds that we plant that determine our harvest!

If we want a better, more fruitful harvest in life, we must learn to plant better seeds. This happens by uprooting the weeds of limiting beliefs and planting new, fruit-bearing beliefs in their place.

We can't plant crabgrass and expect to harvest peaches. Likewise, we can't plant the belief, "I'm not worthy to make money," and expect to harvest a million dollars.

Case Study: Jayson Breaks Through the $1 Million Barrier

Jayson is a member of the Limitless Inner Circle and a business owner. He's been trying for five years to get his business to make $1 million a year. He recently surpassed that mark after experiencing some major belief breakthroughs. Here is his story in his own words:

"I own an appliance repair franchise servicing two counties. I've been frustrated for years because other franchise owners in my company with the same population base earn over $1 million, but we haven't been able to break through that ceiling. We tried everything we could think of but kept falling short. Last year we fell short by just $30,000.

"When my wife and I came to Limitless and joined the Inner Circle, I had some major breakthroughs. I uncovered a lot of limiting beliefs I had created as a result of being abused by my adopted father as a child. I had put up walls and never let anyone get too close to me because I didn't feel safe. I had tons of self-doubt and a very negative view of the world and other people. As I changed my beliefs, I learned to open up. I learned to love myself and love others where they were. I let go of the hatred I held in my heart. I forgave myself for choices I've made in the past as a result of that hatred.

"These breakthroughs and insights started to have a clear and direct impact on the way I ran my business. Before, I would be very critical of my technicians. I always focused on the things they did wrong, instead of noticing what they did right. Because I didn't feel worthy myself, I projected that onto them and didn't feel like they were worthy either.

"Those seeds of negativity and criticism I planted had very real and tangible results on my business. Because my technicians didn't feel appreciated by me, they wouldn't put their heart into their work. Instead of selling customers on a job they would often just take a diagnostic fee and tell them to buy a new appliance. They were doing minimal work because they figured, 'I can't do it right anyway so why should I even try? If he's just going to complain about what I'm doing wrong, why should I even do the repair?'

"Without change, something sleeps inside us, and seldom awakens. The sleeper must awaken."

–FRANK HERBERT

"After my breakthroughs, I started focusing on the positive. I saw everything that people were doing right, and I complimented them often. Because of this shift, they're now eager to do jobs right the first time. They ask more questions. They call me if they're stuck with troubleshooting. They never used to call me. Now they call me all the time. They also open up and talk more to each other as a team. Whenever we encounter problems, we don't point fingers but instead we lift each other up. And now, when they do mess up, they own it.

"I've been amazed by how quickly things shifted after I replaced my seeds of self-doubt and criticism with self-confidence and praise. In less than a year we surpassed our goal and exceeded $1 million in revenues for the first time. Our harvest changed because I started planting different seeds."

TAKE ACTION AND APPLY THE LAW OF THE HARVEST

Consider your next creation. What results do you want to manifest that you have not created yet?

Journal a list of all the beliefs (seeds) you get to choose (plant) to make your desired outcome possible, with proper gestation.

Write down your beliefs:

CHAPTER 18

THE LAW OF PURPOSE

We all have our own unique purpose on this planet. Our desires and actions must be in alignment with our purpose and our sacred self to achieve our highest potential. Our sacred self embodies the highest, most accurate truth from which we can create at our greatest potential. Conscious Creators seek to know who they are and how to fulfill their purpose.

For you to achieve your highest potential, your desires and actions must be manifestations of your True Self and True Purpose. Your True Self embodies the highest, most accurate truth from which you can create at your greatest potential. Conscious Creators know who they are and what they were born to accomplish.

The Law of Purpose is based on three premises: First, that you were born for a specific reason. That there is an innate purpose to your life, unique to you.

Second, that your highest potential can be achieved only by aligning with your inborn purpose. As long as you're ignorant of or resistant to your calling, you will never feel satisfied or perform at full capacity.

Third, that following your bliss is the doorway to your unique path of purpose. Follow it to pursue those things that give you the highest and purest feelings of joy and satisfaction. Your bliss is like clues placed

> *"Everyone has his own specific vocation or mission in life; everyone must carry out a concrete assignment that demands fulfillment. Therein he cannot be replaced, nor can his life be repeated. Thus, everyone's task is unique as is his specific opportunity to implement it."*
>
> —VIKTOR FRANKL

strategically in your heart by your Creator. As you follow the trail of clues, not only do you become happy, but you also serve others better.

The Law of Purpose states that for you to achieve your highest potential, your desires and actions must be manifestations of your True Self and True Purpose. Your True Self is who you really are at your highest and deepest spiritual core, beyond ego, vice, and self-deception. Your True Self is your conscience; it gives you satisfaction when you do right and distress when you stray off your right path.

> *"Follow your bliss and don't be afraid, and doors will open where you didn't know they were going to be."*
>
> –JOSEPH CAMPBELL

Your True Purpose, then, is your True Self in action. It is manifested by the things that come naturally to you, the things that make you lose all sense of time doing them, the things you would do even if you never got paid a dime or if no one ever noticed, the things you can't *not* do, because they are so compelling and irresistible to you. It is who you were born to become. It is your exclusive combination of interests, passions, gifts, talents, values, knowledge, and skills leveraged to create value for others.

Simply put, this law says you need to know who you truly are and what you were born to do, and you need to follow that knowledge with commitment and integrity.

You don't have to have absolute clarity on your purpose in order to take action. You don't have to wait for the heavens to part and a choir of angels to sing while a voice reveals your purpose. It's something you can ask through intuition (see the next chapter) each day to uncover a little more. What you know about your purpose now is the perfect amount you need to fulfill it today. And I'll leave you with this clue: If you desire to retire, then you have not found your passion.

Our Gifts *and* Our Limits Point to Purpose

Despite our ability to choose, imagine, and create, we have to be clear on our gifts and realize our personal limitations. There is a common belief that we can do and become anything we want, if we're just willing to make the effort. That is simply not true, and this type of belief can be as misleading as limiting beliefs that hold your potential hostage.

Usain Bolt was born with specific physical capabilities, which enable him to be the fastest runner in the world. No matter how much I believe, and no matter how much effort I put into it, I can't transform my body to run like him. Steve Jobs, John Lennon, Ernest Hemingway, Pablo Picasso, and Mozart were each born with their own unique gifts that none of us can duplicate.

"Man's ideal state is realized when he has fulfilled the purpose for which he is born. And what is it that reason demands of him? Something very easy—that he live in accordance with his own nature."

—SENECA

Our purpose is defined as much by our gifts as by our limitations. In this sense, understanding our limitations is actually liberating, rather than constricting. It keeps us from doing things we don't enjoy, that aren't a full expression of our unique gifts and True Purpose. As author Parker J. Palmer explains in his book, *Let Your Life Speak: Listening for the Voice of Vocation,*

Each of us arrives here with a nature, which means both limits and potentials. We can learn as much about our nature by running into our limits as by experiencing our potentials. If we are to live our lives fully and well, we must learn to embrace the opposites, to live in a creative tension between our limits and our potentials. We must honor our limitations in ways that do not distort our nature, and we must trust and use our gifts in ways that fulfill the potentials God gave us.

There's only one you! Being limitless isn't about using the power of your thoughts to become someone or something you're not—it's to become the best and highest version of *you*. It's about maximizing your natural talents and gifts and manifesting them to their fullest expression.

How the Law of Purpose and Belief Breakthrough Work Together

One of the most common struggles people experience is trying to find their purpose. They don't have enough self-awareness or experience to see their gifts and how to apply them to create value for others.

One of the reasons for this is that their perception of themselves is clouded by false and limiting beliefs. How can you see that you have natural gift for investing if you carry the false belief, "I'm bad at managing money"? How can you recognize your natural talent for writing if you believe, "No one values what I have to say"?

When our purpose feels concealed, belief breakthrough is vital. It helps us to cleanse our lens of perception so that we can see ourselves more clearly. The more belief breakthrough work we do, the clearer our purpose becomes.

Case Study: Veteran Mitch Finds His Purpose

Mitch is a military veteran who found his purpose in belief breakthrough work. Here is his story in his own words:

"I served in the Army for a few years, including tours in Iraq from 2010 to 2011. After experiencing significant health issues, I came home with the label 'disabled veteran.' The struggle of veterans coming home and trying to reintegrate into life after combat is very real and personal to me.

"I attended my first Limitless seminar and was blown away by the belief breakthrough process. After the second day I realized how deeply the work was changing me, and I knew I had to take it to my brothers in the military. Twenty-two veterans are committing suicide every day because of struggles with PTSD, addictions, and integrating back into home life. It's all in reaction to their environment, what's going on in their minds, and their sense of hopelessness to change.

"So after getting home from Limitless, I sat down and started drawing out an intention. I wanted to take Limitless and the belief breakthrough process and adapt it to serve military families. I wanted to help the soldiers and spouses coming home to each other.

"When I made that intention clear, things just started happening. A friend of a friend on Facebook happened to see what I was doing. She reached out to me and told me she used to run a PTSD retreat. She had to close her doors because of failures, but I was able to interview her and find out what worked and what didn't. She mentored me on how to set up a non-profit to access government grants and get this message on military bases, where a corporation wouldn't be welcomed.

"The thing is to understand myself, to see what God really wants me to do, to find the idea for which I can live and die."

–SOREN KIERKEGAARD

"Then I started finding other people in alignment with this goal. More opportunities kept showing up. One gentleman reached out to me who used to be the vice president of the Boy Scouts organization. He had spent nineteen years in the non-profit world and knew all the ins and outs. We met several other families involved with Limitless who all shared the ambition to help veterans and their families, though they hadn't thought of using belief breakthrough to do so.

"I found myself leading this charge of this idea. Belief breakthrough has the ability to help with PTSD, disabilities, and the wounds that our soldiers and their families are carrying. Everything is a perfect structure to take it and really do some good.

"I personally owe so much to belief breakthrough. My first breakthrough was to realize that I'm a 'fixer.' I see problems and try to fix them—even when it hurts people's feelings. I haven't often been loving when offering advice. Through belief breakthrough, I'm learning to show love first before teaching. I now strive to never raise my voice.

"If a man hasn't discovered something that he will die for, he isn't fit to live."

–MARTIN LUTHER KING, JR.

"I use my Limitless wristband every day to keep myself in alignment with my purpose. My purpose is to be an expert in military family reintegration. We are currently forming the non-profit organization. We've built our team and have the board. We're writing our program so we can run it through the military as a treatment and reintegration process.

"I've gone through multiple integration processes myself. They were all 'death by Powerpoint.' They would just read presentations to us and never gave us any tools that we could really use in our daily lives. But belief breakthrough is something you can use to change any situation."

TAKE ACTION AND APPLY THE LAW OF PURPOSE
Ponder these five questions and journal as much information you can to gain clarity on your purpose:
1. Talents: What are my natural gifts and strengths?
2. Passions: What things bring me joy?
3. Freedom: If money were of no concern, what would I love to do?
4. Problems: What challenges have I overcome?
5. Service: Whom would I love to serve based on my abilities?

CHAPTER 19

THE LAW OF INTUITION

 We are infinite beings with access to limitless wisdom and insight. We can access this wisdom by listening through intuition to our sacred selves and to the divine.

There is so much we don't know. Our lack of knowledge, and the uncertainty it creates, can seem so daunting. This is particularly true when we're trying to make major decisions, and we don't know how things will turn out. We get stuck in "paralysis of analysis." Oftentimes, we fail to make a decision either way and thus remain stuck.

> *"I believe in intuitions and inspirations...I sometimes FEEL that I am right. I do not KNOW that I am."*
>
> **—ALBERT EINSTEIN**

To live a limitless life, you must become an expert decision maker. One of the keys of success correlates with the number of decisions you make. Successful people make way more decisions than unsuccessful people. If you wait for all the analytics, data, and factors to come before making a choice, you will never make enough choices to achieve your dreams.

The Law of Intuition is how we break free from vacillation and paralysis and make decisions with absolute, unwavering confidence. It is the key to accessing infinite storehouses of knowledge and wisdom. Success is a function of decision making. Poor decisions will get you further than indecision. Limited people are stuck and do not make enough choices to be successful. Belief breakthrough changes that.

We get stuck when we try to make decisions from our heads. Intuition is accessing higher truth and wisdom from our heart. The Law of Intuition says that the information we need to make the decisions that will best serve us is always present, always available at a moment's notice. We simply need to know how to tap into it.

The six steps for tapping into intuition are as follows:

1. Ground
2. Ask
3. Listen
4. Receive
5. Trust
6. Take Action

Step 1: Ground

Grounding means to clear your mind, get into a meditative state, and prepare space to receive information.

To get grounded, close your eyes. Breathe deeply. Completely fill your lungs, hold it for a moment, then release the air completely. Do this several times until you feel completely relaxed. Clear your mind of all thoughts. As thoughts arise, just let them go effortlessly. Get completely present with the moment, releasing all worries and anxiety about the past or the future.

Step 2: Ask

Once you're grounded, then ask the pressing question that you're struggling with. Is there something you want that you haven't been getting? Where are you blocked and stuck? Where would you like a breakthrough? You can ask your questions as "yes" or "no" or open-ended.

Here are some examples of possible questions to ask:

- "Should I accept that new position at work, or stay where I am?"
- "Should I invest this money/build this business?"
- "What is the number one limiting belief that is blocking my progress?"

- "Why am I reacting to this person or situation this way?"
- "What's my next step to make _____ happen?"

You can literally ask anything you want. So many people wear calluses on their knees in prayer asking these big questions. They think they have to wait a certain amount of time to receive an answer from God. I'm here to tell you that you can receive an *immediate* answer on *every* single question you have. The information is *always* available.

Step 3: Listen

Once you've asked your question, you're ready to receive an answer. Remember: This is not a logical process. We're not trying to think more clearly—we're transcending our thoughts completely. So you're not looking for the answer you think in your head; you're looking for the answer you feel in your heart.

Step 4: Receive

Answers can come very subtly, or very clearly and powerfully. It's the right answer, either way. Don't try to think your way to an answer. Just sit still and listen and feel. Even if it comes as the slightest leaning toward one path over another, that's your answer.

Step 5: Trust

As answers arise, grab onto the first thing that comes up. You're going to be tempted to doubt it, or say, "That can't be it." Don't do that. *Never* doubt intuition. Stop second-guessing yourself.

Step 6: Take Action

Finally, be willing to follow whatever answer that comes. This is how you prove that you're worthy of receiving inspiration. The more you follow intuition, the more in tune you'll become and the clearer and more immediate your answers will come. Conversely, the less you follow it, the less in tune you will be.

I live, breathe, and grow my business by this process. My companies have processed hundreds of millions in business, and this is my core operating system for making all decisions.

How the Law of Intuition and Belief Breakthrough Work Together

"Be brave enough to live creatively. The creative is the place where no one else has ever been. You have to leave the city of your comfort and go into the wilderness of your intuition. You cannot get there by bus, only by hard work, risking and by not quite knowing what you are doing. What you will discover will be wonderful; yourself."

–ALAN ALDA

The Law of Intuition plays a vital role in belief breakthrough work. It's how we identify false beliefs when going through steps two through four of the belief breakthrough process (Identify a Limiting Belief, Explore Your Memories, Identify the Deeper Limiting Belief). We ask our intuition to help us identify the number one belief limiting our results right now, and our intuition answers. We can trust that whatever arises is precisely what we need to work on. We continue trusting intuition as we dig deeper through our memories, then to find the deeper limiting belief.

Our logical mind can often get in the way of this process. It's critical that we trust our intuition—to feel more from our heart than think from our head. Intuition can give us much better insight into our limitations than logic can.

Case Study: Desiree Dodges a Bullet by Trusting Intuition

Desiree is a member of the Limitless tribe who learned the importance of trusting intuition in powerful way. Here is her story in her own words:

"When I was pregnant with my fourth child I started noticing issues with my body. I would experience blurred vision, numbness in my extremities, and other symptoms. I tried to just push them aside and ignore them.

"One night I was putting my son to bed when I suddenly had an overwhelming feeling that something was terribly wrong. I was a week away from my due date so again I tried to ignore it. I didn't want to be worried going into labor. But that feeling that something was wrong wouldn't go away.

"A week later I delivered a healthy baby. Everything went fine with the delivery. But that night, when I started falling asleep I would jerk awake gasping for air. I couldn't breathe and I felt very weak. I went to see the doctor about the symptoms I was experiencing. He automatically concluded it was postpartum depression and anxiety. I said it was different. I just knew. But he just laughed, prescribed Xanax, and sent me out the door.

"When you reach the end of what you should know, you will be at the beginning of what you should sense."

–KAHLIL GIBRAN

"This went on for quite a while. My symptoms were getting worse. On one occasion, I completely lost my vision for several minutes. I couldn't fall asleep. My memory started failing. I went to see the doctor again and told him I thought I had a brain tumor. He said, 'Desiree get real, you don't have a brain tumor.' None of my family or friends believed me either. They all thought I had lost my mind. I felt so alone. The feeling that I needed to take action continued to overwhelm me. I started eating a raw food diet because I didn't know what else to do.

"One day I was looking in the mirror and I noticed that my pupils were different sizes. I called my ophthalmologist and he said that could be a sign of something serious and ordered an MRI. The MRI showed a small cyst in my brain. The doctor said they'd just watch it to see if it grew. I said, 'No way. I've known for months that something is there. We're doing something about it now.'

"If the single man plant himself indomitably on his instincts, and there abide, the huge world will come round to him."

–RALPH WALDO EMERSON

"So I contacted a neurosurgeon. His test showed that the cyst was large and he said I needed to get it out. The surgery wasn't covered by my insurance and was going to cost me $80,000, and I didn't have that kind of money. So we did our best to raise funds. We couldn't raise enough and I became discouraged. But then intuition led me to a new doctor who was within my insurance network. We scheduled the surgery and he performed it. He later told me that the surgery felt miraculous. He said it was like my brain opened up to remove the cyst.

"This experience was such a confirmation to me to trust myself and my intuition. Throughout the process, I kept seeking outside approval. I wanted everyone to agree with me. I had this overwhelming feeling to act and no one believed me. What I learned is that only you know you. Only you can receive that inspiration or intuition for yourself. No one knew what I was experiencing. I didn't know how it was all going to work out. It really taught me to listen to intuition and to pay attention and not give up just because people don't believe me or tell me to do something else."

TAKE ACTION AND APPLY THE LAW OF INTUITION

Practice developing your intuition by asking the following questions using the six-step intuition process you learned above:

1. What is the number one limiting belief that has been holding me back?

Replace this with a new empowering belief:

2. What is an important question that has gone unanswered for a long time?

Ask what your next step is in relation to an active goal you are pursuing. Write down the answer you receive

THE LAW OF CONNECTION

Our ego creates separation through comparison and competition, and our sacred self recognizes that we are all one. We cannot hurt another without hurting ourselves; we cannot bless another without blessing ourselves. The shadow that we judge or the greatness we see in others is simply a reflection of aspects of ourselves. The more we live with unconditional love and acceptance for ourselves, the more we unconditionally love others.

In 1957, a Buddhist monastery in Thailand was being relocated. Along with everything else, a giant clay statue of Buddha had to be moved. While the monks were moving it, one of them noticed a crack in the statue. Concerned about damaging the statue, they decided to wait a day before continuing the move.

During the night, one of the monks checked on the statue, shining his flashlight over the entire Buddha. When his light swept over the crack, a glimmer of light reflected back at him. Curious, the monk got a hammer and chisel and chipped away the clay. As he knocked off piece after piece of clay, the Buddha got brighter and brighter. After hours of work, the monk was astounded to realize that the entire statue was solid gold.

> *"Rough diamonds may sometimes be mistaken for worthless pebbles."*
>
> —SIR THOMAS BROWNE

Historians believe the Buddha had been covered with clay by monks several hundred years earlier, before an attack by the Burmese army. The monks had covered the Buddha to protect it. All the monks were killed in the attack, however, so it wasn't until 1957 that the great treasure was discovered.

This story illustrates what happens inside each of us. As mindfulness teacher Jack Kornfield explains in his book, *The Wise Heart*, "In much the same way, each of us has encountered threatening situations that lead us to cover our innate nobility. Just as the [monks] had forgotten about the golden Buddha, we too have forgotten our essential nature. Much of the time we operate from the protective layer."

The protective layer is our ego. Underneath the ego lies the gold of our true self. Our essential nature is that we are priceless, precious, and enough. As spiritual teacher Deepak Chopra explains, "The ego is our self-image. It is not our true self. The ego camouflages our true self by labels, definitions, evaluations, analysis, masks, images, and judgment. The true self is the field of possibilities, creativity, intentions, and power. We can go beyond the ego through self-awareness—awareness of our thoughts, feelings, behaviors, and speech. Thus we begin to slowly move beyond the ego to the true self."

The greatest suffering caused by the ego is separation. When we operate from the ego, we see ourselves as separate and isolated from everyone and everything else. The ego is by definition self-centered and selfish. It is driven by greed, desire, and fear. It wants what it wants regardless of the impact on other people or the environment.

Man's ego is the cause of conflict and war. It generates pride. It creates racism, sexism, and every other "ism" that creates division and strife. It is responsible for the degradation of the environment. It views life through the lens of win-lose competition. It strives to win at the expense of others.

In contrast, our true self, our authentic nature, is to be connected, caring, compassionate, and loving. When we operate from our true self we don't fight with others because we see everyone as connected; fighting with others is essentially fighting with ourselves. As the Buddha said, "We are not separate, we are interdependent."

While our ego tries to tear others down to elevate ourselves, our true self seeks to serve and uplift others—knowing that in serving others, we also serve ourselves. When Gandhi was praised for his work in India he responded, "I do not do this for India, I do this for myself." The renowned

Buddhist monk Thich Nhat Hanh adds, "When you are well, your wellness spills onto others."

The ego constantly judges other people for their flaws and weaknesses. We do this because of the psychology of projection—we see in other people the things we don't like about ourselves. Our true self judges neither ourselves nor others. It holds ourselves and others in unconditional love, acceptance, and compassion. As we learn to accept, embrace, and love ourselves in spite of our flaws and weaknesses, we're able to do the same for others.

The sixth-century sage Shantideva summed up the attitude of one who understands and lives the Law of Connection:

May I be a guard for those who need protection
A guide for those on the path
A boat, a raft, a bridge for those who wish to cross the flood
May I be a lamp in the darkness
A resting place for the weary
A healing medicine for all who are sick
A vase of plenty, a tree of miracles
And for the boundless multitudes of living beings
May I bring sustenance and awakening
Enduring like the earth and sky
Until all beings are freed from sorrow
And all are awakened.

How the Law of Connection and Belief Breakthrough Work Together

The Law of Connection helps us to connect to our True Self underneath all our layers of limiting beliefs. When we're struggling with our self-worth, we can remember the Law of Connection and know with certainty that we are more than our limiting thoughts and beliefs about ourselves. We are more than our failures and shortcomings. We are more than our ego. Underneath all of the junk that limits us is a divine, limitless, and pure being. Thus, the Law of Connection gives us motivation and inspiration to do belief breakthrough. As we understand and apply the law, we're driven to become our best self.

Belief breakthrough is the process by which we chip away the clay to reveal the gold of our essential nature.

Then, as we learn to see our true selves, we also learn to see others in their goodness beneath all their protective layers. We become less judgmental and more compassionate. We're then able to work with people more effectively to achieve our dreams and goals.

Case Study: Bill and Julia Save Their Marriage

Bill and Julia are members of the Limitless tribe. Julia had been divorced and single with two children for thirteen years, and Bill had been widowed and single with four children for seven years when they married in 2007. They both came into their marriage with certain expectations. When those expectations were not met, their hope was shattered and they drifted further and further apart. But everything changed when they learned the laws of creation. Here is their story in their own words:

"We came together very excited to start a new relationship. As we got into it, we found it to be a whole lot harder than we ever imagined. Bill had had a fabulous marriage and thought he just had to do the same things as before to have another great relationship. It didn't turn out that way. We both discovered that we were both carrying a lot of baggage, which led to a lot of misunderstanding and misperceptions.

"It wasn't long before we found ourselves being very disconnected. We seemed to have constant conflict. We felt like we were walking on eggshells around each other. We could hardly even talk to each other. There was so much silence and fear. We both got stuck in a lot of pride and ego. We were blaming each other for all that was going wrong. It got to the point where Bill actually left for three days one time.

"Neither of us wanted divorce, but we started considering it, thinking it might be the only way to feel peaceful again. We went to see a counselor and, shockingly to us, he told us we should consider divorce. He said he'd never seen any marriage overcome challenges like ours. But we both had a fear of being alone and having to start all over again, so we stuck with it.

"In 2013 we met Kris and got involved with his company. We read his book, The Conscious Creator. It was the beginning of dramatic transformation in our marriage. It gave us hope that if we could just live the laws, progress could happen.

"The first thing we recognized was that we could not connect with each other until we connected with ourselves. We put effort into loving ourselves unconditionally and connecting more with our Higher Power individually. This began breaking down the barriers of ego and pride. It allowed us to get vulnerable with ourselves and with each other. Being true and authentic was a key element for a needed turnaround.

"Another critical thing we had to learn was to take accountability for our own feelings and actions, instead of blaming one another. We used to come into an argument with the belief that it was the other person's fault. We would say things like, 'You shouldn't have done that,' or, 'You make me angry.' Now we know that no one makes us feel or do anything but ourselves. We are responsible for our own feelings and behavior. It was hard at first but soon became liberating. We found freedom in taking personal accountability.

"Real connection was made possible by accountability. Then we started building on that connection. We started focusing on meeting each other's needs, instead of just our own. We learned to negotiate and compromise. There was a lot of trial and error. We made it a point to create a safe space for each other, and set aside dedicated time to talk and work through our issues.

"Once we learned how to love each other selflessly and unconditionally, everything shifted. We found this great joy surfacing and blossoming as we got to see each other being happy. We now experience an amazing unity physically, mentally, emotionally, and spiritually.

"We describe it as like having been in two separate bubbles that were constantly colliding. Now it's like we're inside one bubble together. It has been a gradual process but we are now experiencing the most connected marriage we can imagine. Everything has shifted. We find joy together each day as best friends."

TAKE ACTION AND APPLY THE LAW OF CONNECTION

Develop unconditional love over the next thirty days by selecting a relationship you wish to improve and playing the "Unconditional Love Game." Follow these four daily steps for the next thirty days:

1. Ask this person what you can do to show love to him or her.
2. Do what he or she asks, no matter what.
3. Have no expectation of love in return.
4. Check back at the end of each day for feedback

CHAPTER 21

THE TOP CREATION KILLERS

There's something else to understand about the laws. Inherent in each law is a counterfeit, or an opposite principle or behavior, which kills creation. So not only do the laws reveal the biggest factors that create success, but they also reveal the biggest factors that limit success.

So now that we understand the laws, we can explore each further to find how misapplying each kills our efforts to create.

Law of Attraction Counterfeit: Attracting More of What You Don't Want

The counterfeit to the Law of Attraction is attracting what you *don't* want because you don't know what you *do* want. The Law of Attraction works! It will give us what we think about the most.

To counteract this counterfeit, make sure you're not just complaining about what you don't want, but rather focusing on what you really want.

Law of Alignment Counterfeit: Clinging to False Beliefs

The counterfeit to the Law of Alignment is simply being okay with living with your limiting beliefs. It's allowing false beliefs to dictate your choices and results.

To counteract this counterfeit, go on a conscious search-and-destroy mission to identify and change every limiting belief you can find in yourself.

Law of Choice and Accountability Counterfeit: Blame

The counterfeit of the Law of Choice and Accountability is blaming other people and circumstances for our results in life. It's holding other people accountable for all our failures.

To counteract this counterfeit, accept full responsibility for your behavior and choices. Empower yourself to respond more appropriately to other people and circumstances.

Law of Gestation Counterfeit: Unrealistic Expectations

The opposite of the Law of Gestation is not allowing adequate time for creations to manifest. It's having unrealistic expectations on the timing.

"Whatever the mind of man can conceive and bring itself to believe, it can achieve."

–NAPOLEON HILL

Just because something doesn't manifest on our expected timeline doesn't mean it's not going to. It just means that it hasn't yet and that our guess on timing was off. Instead of giving up on our dreams and goals, we simply need to adjust our timing, look for the lessons we need to learn, and continue working for our goals in complete faith.

Law of Faith Counterfeit: Seeing Before Believing

Lack of faith kills creation perhaps more than any other factor. The Law of Faith works against us when we wait to see our creation before really believing that it will happen.

To counteract this, we have to learn to believe things before we can see them.

Law of the Harvest Counterfeit: False Expectations

We kill our creations when we expect a specific outcome and become attached to that outcome. Then, we become disillusioned and even bitter when things don't work out exactly how we wanted or expected them to.

To counteract this, we have to learn to release attachment to outcomes. We have to work towards our dreams and goals with detachment, trusting that whatever outcome we experience is for our best benefit.

Just because things don't turn out how we expected them to doesn't mean that we did something wrong or that a law didn't work. It means that we didn't know the results that would flow from our choices—we had hope for an outcome, but not certain knowledge.

We *do* reap what we sow, but sometimes we just don't fully understand what seeds we're planting in the moment. It's like a farmer throwing unidentified seeds in the ground. Something *will* grow, even if he doesn't know what seeds he planted.

Law of Purpose Counterfeit: Satisfying the Ego

The Law of Purpose works against us when we try to be something we're not in order to satisfy the ego. We seek fulfillment in external things that feed ego, such as status, prestige, money, comfort, etc. We pursue the wrong opportunities because they feed our ego. We don't follow the right paths because they don't seem important, conspicuous, or "sexy" (the ego craves the limelight). We compare ourselves to everyone else, we judge others, we compete with each other.

To counteract this, we have to learn to be at peace with who we are and our true purpose. We have to follow what makes us truly, deeply happy, not just what feeds our ego.

Law of Intuition Counterfeit: Relying on Logic

We get stuck when we try to solve our problems and get breakthroughs through logical thinking. But our logical mind is quite limited. To get deeper breakthroughs, we have to go deeper than logic to intuition.

Logic can be a great servant, but it's a poor master. We want to trust and follow our hearts, while using logic to be

"No problem can be solved from the same level of consciousness that created it."

—ALBERT EINSTEIN

practical in doing so. But never do we want to make decisions through logic alone.

Law of Connection Counterfeit: Pride and Selfishness

We kill connection when we live life as a solo journey. We live the Law of One, living just for ourselves. Have you ever heard the term "self-made millionaire"? It's a misguided term because such a thing doesn't and has never existed. Nobody becomes wealthy on their own. Wealthy people become so precisely through relationships and by leveraging the abilities of other people.

The Law of Connection shows that you can't manifest your creations on your own. You need other people. This journey isn't about you or me—it's about all of us. It's a journey where we support, uplift, and inspire one another, and receive that from others.

PART IV

Manifesting Your
Limitless Life

You've learned the power of belief breakthrough and how to do it. You've learned the 9 Laws of Conscious Creation. Now it's time to put them together in a formula that literally enables you to manifest breakthrough results at will.

Your whole life, you've accepted things as reality that were really just created by your beliefs. You've told yourself, "That's just the way it is, and there's nothing I can do about it." Your challenges have seemed insurmountable.

Perhaps you've buried yourself in debt, or have never been able to break through the ceiling of your income. Maybe you struggle with obesity or a chronic illness. You may be on the brink of divorce. You may feel so emotionally wounded and scarred that you'll never be able to heal.

You *do not* have to accept these things as your reality. You have the power to manifest a new reality. You have the power to make things happen that previously you would have thought to be impossible.

Welcome to a new world of possibility...

CHAPTER 22

THE FORMULA FOR MANIFESTING LIFE-CHANGING BREAKTHROUGHS

Y ou are worthy of experiencing life-changing breakthroughs, which can be nothing short of miraculous. You are capable of producing them. The Divine *wants* to give them to you. But you have to believe and do your part.

I'm not talking about you flying, walking on water, or transforming substances. I'm talking about accessing and harnessing divine power—your own and God's—to manifest things in your life that you previously never thought yourself capable of.

For example, consider a man who has weighed 300 pounds for twenty years, and never believed it was possible for him to get down to a healthy weight. He experiences belief breakthrough work and loses 110 pounds in nine months. A woman who never believes she can get married breaks through her limiting beliefs and marries the man of her dreams. A man who never believes he could earn more than $100,000 eclipses this mental ceiling through belief breakthrough and earns $250,000 the year after his breakthroughs. These are all miraculous breakthroughs and manifestations!

> *"Life has no limitations except the ones you make."*
>
> –LES BROWN

When we experience extraordinary breakthroughs in our thoughts, we manifest extraordinary results.

When you believe you're worthy and capable of achieving life-changing breakthroughs, there is a formula to follow. Once you know the formula, you can manifest your desires predictably and at will. Manifesting becomes something that happens regularly in your life, rather than unexpectedly, unpredictably, and sporadically.

Within each step of the formula, specific Laws of Conscious Creation are leveraged. You'll notice that there is overlap in some steps, as the laws are all interrelated.

Here's the formula:

Step 1: Clearly Define What You Want

Surprisingly, very few people know what they actually want. They can give you a long laundry list of everything they *don't* want, but ask them what they actually *want* and they go blank.

When you focus on what you don't want, all your energy stays there, so that's what you manifest. You attract what you think about most, which explains why people who constantly complain about everything they don't want keep getting it.

"There is great treasure there behind our skull and this is true about all of us. This little treasure has great, great powers, and I would say we only have learnt a very, very small part of what it can do."

–ISAAC BASHEVIS SINGER

You have to get crystal clear on exactly what you want to gain and achieve. What are you trying to make happen? How will you measure success? Can you see it in your mind's eye? Can you feel it?

Once you've defined what you want, you must write it down. In 1979 the Harvard MBA program performed a study in which graduate students were asked "Have you set clear, written goals for your future and made plans to accomplish them?" They found that 84 percent of students had no goals at all, 13 percent had goals but they weren't in writing, and only 3 percent had written goals and plans.

Ten years later, the same group was interviewed again and the results were stunning. The 13 percent of the class who had goals, but did not write them down were earning twice the amount of the 84 percent who had no goals. The 3 percent who had written goals were earning, on average, ten times as much as the other 97 percent of the class combined!

The goal must also be believable to you. This may sound contradictory, given that breakthrough goals by definition seem unbelievable and unattainable. But if you don't believe to your bones that the goal is possible, you'll never achieve it. Choose goals that stretch your mind without breaking it.

Active Laws in Step 1

 The Law of Attraction: We attract into our lives what we think about the most. Most people attract more of what they don't want because that's what they think about most. By clearly defining what you want, your mind begins broadcasting your desire to the universe.

 The Law of Purpose: Make sure that what you want is in alignment with your True Purpose. Do you want this because it strokes your ego, or because it really is a manifestation of your True Self?

 The Law of Connection: Is what you want in the best interests of other people and the planet? Will it serve and uplift others and make the world a better place? Or is it based on greed and competition, and will it create conflict, strife, and suffering?

Step 2: Take Bold Action Toward Your Goal

You've heard the phrase, "Pray as if everything depended on God, and work as if everything depended on you." It really is true. Set your intention, and then give everything you have to make it a reality.

It's not enough to set a goal—you must also create a plan. Map out exactly what needs to happen in order for your goal to manifest. Detail precisely what you plan on doing to achieve your goal. Set benchmarks to track your progress.

Having said that, remember the mantra, "Goals in stone, plans in sand." Plans must be adaptable. When you set out to create something new and big in your life, by definition you don't know how to achieve it. If you knew exactly how to achieve it from the start, it wouldn't be a breakthrough! You don't know everything you'll encounter along the way. You don't know whether your plans will actually give you the results you want or not.

"Mistakes are the portals of discovery."

–JAMES JOYCE

You have to be persistent, buoyant, and flexible. Get up every time you get knocked down. Learn from your mistakes and failures. Don't get bitter—get better. Use the Law of Intuition to make decisions along the way. Trust and follow your intuition—even and especially when it seems crazy.

The path to a life-changing breakthrough isn't a straight line. It winds and twists its way through dark forests and long stretches of desert. You have to course-correct constantly.

Active Laws in Step 2

The Law of the Harvest: This is the stage where you plant your seeds. If you don't plant any seeds now, you'll have nothing to harvest later. And if you don't plant the right seeds, you won't harvest what you really want.

The Law of Intuition: Along the journey a million and one decisions will arise that you will have to make. Use your intuition to make these decisions, fully trusting that whatever decision you make is the right one to give you exactly what you need to progress in any given moment.

Step 3: Believe and Act as if Your Goal Were Already Reality

When you start to create a transformational breakthrough, you won't have any evidence that it's possible. This is where you use the Law of Faith. You have to believe to see.

Live as if your breakthrough is a reality, as if it were already happening. Feel it as if it were real. Use your imagination. If your breakthrough goal were to manifest right now, how would it feel? Conjure those emotions and bask in them. Your emotion is based on your "why." When your why is big enough and you want something bad enough, those emotions drive your behavior, not your logic. You can spend as much time with your manifestation in your mind as you would in reality. Either way is real to your mind.

As you move toward your goal, evidence will appear that can either be perceived as your efforts working, or not. Whatever the evidence, celebrate it as if everything is going your way. I mean this! Celebrate every tiny step of progress, every new dollar earned, every ounce of joy you experience. It all matters. Do not recognize counter-evidence as counter anything. See not opposition, but vital lessons that must be learned along the way.

Active Laws in Step 3

 The Law of Faith: You must believe your breakthrough goal before you can manifest it. Remove all doubt from your mind.

 The Law of Attraction: Believing as if your breakthrough goal were a reality broadcasts a strong signal to the universe.

 The Law of Alignment: Everything you think, say, and do must be in alignment with what you want to manifest. Fear and doubt cause misalignment.

 The Law of Choice and Accountability: Regardless of what happens along the journey, take responsibility for your results. Never blame circumstances or other people when things don't go your way. Own your life and your choices. Perceive all evidence that everything is working in your favor. Choose into your breakthrough goal!

Step 4: Master Belief Breakthrough

Nothing brings out your false and limiting beliefs out of the woodwork like setting an intention to manifest a breakthrough goal. Thoughts of unworthiness will erupt inside you. Self-doubt will ooze from every pore. Fear will leap out at you from the darkness.

This is when you put your belief breakthrough work on hyperdrive. Go on a search-and-destroy mission to uncover and change every false belief that arises. Your goal is less dependent on hard work than it is on purifying your beliefs.

Install a Limitless filter in your mind. Let every thought and spoken word represent an investment into what you want. Never invest in what you don't want. Enough breakthroughs equal transformation. Enough transformation equals a life-changing breakthrough.

Active Laws in Step 4

 The Law of Alignment: Your "search-and-destroy" mission to remove all limiting beliefs aligns your beliefs with the reality of your goal. Life-changing breakthroughs cannot manifest in the presence of any degree of misalignment!

 The Law of Choice and Accountability: The first and best place to own our life and our results is to change our beliefs. The very act of changing our beliefs from limiting to limitless, from disempowering to empowering, *is* taking accountability for our choices!

Step 5: Do Your Part and Trust God to Do His

Your part is to know the why and what. God's part is to do the when and how. Have faith that God is manifesting the how, whether it looks like it or not. You don't know how your goal will be manifest—and you don't need to know. You simply need to live the laws and take action toward your goal.

YOUR PART   UNIVERSE PART   DESIRE
(What + Why)   (When + How)   MANIFESTED

At times, you'll get to the end of the time frame you had set for yourself and your goal hasn't manifested yet. All this means is that your guess on gestational timing was off. The calendar was for you, not the goal.

The worst thing you can do is beat yourself up for not achieving your goal. Celebrate your progress. Remind yourself of how far you've come and how much you've learned in the process. What you're really celebrating is who you're becoming. Who you become is more important than anything you ever achieve because *you* are the true miracle. Reset the gestational period and keep moving forward with absolute faith and trust.

Active Laws in Step 5

 The Law of Faith: Trust the laws, trust God, trust the universe. Believe in your goal with unwavering faith.

 The Law of Gestation: Trust that your goal will appear in its proper gestational time.

 The Law of the Harvest: You've planted your seeds. Now cultivate them and trust that they will sprout and generate a bountiful harvest for you.

THE MECHANICS OF MANIFESTING BREAKTHROUGHS

 **Step 1:** Clearly Define What You Want

 **Step 2:** Take Bold Action Toward Your Goal

 **Step 3:** Believe and Act as if it Were Already Reality

 **Step 4:** Master Belief Breakthrough

 **Step 5:** Do Your Part and Trust God to Do His

My Personal Breakthroughs

I've used this manifesting formula to create many breakthrough results in my life. I don't share this with you to brag, but simply to affirm that it works. Here are two such experiences:

Shifting My Son's Autism

When our second son, Kaiser, was born, we didn't notice anything out of the ordinary. Starting at about the age of one, he was slow to progress. He didn't walk until sixteen months and wouldn't say "mama" or "dada" until after age two. He started really falling behind normal milestones of child development at age three. By the time he was four he wasn't potty trained, he didn't speak, and he wouldn't even respond to his own name and very little else. We took him in for testing and he tested moderate on the autism scale.

The common perception of autism is that it's incurable. But Kalenn and I were willing to hold space that something could be done. We envisioned it. We believed it.

We were on a business trip in California one time. We talked to a friend who happened to be dating a woman who had worked four years as a secretary for a Doctor Buttar in North Carolina (www.DrButtar.com). She had watched this doctor dramatically help many children on the autism spectrum. We immediately scheduled an appointment with him and started Kaiser on treatments.

On the scale of autism, 100 to 200 is normal and 1,000 is profoundly autistic. Kaiser initially tested at 436. It's extremely rare for anyone to move on that scale, especially without treatment.

Autistic children have inhibited social function, which makes it difficult for them to learn. It usually takes a few years for the treatments to start showing results. But Kaiser responded within a couple of months. Within the first four months he started responding to his name, speaking, and he potty-trained—all things he hadn't done in his first four years. After treatment, Kaiser has vastly improved. He attends school. He socializes. Over a period of about three years, Kaiser dropped to 182 on the autism scale, which is considered normal. We couldn't feel more blessed.

RAP-TD RESULTS FOR KAISER KROHN

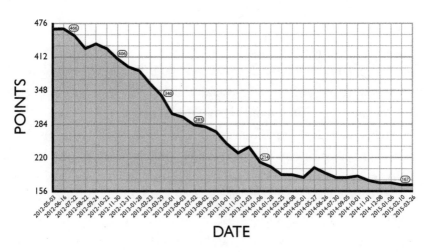

I'm not saying that something magical occurred to give Kaiser a more normal life. These treatments have worked for many children, and they're available. But because of the perception that nothing can be done about autism, very people know that options exist. (Dr. Buttar's treatment has been available for less than fifteen years.) What catalyzed the result for us was simply the belief and faith that there was something that could help our boy. All breakthrough results start with belief, and we couldn't be more grateful that we held space for this one.

Manifesting a Retreat Center

I'm from Washington state. Living in Utah now, I miss the evergreen trees. My wife and I had lived in Utah for ten years before fully committing to stay. We decided years ago that we'd love to have a getaway in a beautiful place with lots of evergreen trees.

We've traveled through every corner of Utah looking for a place. We finally found the perfect location, which just happened to be within fifteen minutes of our home in Sundance. When we looked for property there years ago, I initially wrote it off because lots there easily go for $1 million or more. But we created an intention to own a cabin in Sundance. We went up there and made a video with our family. We envisioned it as if it had already happened. We celebrated it together.

In 2014 we found the perfect lot. It was secluded, it had a stream on it, and it was surrounded by evergreen trees. It was worth about $1.3 million at the time, but it was listed at $950,000. The lot was right but the resources were not immediately available and the timing was off. But we made an energetic claim on the lot. We just knew it would be ours.

When we created the Limitless Inner Circle a couple years later, we began envisioning a getaway retreat center wherein we could take our top leaders and mentor them. We knew it was time. I still wasn't able to pull it off alone, so I decided to find the perfect partner to help me make this a reality.

Three days later I received a random text from a friend who I hadn't talked to for five years. In that time he had become incredibly successful in network marketing. Amazingly, he told me he was looking for a partner to create a cabin for doing transformation work in Sundance. Here's a screen shot of that text:

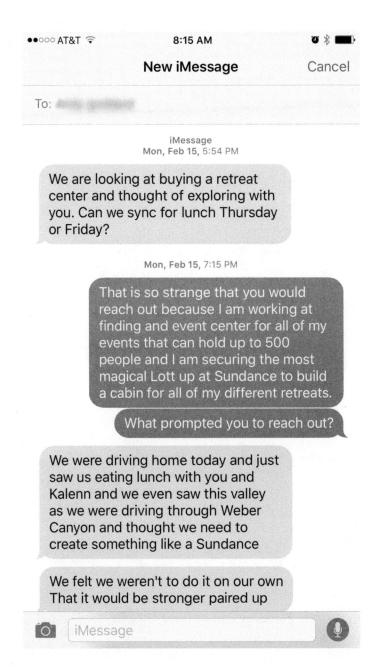

Remember that lot we had found in 2014? We partnered and bought that exact lot in 2016. Now we are working on our plans for construction.

Breakthrough goals really can be achieved. And *anyone* can achieve them. It's not about being special or uniquely endowed. It's simply about following the formula.

When desired resources present themselves, we often perceive this to be a miracle. In truth, it's a natural result of following the formula. This formula is all about intentionally manipulating the resources of the universe by making good choices in alignment with this formula to consciously create your ideal life.

CHAPTER 23

REAL-LIFE BREAKTHROUGHS

I've been privileged to facilitate belief breakthrough work with thousands of people. There are many, many stories I could share of people experiencing life-changing breakthroughs through these laws and principles. Here are just a few, in each of the four domains of Limitless living, and in people's own words:

Personal Power Breakthroughs

Kristen Overcomes Her Shyness

"For as long as I can remember, I've always been extremely shy. I hide in social settings. I'm never the one who reaches out to meet new people. It takes me a long time to feel comfortable being myself with people. As a result, I've missed out on so many things in my life because I choose not to put myself out there. I've lost out on going on trips and promotions at work. I've missed having fun in group settings. My shyness has really held me back in so many areas.

"When I attended my first Limitless event in August of 2016, I started out as I always have been. During exercises I would hold back, or just stay with my husband because I didn't want to work with anyone I didn't know. But over the course of the three days I started opening up a little more. I actually ended up speaking on stage and sharing an experience from my life. I was shocked that I could even do it—it's so unlike me.

"Truthfully, I know that the person that's always been inside of me is completely different than what I show. I'm actually super fun and outgoing.

After that event, I knew I wanted to be different. I set out to change and improve that about myself.

"My husband and I joined the Limitless Inner Circle, which required even more group interaction. At first I had no intention of being up in front of anyone. I just wanted to be behind the scenes and to support my husband. But after attending the Limitless event that October, I set the intention to become breakthrough certified. It took me a while to complete, but I did it.

> *"Life is either a daring adventure or nothing. Security does not exist in nature, nor do the children of men as a whole experience it. Avoiding danger is no safer in the long run than exposure."*
>
> –HELEN KELLER

"A while later we came to another Inner Circle event. As before, I had no intention of engaging. I was just going to listen. We broke off into groups and were supposed to share 'signature presentations' with everyone. I didn't have one prepared. But after all I'd gone through, I didn't want to regret not stepping up. So I did it. I delivered a fifteen-minute presentation with ease, without even preparing. People in my group said I was a natural.

"I know that may not sound like a big deal, but it was monumental for me. It really was a miracle! Before my breakthroughs I would have been absolutely terrified. I wouldn't have dreamed of doing something like that. I would have escaped out the back and just sat out the exercise.

"One of the biggest things I've worked through is fear of failure, fear of doing it wrong. I thought I would do everything wrong and I didn't want to be judged. I've worked with getting over that and sharing regardless and going with my intuition. So often I encounter things I know I can do but I choose not to try because of fear of failure. I decided I would no longer be held back by that.

"My old crippling belief was, 'I don't do anything right.' I've changed that belief to, 'I succeed in what I try. I am powerful. I have a message to share. I trust myself.' I have stepped into my power. I've always known I have a message to share and an ability to connect with others. I've gone from being a completely shy introvert to reaching out and doing adventurous things and sharing my message."

"I recall a time in my business career when I was in line to become the CEO of a multi-million-dollar company. The CEO had named me as his successor as part of his exit plans. But when the president of the company disagreed and gave him an ultimatum, I was let go. It was a huge shock.

"But I left with a lot of confidence in myself and my ability to find a new management job. I was quickly hired by another company. They didn't hire me as a manager, but they saw my value and promised me a lot of upward mobility. Although I had taken a huge pay cut, I jumped in and gave it everything I had.

"My experience in this new company was much different. In my previous company, my input and ideas were welcome and my voice was heard. In this new company I tried to make helpful suggestions. That ended when the owner of company reprimanded me for speaking out of turn and sticking my nose where it didn't belong. I stayed there for a year thinking I could make a difference. But every time I tried I got shot down. I ended up getting fired a week before a promised raise.

"I'd never been fired before. It was a huge blow to my self-esteem and self-confidence. I really started questioning my value, not only as an employee, but also as a leader and as a human being. I was forty-eight years old. I remember coming home the day I was fired and feeling defeated.

"I had no desire to go back to work. For a couple weeks I just hung around the house. I had completely lost my drive. I started feeling a lot of self-pity. I also started resenting my husband, who was disabled. His fixed disability income wasn't enough to support our family and I had to work to make up the difference. I was really stuck in victim mode.

"After a few weeks reality kicked in and I knew I needed to bring in income. I found a job as a shipping manager starting at $12 an hour. My self-worth was at an all-time low. I believed I was only worth doing what other people told me to do, just clocking in and getting a paycheck. I didn't trust that my employers would take care of me. I had made a decision that I was just going to get let go again anyway and nothing was secure. As a result, I didn't give as much. I wasn't as dedicated to my job as I had been in the past and it wasn't as fulfilling. That was out of alignment with who I really am.

"After working at this job for a month, on February 2, 2013, I had a heart attack at the age of forty-nine. I was told it was caused by stress. The doctor told me I needed six to eight weeks of recovery with no stress or physical activity. I took the time off and then returned to work.

"It was at this time that I was introduced to a new entrepreneurial opportunity that I began building part time. Though excited about the business, I feared that if I were to put my heart and soul into it, I would have another heart attack. I started working with Kris Krohn as a personal mentor. We addressed this fear head-on.

"No one will act for you. Your plans will remain no more than an idler's dream until you rise up and fight against the forces that would keep you small. To take action is always dangerous, but to sit and wait for the good things of life to fall into your lap is the only calling where failures excel."

—OG MANDINO

"I discovered that my heart attack was not caused by outside factors, but because I was living an inauthentic life that wasn't aligned with my values. I was able to change my beliefs and become aligned with my truth. I accepted there was more to me than I was giving myself credit for. Within two months of starting my new business I made twice the money I was making in my full-time job. A month later I quit my job with absolute faith that I could continue making the income I needed for my family.

"In that first year I earned $40,000 from my business, which was more than double the amount I had been earning in my job. I very soon had many opportunities to speak on stages. I had never been much of a public speaker, but my ability to inspire and transform audiences improved dramatically. I have had countless individuals tell me that something I said from stage totally changed their lives. I've been able to help hundreds of people launch their own businesses. I'm far beyond where I ever was before as a leader. People now look to me for mentorship and inspiration.

"I've continued supporting our family and we live a comfortable life. Through my business and investing, we've become financially free. Our residual income exceeds our monthly expenses. I mentor other people to help them create major transformation in their lives."

Wealth Breakthroughs

Irina Climbs Out of a Financial Hole

"Before Limitless I was a stay-at-home mom and my husband and I were really struggling financially. I have studied personal development for years. I understood the idea of abundance and the principle that you create everything in your mind before it manifests as reality. But I was frustrated because nothing was showing up in my life. I was watching other people thrive, while we could barely make ends meet.

"I wanted to get a job to bring in additional income. I got a job with a training and coaching company where there was the possibility of making a lot of money by selling programs. But I wasn't making much at all to begin with.

"We received an invitation to Limitless about the same time my husband lost his job. So we went to the event in a worse position than we'd ever been in. After the event I knew this was exactly what we needed, so we signed up for ongoing training in the Inner Circle program. This in itself was a miracle because we were only able to do it by finding a resource we didn't know we had.

"I started learning how money is connected to living purpose. I started getting more intentional about my purpose and what I wanted to create. I wanted to mentor other people to heal and break through their limitations as I had. I had tried to do that prior to experiencing Limitless. But I was struggling to get people to sign up. Previously, I didn't believe it would be possible to find anyone willing to mentor with me.

"This is my world, my stamping ground. I must run free, mad-hearted, bellowing with pain and ecstasy, charging with lowered horns, ripping up the barricades that hem me in and stifle me. I must have room to expand."

–HENRY MILLER

"In my position as a mentor within my company, they set the prices, which made me so scared I would stop breathing just thinking about it. I knew I had the talent and skills but just imagining that someone would pay me so much money was very hard to accept. But it actually didn't take long for me to sign up my first $10,000 coaching client. This was my first big awakening.

"My boss started asking me to do discovery sessions for company seminars we were doing. On our very first event, I closed $50,000 in training programs in one day, signing up three personal clients and two company clients. This was a company record and far beyond anything I had achieved before. (In fact, I had been fired from another training company for not being able to sell the required $800 per month.) And it didn't stop there. I continued breaking records, including closing $100,000 of business in one day, and later $250,000 in one month.

"The year before attending Limitless, in 2015, my husband and I made about $35,000. As of writing this in the fall of 2016 I have personally made more than $95,000 this year—and the year isn't over yet!

"It feels incredible and liberating. I'm in a space where I know if I need money for something it's going to show up. There's nothing I cannot do. If I want to purchase a program but don't have the money, I know I can manifest it. If we want to go on vacation, I know we can manifest it. It's never about the money any more. Money has been taken out of the decision-making process.

"It's an amazing way to be with money, to know money will show up whenever you need it. I used to view money as a scary thing, a monster that can chew you up and spit you out and is always controlling you. Now I view it as a friend that shows up to support me any time I need it.

"The real miracle for me has been less the money itself and more about my mindset. If my money were to disappear today, I wouldn't feel any less content or happy. That's been the most important shift in my life as regards to wealth. I know it's going to keep growing and I don't have to worry about how and when and what. It's just there."

Eric Goes from Rock Bottom to $100,000/Month in Three Years

"I took a major leap of faith a few years ago. I had been waiting tables full-time to support my family. I had become certified in a holistic healthcare technique that I loved and dreamed of being able to practice full-time. I felt impressed to quit my job, even though I had no office, no steady clientele, and no real outside income coming in.

"Because of my lack of entrepreneurial experience, my business floundered for several months. Things became so bad that I finally had to sit my wife down one day and explain to her that I hadn't even made enough money to buy food for us for that month. I had hit financial rock bottom.

"Because we were desperate to get out of the financial hole that we were in, we started looking for answers. We attended a seminar that gave us much-needed hope and real-life skills that we could begin to implement immediately. On the final day of the seminar, the presenter offered a six-month group coaching program. I felt myself get more and more excited as I listened to the details of this program. I knew in my heart that if I could somehow receive the training, I could get us out of the rut we were in.

"There was just one problem: the cost of the program was $5,000 which we certainly didn't have at the time. So I sat down feeling dejected.

"My wife urged me to sign up for the program. I protested, not knowing how I could pay for a course with money I didn't have. She then asked me a simple question: 'Is it right?' My logic told me 'no,' but my intuition told me 'yes.'

"Life is too short to be little."

—BENJAMIN DISRAELI

"She responded with what has become one of our life mantras: 'If it's right, what else matters?'

"So I went to the back table and picked up a registration form. I was freaking out so bad I was hyperventilating. Thankfully, my wife came up to me again and said, 'Is it right?' I nodded my head. 'Then what else matters?' I maxed out every credit card we had and signed up for the mentoring.

"It paid off immediately and in a big way. My income quintupled within four months. Then I hit a plateau for about three months. I told my wife I needed a personal mentor. I found one and we maxed out another credit card. Immediately after, I felt prompted to approach my original mentor for a more personal relationship. He told me it would be $25,000 and then asked, 'How soon can you have the money?'

"Without thinking I said, 'Tomorrow.' I had no idea how I was going to come up with the money, but I did it. Creative ideas kept popping into my head. I followed all of them and within twenty-four hours I created

$25,000. From that personal mentoring, my income jumped to between $20,000 and $30,000 per month.

"But then I hit another plateau. I made several business mistakes. I decided it was time to seek out another mentor. In early January of 2016 I felt prompted to reach out to Kris Krohn on Facebook. I had never met him, so the prompting was totally out of the blue. We spoke and he invited me to Limitless. On the first day I told my wife that it felt right to seek him as my next mentor.

"Once again, I followed my intuition. I met with Kris and he made an offer for personal mentoring. Again, the number made me gulp. But with my wife's counsel in the back of my mind, 'If it's right, then what else matters?', I moved forward and again figured out how to come up with the money.

"When we started working together I was averaging $20,000 per month. Now I'm averaging $100,000 per month. This has happened because I've been willing to follow intuition, take huge leaps of faith, and work with mentors.

"My wife's statement was a major breakthrough for me: 'If it's right, what else matters?' Before that, one of my biggest mistakes used to be saying, 'I'll think about it.' I know from personal experience that we often logic our way out of manifesting miracles. The path to manifesting major miracles usually doesn't make a lot of sense to the logical brain. It didn't make logical sense to invest what I've invested in mentors. It didn't make logical sense to quit my job when I don't have the resources. But I did it, simply because I felt in my heart that it was right for me, and I will forever be grateful that I did.

"To manifest miracles, you have to trust your intuition and your heart, versus doing what your logical brain says to do. It makes such a huge difference. It allows you to open up to inspiration, which will tell you how to manifest your own miracles in your life."

> *"Ask no one for permission to perform that which is within you to do. Boldly strike out upon your own initiative and DO while the multitude stand by in mouth-stretched awe. The reliant, the bold—the Conquering Chief steps forward and plucks the prize while all the others stand by and marvel at his daring."*
>
> –ALBERT LEWIS PELTON

Health Breakthroughs

Kara Overcomes Chronic Illness and Pain

"Before learning belief breakthrough, I suffered from chronic illness for twenty-two years. I was diagnosed with fibromyalgia, which is a condition similar to arthritis. It affects the central nervous system and creates intense physical pain, chronic fatigue, depression, and an inability to lose weight, among other symptoms. The only thing doctors can do for it is give you medication to alleviate the pain. But these medications have a long list of intense side effects, and they don't fix anything anyway.

"I tried a lot of things to get rid of it over the years, including things like energy healing. Some of them would create temporary relief from the symptoms, but I would still have cycles where I would sink back to rock bottom. Nothing worked permanently. I realized I was just treating symptoms instead of getting to the root of the problem. I understood that emotions could affect the physical body. But it wasn't clear to me how the stories we tell ourselves and the beliefs we have are the seeds that create 'fruit' in our lives, whether good or rotten.

"When I attended my first seminar with Kris, he taught about roots and fruits and about the stories we tell ourselves. I had a huge epiphany. I spent the next few months becoming aware of the stories I had created from my perceptions of my childhood.

"In that time, my mind and body really resisted the idea that I could be responsible for my own pain and symptoms. I shut down big time. My body got worse than it had ever been. I went into a dark place that summer. I wasn't clear on how to clear and release the emotions and physical symptoms.

"But when attended my first Limitless seminar and learned the belief breakthrough process, everything became clear to me. It was so simple, and I love simplicity. I immediately joined the Inner Circle because I knew I needed support. I had been doing my healing journey by myself for so long. I wanted to surround myself with like-minded people who would love me no matter what and would create a place of both safety and honesty.

"After about a month of being in the Inner Circle, I attended a training where we did a specific exercise intended to break through the stories in our heads. I was in so much physical pain that day that I could hardly stand. I put on a brave face and no one knew how badly I was struggling.

"One of my beliefs was, 'I don't have any control over my body.' Kris was talking about stories and how they create evidence in our lives. He then looked me in the eyes and said, 'Evidence like fake diseases.' It hit me to my core because I had been to multiple doctors and none of them could tell me anything. They told me it was all in my head.

> *"If any organism fails to fulfill its potentialities, it becomes sick."*
>
> –WILLIAM JAMES

"I realized that my illness was a product of shame and guilt I had carried from my childhood. I thought I must have done something to deserve it. It was a lightning bolt moment for me. My perception was no longer the shame, guilt and victimhood. My perspective was if it's all in my head then I have the power to change it.

"For next three weeks I spent every possible free moment writing down all my limiting beliefs and stories and turning them around. For first time in my healing journey I was choosing something different. Within three weeks I was completely pain free. I'm now functioning on a level that I've never experienced in my life. Occasionally my body will speak to me and tell me something is out of alignment. But I'm able to shift it and I don't experience discomfort for more than a few minutes. The anxiety, depression, and paranoia, which I've lived my whole life, no longer control me.

"Because of my miracle, I'm now super passionate about helping people with chronic illness and pain. I'm living proof that miracles are possible, and that with the right knowledge and process, real physical healing can happen."

Jennifer Loses Seventy Pounds in Eight Months

"As a child I was an active, vibrant, bright, and passionate girl. I started dancing at age three and acting in plays by age ten. As a teenager I was a cheerleader and on the drill team. I was always super skinny and fit. At age fourteen I won the title of Miss Teen Utah.

"But that year, after winning the pageant, I broke my back. I had to lay in bed for months to heal. During that time my muscles all atrophied. As a result, my body shape changed dramatically. My body was never the same from that point. I also felt very alone during this time. Few people came to visit me. I didn't know if I would ever walk or dance again. It started a ripple effect of self-doubt and feelings of unworthiness.

"As I grew, I kept gaining weight. It seemed like no matter what I did it was impossible to lose it. And even if I could, it was tiny amounts and would only last a short time. As an adult I ended up at 230 pounds and size 20 pants. This was a lot of weight for my petite dancer frame to carry.

"I also developed depression, anxiety, and diseases. All my false beliefs and perceptions compounded until I felt buried alive. I was so depressed that it was a struggle to get out of bed in the morning. In fact, I got to a point where I no longer wanted to live. I would put on a fake mask every day. I hated my life and who I was. I was in an abusive marriage to a man whom I had attracted because of my feelings of unworthiness.

"In January of 2016 I came to my first Limitless event and learned about belief breakthrough. I realized I had been starving myself of food, connection, life, joy, personal power, and freedom. As I learned to love myself, I fed myself with healthy food, connection, and positive thoughts. I finally started to live again.

"May you live all the days of your life."
–JONATHAN SWIFT

"The pounds just started falling off. In March I came back to my second event and that weekend alone I lost five pounds. As I used belief breakthrough to forgive and let go of things from my past, the weight that was resonating with my negative thoughts just fell away as my thoughts shifted.

"I had developed hundreds of limiting beliefs about myself from the age of fourteen. 'I'm not lovable.' 'I'll never be enough.' 'I'm not capable.' 'I'm not pretty.' 'I will always be fat.' 'I'm not desirable.' 'I can't connect with people.' 'I can't make friends.' 'No one wants to be around me.' And on and on. The list was daunting. I started processing and changing all of them relentlessly. As each belief would come up, I wouldn't let it sit for a minute. I saw these lies that had taken such a strong hold on my mind to the point that I lost every ounce of belief in myself.

"I started to believe in myself again and to see who I really was. I let go of negative thoughts and beliefs. I fed my mind positive words and affirmations. I now know I am beautiful, smart, strong, and capable. I connect deeply with people. I make friends easily. I have the light back in my eyes and passion back into my life. I have chosen to live with joy and passion.

"I now eat whole, healthy food. I don't feel the need to starve myself and then gorge on empty calories to try and fill myself. I had starved myself fat and sick. Now I am feeding myself whole and thin. When I chose to live again, I started moving my body. I started exercising and working out at the gym. I discovered that I love to run. I also hike a lot. My favorite thing is that I've started dancing again!

"With all these changes, the weight has been melting off. I watched the scale as I lost twenty, then thirty, then forty pounds and more. Within eight months of my first Limitless event I had lost seventy pounds. As of writing this I weigh 161 pounds and am down to a size eight. And the weight continues to fall off.

"I also chose to leave my husband after seventeen years of abuse. I have been dating again and creating healthy relationships. That vibrant, beautiful, passionate girl who I thought I had lost forever is back! I can't express how good it feels."

Connection Breakthroughs

Marianne and Anthony Overcome Addiction
and Infidelity and Create a Limitless Marriage

"We met at a dance when Marianne was fourteen years old and Anthony was fifteen. We got married when we were eighteen and nineteen. We were just kids. We really had no idea what we were doing. We were blissfully ignorant of what lay ahead. After all, the fairytales end with the wedding day 'happily ever after.'

"Our relationship disintegrated over time. We drifted apart with the usual busyness of going to school, getting jobs, and trying to build a home and family. The happily-ever-after storybook ending we had envisioned turned into a nightmare instead. We did our best to keep it together, but we weren't equipped at all. We had no idea what we were doing, and no handbook to guide us. We were shooting in the dark, with limiting beliefs as ammunition.

"Statistically, our marriage didn't stand a chance. From the age of eight, Anthony had an addiction to pornography, which led to repeated infidelity in our marriage. Over time, it became obvious how that story was going to end. After one of the affairs, we hit D-Day. It was time for a decision to be made. We both had to choose, once and for all, whether we were in or out. Anthony was feeling so low that he even wondered if it was even worth living any more.

"Even through all that, we loved each other. Marianne told Anthony, 'I love you so much. And this self-destructive tendency on both of our parts needs to stop. I have appointment with lawyer tomorrow. Are you in or out? No matter what you choose I'm okay.'

"Everything will change when your desire to move on exceeds your desire to hold on."

–ALAN H. COHEN

"For Anthony, this was a huge and scary moment. It was the pattern interrupt he needed to stop blaming Marianne. For her part, Marianne stopped thinking that something in her had to be fixed and stopped blaming herself. She also admitted that she had her own addiction: She was addicted to creating drama and crisis in her life so that people would buy her story and give her sympathy. It felt like the only way she could ever get the love and attention she was craving.

"When we discovered belief breakthrough, we were given the tools we had desperately needed for so long. We both experienced a complete 180-degree turnaround. We stopped blaming ourselves and each other, and instead took accountability for what each one of us had created. Not everything changed overnight. It took commitment and time. But the changes did happen much faster than we ever thought possible. And we found that it doesn't have to be a hard journey. It can be full of joy. It can even be fun. You can make any bit of the experience what you want it to be. You get to pick the emotion you attach to whatever your experience is.

"We took the opportunity to start completely over. After D-Day, the relationship as we knew it was gone, and we got the opportunity to start fresh with one another. To restart and recommit. We are even planning a renewal wedding ceremony.

"After belief breakthrough work, our marriage no longer suffers from the effects of addiction. Anthony was able to figure out the emotional and circumstantial triggers attached to the addiction, which were causing him to repeatedly go back to the addiction as a source of comfort or medication. Up until Anthony discovered belief breakthrough work, he never thought he'd be able to conquer his addiction for good. He had been through many recovery programs and they all told him, 'Once an addict always an addict.' He thought white-knuckling it through life was the best he could hope for.

"Our connection and intimacy are phenomenal. Our intimacy goes so much further than simply physical intimacy now—it encompasses spiritual, emotional, and mental intimacy. We've learned to become unconditional with sex and to be intimate without necessarily being sexual. We've learned that sex is the *result* of ultimate connection and intimacy, not the source.

"Because of belief breakthrough, we have our fairytale marriage and we're living it every day."

Michelle Reconnects with Her Estranged Father-in-Law

"My husband and I have always loved each other. But like all couples, we have had our struggles. We used to fight a lot about money and the typical things like how to run a household and parent.

"My husband would tell his father about some of our struggles. His father was very blunt in his advice. He would tell my husband things like, 'You need to strap on a pair. What kind of a man are you?' He told my husband to tell me, 'If you don't like how things are going, then here's where you can go and here's how to get there.' He basically told my husband to divorce me. It was so hurtful.

"This obviously caused a ton of conflict between all of us. When my father-in-law tried to drag our kids into the fights and manipulate them, that's when I drew a line and cut him off. He was no longer welcome in our family. Thankfully, my husband supported my decision.

"After being estranged for five years, my husband and I discovered Limitless. We started having major breakthroughs and our relationship got stronger and stronger. Nine months after our first Limitless event, we attended a retreat where we performed a forgiveness exercise. The person who came up for me was my father-in-law. I did a lot of deep forgiveness work and was able to completely let go of all my resentment toward him.

"We live in Idaho and my father-in-law lives in Wyoming. Amazingly, while we were at that retreat in Utah we just happened to run into my father-in-law. We were able to spend a couple hours talking and reconnecting. My father-in-law genuinely apologized for the first time.

"If I hadn't have done that forgiveness work, I wouldn't have been in a position to reconcile. It opened my heart to see things from his perspective. Looking back, I now understand that he was sincerely trying to help his son, however misguided it may have been. His wife had left him and he was completely blindsided by it. So he was trying to protect his son from being hurt in the same way he had been. In his mind, he was trying to be empathetic to my husband when he would talk about our marital struggles. I see now how the whole thing came from my husband seeking empathy and his dad trying to give him empathy. It became an ugly triangle of 'he said, she said.'

"We make a living by what we get, but a life by what we give."

–B.J. PALMER

"Through belief breakthrough work my husband and I realized we are different, and because we are different the relationship with his father needed to be different. We have a greater understanding. The one thing you can't replace in life is time lost with loved ones. I can step back and recognize how all of us have been reactionary.

"It has truly been a miracle. I was in a place where I was content with never seeing him again in this life. I figured it would all get worked out in the next life. I'm so grateful it is getting worked out now."

CHAPTER 24

ENSLAVED TO ENLIGHTENED

How Belief Breakthrough Liberated My Life
Through Forgiveness and Love

By McLean Taylor

I never thought I would lose trust in God. But I did. I didn't trust Him for a long time. I didn't trust myself, either.

My Story

I've always been a very religious person. I believe in God and in my Savior Jesus Christ. For as long as I can remember, I went to church every Sunday. I even served a two-year service mission for my church. So when I met my wife, marriage was definitely something I wanted and something I deeply believed in.

After prayer and careful thought, I asked her to marry me. We were in love and I knew this was the right course for me and my future. I was excited and looking forward to many years of happiness.

Over time, the trust my wife and I shared at the beginning of our marriage became frail. Many of her actions went against my standards and beliefs, and began to wear down my trust in her. I wanted to trust her. I wanted to trust that the inspiration I'd received to marry her was in alignment. I wanted to trust that our marriage would make it through these rough patches. But there came a point when my trust weakened beyond repair. I was afraid for my emotional health, and I knew that I couldn't, in good conscience, bring children into such a dishonest and unhealthy environment. It may seem like a given, but I wanted children at some point.

After we divorced, I fell into a deep depression. I went two weeks straight without functioning; all I could do was think about what went wrong in my marriage. My family worried about me and took care of my needs. My mother came over daily during those two weeks, bringing meals and a smile, though it was hard for me to smile back. My brother was central in helping me pass my classes that semester; I'll always be grateful for his assistance.

Panic attacks were common during this time, and eventually I took medication to combat them. I couldn't stop feeling like I was a slave to bitterness, resentfulness, and anger. I wondered if God even loved me. Why would He tell me to marry her and let this happen? While I knew He was there, I didn't want to trust Him anymore. Eventually, I chose not to trust Him. Frankly, I didn't trust myself either.

I took on a very deep and dark limiting belief at this time: "I am not worthy." I felt I wasn't worthy of a good marriage and the blessings that come from a happy union. I felt I wasn't worthy of happiness because I must have done something wrong to cause my divorce.

Subconsciously, most things made me feel unworthy. I thought I was fine consciously, and I even told people I was worthy of a better life. But I didn't truly believe it. I couldn't. This belief was so deeply rooted that it was easy to ignore and live life as if everything was fine, even if I wasn't truly happy or fulfilled.

This subconscious belief, along with my bitterness, resentment, anger, and feelings of unworthiness spurred on self-deprecating habits. I wasn't proud of these habits; I knew they were against the standards and commandments I had always been taught. But I didn't care. I didn't want to listen to any of God's commandments or counsel. His counsel had led me to a painful marriage. I did not want to trust God with my happiness again. Ultimately, I just didn't care to feel the heartache and pain I felt God placed upon me, and these choices seemed like the best escape.

These habits took their toll on me emotionally and spiritually, just as they would on anyone who held my same standards and beliefs. Maybe it was so devastating to me spiritually because I was so religious and knew deep down that what I was doing was wrong. Regardless, I felt trapped and enslaved to my beliefs and to the actions and habits that resulted from those beliefs. Finally, I came to a point when I knew it was time to change.

Beginning to Change

I was terrified to go and meet with my ecclesiastical leader and make the changes I needed to make. So many thoughts raced through my head: *I can't be forgiven. I've gone too far. I'll never be worthy.* I believed God would just expect me to mess up again, so why would He forgive me THIS time?

Of course, that's not how God handles our mistakes. Eventually, I worked things out with my ecclesiastical leader and God and moved forward with my life. I thought I was making good progress—then I was invited to Limitless. At Limitless, I quickly realized that my progress would be stunted without working out the beliefs I still held about myself because of my mistakes.

Limitless

I attended Limitless for the first time in August 2016. I enjoyed what I heard and experienced during the general sessions, but the real shift came when I had an angel breakthrough session.

The limiting belief that came out when I sat down with one of the breakthrough specialists was, "If I quit my current job and pursue a career in building my own mentoring business, doing seminars, humanitarian work, etc., then I will lose stability. Maybe I might even lose all my money and opportunities for success in the future."

That belief was really specific, so the angel asked me to ground and find the number one limiting belief holding me back. What I identified as my number one limiting belief was, "I'm not worthy. I'll never be enough."

My breakthrough was special and profound. I walked away with a new vision of who I am. I saw myself on a completely new level. I saw myself as powerful and worthy, stable and divine. I saw myself in my greatness. I saw my purpose.

My new belief wasn't just, "I AM worthy; I AM enough," although I fully believed I was worthy and enough in that moment. My new belief was deeper than that: "I am liberation."

When I spoke those words, I felt lighter, I felt free, empowered, and liberated from all that was holding me back, and I saw myself worthy to be the man I always wanted to be: a liberator for those around me.

I am Liberation.

Another Layer

After my breakthrough, I thought I had moved beyond my belief of unworthiness. I joined the Limitless Inner Circle and started working on my limiting beliefs with a vengeance. First, I worked through my feelings of victimhood left over from my divorce. Then I found my message and launched my own mentoring platform helping people take ownership of their lives.

Result after result showed up to parallel my increased belief in myself. In four months, I earned the equivalent of my previous yearly income. I stopped having panic attacks, got rid of my anxiety, and left depression behind. I committed to my long-time girlfriend and asked her to marry me. I thought I had found happiness and joy.

And I had. I *was* happy. I was fulfilled. I was doing everything I had always wanted. But there was still work for me to do.

The January 2017 Limitless Inner Circle weekend was another game changer for me. Kris introduced a new process that freaked me out. This process involved trusting someone to verbally guide me through a maze of mouse and rat traps while I walked through the traps to the other side of the room, barefoot and blindfolded. I wasn't allowed to ask questions or speak at all, just walk forward.

I don't usually get scared during Limitless processes, and I've never had a process that I've opted out of before, but this process put me in my place. I was deeply triggered and afraid, and I didn't know why. A Belief Breakthrough Coach took me aside for a breakthrough. I was so grateful, as I was crying and very embarrassed. In that breakthrough, I discovered that I was afraid of what I cannot see. If I can't see something, then it is hard to believe it is true.

There were lots of areas in my life where I didn't believe because I couldn't see. I lacked faith. That January, the concept I struggled with was forgiveness. I can't see forgiveness. Therefore, how can I know that I am truly forgiven?

Years after working through my divorce and my subsequent rebellious phase, I still didn't feel forgiven, because I couldn't see it. And part of me didn't want to believe I'd been forgiven, if that really was the case, because I wasn't worthy of forgiveness. I could never be enough, never be the man God wanted me to be. I still felt trapped and powerless. How could God forgive me for what I had done? How could I forgive myself, too?

My breakthrough that day was even more powerful than the one at Limitless. It healed a hole in my heart that had been in a blind spot, hidden, for a long time. My new beliefs that night were numerous and powerful: "I am forgiven." "I forgive myself." "I am a leader." "I have always been the man He wants me to be."

I am Liberation, and I felt I had finally liberated myself.

Limitless Lessons

After attending Limitless and joining the Limitless Inner Circle, I learned many valuable lessons which have brought me to my liberated life of happiness, contentment, and peace. The following are some of the vital principles which have led to my success.

Integrity – During the many mornings I was working out with Kris, I would arrive late. Five o'clock in the morning is early, and I would regularly arrive 10-15 minutes late. I justified my tardiness by telling myself I didn't need as much time at the gym since I didn't want to run as long as Kris. But Kris nailed me hard on this lack of integrity. He told me that if I cannot be relied upon in the small moments, how could I be relied upon in the moments that really mattered? THAT got to me. I wanted to be known as the man that people can always rely on.

Since that discussion, I am always on time. When I give my word, I keep it. As I have kept myself accountable to the things I've said or agreed to, I've noticed people's attitudes towards me have changed for the better. And I feel a higher level of self-respect for myself knowing I have raised my level of integrity.

To me, raising integrity is just a matter of keeping your word in the big but especially the little things, at all times and in all places. Are you keeping your word in every aspect of your life, in both the big and the little areas? What can you do to raise your integrity level today?

Trust – Before Limitless, I didn't trust others to do a good job. I was in the mindset, "If I want something done right, I need to do it myself." Kris Krohn taught me a different mindset: "If you want something done right, DO NOT do it yourself."

Kris practices the principles he teaches. He *always* hires experts to do the things he either doesn't want to do, or hasn't put the time into being exceptionally good at. As a result of trusting others, his businesses continue to flourish.

My friend Ben Allred took his business to $1 million in nine months, because he learned to let others run his business. He trusted the expertise of his employees, and he reaped incredible benefits.

I cannot do everything, nor do I want to. But there are tasks I need completed to get where I want to go, so I needed to learn how to trust. I've learned to let others do the work when they are more qualified and more passionate than I am, and I am more successful because of it. As I have applied this level of trust with those around me, I have stepped into a higher level of respect and leadership. The people who work with me trust me because I trust them. Learn to trust that someone else will do the job right and watch your success increase.

How You Do One Thing is How You Do All Things – This is a very popular saying at Limitless. And it's true. If someone lets a fear stop them from doing the things they want to do, that same fear will show up in other aspects of life. If someone plays big in their goals and dreams, chances are, they also play big in relationships with money, people, and health.

If someone is shy on a dance floor, where else could they be shy when it matters most?

When I learned this concept, I started applying it into everything I do. When I dance, I dance big. When I do business, I make massive waves. When I write a book, I want that book to be a bestseller, every time! And when I am at home with my wife – I want her to know that she is my everything, my world, and my best friend. As I have applied this, I have been much happier and achieved more peace in my life … and I'm having a lot more fun.

How do you do the little things in your life? Are you playing small and living in fear? Or are you living big and seeing massive results in your peace, finances, fulfillment, and happiness?

Belief Breakthrough – Since joining the Limitless Inner Circle, I have absorbed as much as I can about belief breakthrough. I have learned that not only can it change my life, but it can change the lives of everyone around me. My breakthroughs have a ripple effect. As I break through beliefs, I become more liberated and free from any negativity that holds me down. When that happens, my friends and family step up to that same level of breakthrough and experience their own liberation in their beliefs, behaviors, and results.

Belief breakthrough is a powerful tool, which I believe the world needs to apply constantly. We change our beliefs to align with our desired confidence, happiness, and success. A simple shift in the way we choose to believe manifests our desired results. This is what belief breakthrough does.

Be Present – This is one of my favorite principles. Eternity is a forever of "right now" moments. But Eternity will pass us by if we choose not to live in the present. Too often we live in the future (fear or worry) or in the past (regret). But we only control what is happening right now. You cannot change the past, and you cannot control the future. So why let the past or future affect your emotions or even your decisions?

If you want more out of life, take a deep breath and recognize how alive you are in this moment. Look at the beauty around you. Put this book down and look up for a moment. This moment is unique to you and it will never happen again.

Celebrate the Journey – Part of the beauty of life is the journey—the journey of developing a business or a love relationship or finding the chiseled body you're after. I've taken on a mantra in my life to remind myself to celebrate the journey. I might fall; that's okay. Triumph or defeat is in the eye of the beholder. I choose triumph in my journey, and not just at the end of it. I choose it every step of the way. Let's celebrate each "right now" moment of eternity.

Make More Decisions – If a man wants to be successful in any area of his life, this is the most important lesson I can offer: Make more decisions. When we make a decision, we change our position in life. Whether we fail or succeed, a decision always gives us an opportunity to learn and grow. And eventually, we will succeed, just like Thomas Edison succeeded after trying 1,000 times to invent the lightbulb.

It is better to make 100 quick decisions with 10 bad mistakes and 90 good choices than it is to spend the same amount of time making ONE perfect decision. You'll find your motivation in making decisions, so make more decisions. Trust your intuition, and get moving!

Liberation: The Result of Transformation

I used to think I wouldn't recover from my disastrous life. I didn't believe I could be forgiven. I never thought I could be something more than a disappointment, sinner, and divorcee. I thought I would remain broken and lost for the rest of my life. I believed I was a victim, and that God was a villain. Now I am whole: happy, forgiven, liberated. I am enough, and I am worthy of all God's blessings. I love God again. I love myself again.

If you want to change, you can. You can take ownership of your life and create something better, happier, and more fulfilling.

If you think you're limited, you're wrong. It is possible to become Limitless. It's just a matter of shifting your beliefs.

Anything is possible if you just believe. It sounds cliché, but it's true.

And my life is proof of that.

I am Liberation.

CHAPTER 25

YOUR NEXT STEPS TO A LIMITLESS LIFE

Christopher Crawford said, "Knowledge without application is like a book that is never read." You've read to the end of this book. If you don't want to waste the precious time you've spent reading, here are the steps I recommend you take:

1. Do Belief Breakthrough Work Daily

Remember the first question of the belief breakthrough process: "What is the number one limiting belief keeping me from my greatness?"

Many people worry that they're not actually getting to the core belief. The truth is that it doesn't matter what comes up when you ask that question. It may not be the real root, but it points to the truth. All you have to do is stay consistent with the belief breakthrough work and eventually, everything will be revealed.

Belief breakthrough is like peeling the layers of an onion. Just start with what comes up initially for you. Uncover and reprogram one belief at a time. Then move onto the next one. The longer and more consistently you do it, the more likely you are to uncover the real root fears, wounds, and false beliefs.

> *"A small daily task, if it be really daily, will beat the labours of a spasmodic Hercules."*
>
> –ANTHONY TROLLOPE

This is why I teach people to use the Limitless wristband, where you start each day with the black side showing, then flip it to display the red side after changing a limiting belief. It's a powerful visual reminder to do the work, as well as a way to demonstrate progress and encourage yourself.

As you get skilled with the nine steps of belief breakthrough and have them memorized, you'll find that you can process beliefs much more quickly. When you're ready for that, you can shift quickly using these steps:

1. Ground.
2. Ask, "What is the number one limiting belief keeping me from my greatness?" (Or ask a more directed question in response to a specific struggle or trigger.)
3. What belief would serve me better?
4. State the new belief with conviction.

2. Recite Your "Belief Manifesto" Daily

In Chapter 8, I taught you to keep a daily journal of the limiting beliefs you uncover and the new beliefs you change them to. Next, you'll want to recite your list of new beliefs daily.

This ties back into Johari's Window. Here's another way to look at the four quadrants:

1. Unconsciously Incompetent: You're incompetent in this area, but you're not aware that you are.
2. Consciously Incompetent: You're incompetent in this area, and you're aware of your incompetence.
3. Consciously Competent: You're competent in this area, and you know you are.
4. Unconsciously Competent: You're competent in this area, but your competence has become so second nature that you do it without thought.

Doing daily breakthrough work uncovers the areas in which you're "unconsciously incompetent." After doing the work for a while and recording your new beliefs, your journal will include beliefs that now feel "unconsciously competent." They are voluntarily and chemically programmed to stick and now feel like a natural part of you.

3. Engage with a Belief Breakthrough Mentor

As I mentioned at the beginning of this book, I owe my breakthrough process and my life's results to a number of wise and caring mentors who have helped me break through my ceiling of limitations.

A mentor is someone who has been where you want to go and, because of his or her experience, sees things you can't see. Good mentors point out our blind spots and help us avoid pitfalls. They help us get to the root of what's really happening when we feel angry, upset, frustrated, confused, or fearful. They help us to be self-honest and self-aware. They give us the support we need to cultivate more courage and confidence.

"You become what you think about most."

–EARL NIGHTINGALE

This isn't just my opinion—research proves the value of mentoring. MicroMentor.org connects entrepreneurs with mentors. In 2012, they surveyed users of their service and found that, "those who received mentoring increased their revenue by an average of $47,000, or 106 percent," and, "those who did not receive mentoring only increased their revenue by an average of $6,600, or 14 percent." They also found that 49 percent of pre-launch business that received mentoring actually ended up starting their businesses, and 82 percent survived for one to two years. That's 13 percent higher survival rate than the average new business in the U.S.[1]

In another study, Sun Microsystems compared the career progress of approximately 1,000 employees over a five-year period and found that "employees who received mentoring were promoted five times more often than people who didn't have mentors."[2]

To find and work with a certified belief breakthrough mentor, attend a Limitless event. There are many certified mentors within the tribe.

4. Attend a Limitless Seminar

The Limitless three-day live seminars catalyze life-changing breakthroughs. Live events are so powerful to open your mind and heart, reveal your blind spots, and motivate you to make a change.

These events push you out of your comfort zone while also providing a deep sense of safety and belonging, thus enabling healing through self-honesty and vulnerability. They broaden and deepen your understanding of the Limitless philosophy and methodology. They connect you with like-minded people who can support you in your journey.

In this book I've included two tickets to attend your first Limitless event for free (this event costs $499 per person, so this is a $998 value). To see the dates for the next Limitless Live event, visit www.LimitlessSeminar.com.

Here are just a few raw, unedited testimonials of hundreds we've received from people who have attended the event:

"Limitless was one of the most empowering three days of my life. I do belief reprogramming and breakthrough work with my clients every day, but I know I also need to receive mentoring and breakthrough work to embrace my fullest potential. The biggest 'aha' moments come when we are out of our routine, learning to observe what we have blindly been thinking and feeling, and having someone else guide us to a new way of Being that we couldn't see on our own. I was so thrilled by this experience that I have invited several friends, clients, and family members to join me next time, and most of them have said 'Yes!' I can't wait to see you there!" —JANECE H.

"Limitless was a turning point for me, how I see myself and what I know I am cable of. I already had a very healthy, happy and thriving marriage to my sweetheart, but this event also brought new clarity, vision, and purpose to our relationship than what we have ever experienced so far! I would highly recommend this event to anyone looking to transform their limiting beliefs into Limitless opportunities and success!" —JARED T.

"Limitless has changed my life, my marriage, and my connection with my children. It has transformed my business, and ultimately brought me closer to my highest self, and to my God. It is the best gift I have been given, an answer to prayer, and the best gift I can give." —MARIANNE D.

"Going to Limitless was more than informative...it was transformational! I have been to many seminars and by far this was one of my favorites. With the breakthrough process alone, I was able to take my wifes hip pain that had been around for years and in 15 minutes completely eliminate the pain. Aside from the life transformational content and experience, the people at limitless are amazing to connect with. You will not find a more motivated group to be with. I loved it so much I bought my whole family tickets and they are flying out from Arkansas and Wyoming to come! Rock on!" —TYLER D.

"I went to limitless to break through my weight loss & food blocks. With the help of Kris Krohn & several other members of the tribe, I am LIMITLESS in my weight loss! 18 days after standing on the stage with Kris I am down 16 pounds." —JESSICA L.

"The changes in my life since attending Limitless have been unbelievable. Not only have I already lost 28 Limiting Beliefs but my career is taking off because I accept that I have amazing value to give to others." —BRADY M.

"It sounds cliché, but this program IS LIFE CHANGING!! Limitless mindset training has given me renewed hope!! I understand what being aligned REALLY means. I can now evaluate a set-back with a mindset of 'Great what can I lean from this?' You will never look back again after attending because you'll always be looking forward consciously creating and declaring what you really want in life!!" —JORGINA H.

"I have shed 50 pounds of body fat in 90 days because of my Limitless experience. I'm halfway to my goal of shedding 100 pounds and I've just made the decision to run a marathon in the spring of 2016! That's right, from 290 pounds and unable to jog more than 90 SECONDS to 239 pounds and I'm running for 30 continues minutes just 90 days later! I am Limitless!" —GARY N.

"I had begun learning this process prior to limitless, but limitless helped me to release things holding me back quicker. I came back and brought my husband and 2 teenage boys with me the next month. In just 3 days, we saw more progress in our relationships than several years of working on it. As a couple we have done seminars before, but we haven't been able to sustain the progress because of limiting beliefs. This was an answer to prayers!" —HEATHER W.

"I attended my first Limitless event in March 2016 expecting to take away some nuggets to apply in my quest to improve my life over time and take my business up a notch. I was amazed at the breakthroughs I made in the 3 days. My first breakthrough was on day 1 with the assistance of their facilitators. During the second day I made several breakthroughs and eliminated several limiting beliefs and replaced them with empowering beliefs. I'm accustomed to making rapid changes in my life but this experience exceeded all of my expectations and beliefs, consequently I joined the Inner Circle and am excited and ready to step into my power. Thank you limitless team for making it possible for the miracles that are manifesting in my life. I AM LIMITLESS." —DANIEL L.

5. Get Certified in Belief Breakthrough

Many people who attend Limitless seminars and get involved with the community feel inspired to get certified to do the work themselves. They experience such dramatic improvements in their own lives that they want to share what they've learned with other people.

If this book has really connected with you, I invite you to come to an event and inquire about certification.

Can You Do Belief Breakthrough Work on Your Own?

After giving you those recommendations, I need to clarify something. Yes, it's possible to do belief breakthrough work on your own. You can take what you've learned in this book and uncover and process your limiting beliefs yourself. I've seen hundreds of people do it. They take the same script you now have and step into a whole new limitless world.

However, mastery comes even more quickly and powerfully when you work with certified experts—or eventually get certified yourself. Attending a Limitless event and working with a belief breakthrough mentor helps you really focus and jump-start your breakthrough work.

I'm living my ideal life now. But I could have achieved it even faster had I learned about belief breakthrough work and engaged with mentors sooner. If I could travel back in time and change anything in my life, it would be mastering belief breakthrough much sooner than I did. *Nothing* would have changed my results more quickly and dramatically than that one thing.

I hope this book changes your life. I hope I've given you enough information to help you make dramatic shifts. If it does make a difference for you, my invitation would be to take it to the next level and attend a Limitless seminar. There's just nothing that can replace live interaction with mentors and other people on the same journey as you.

CHAPTER 26

ENJOY THE JOURNEY

If you've ever been to Hawaii, you've probably heard of the famous "Road to Hana." It's on Maui, the north shore. The first time my wife and I went to Hawaii everyone told us we had to drive the road to Hana. We were excited to do it, but hesitated when we learned that it takes all day. We only had a week, and to take a full day out of our schedule to do this one thing was a big commitment. But we decided to go and rented a convertible.

We purchased a guidebook that gave directions to all the attractions along the way. The first stop took us through thick jungle to an amazing waterfall. Two miles down the road we came to a red sand beach, the only one on the planet. Next we saw a black sand beach. That was followed by "Ohe'o Gulch," meaning "something special," and it certainly is. It's seven pools with awesome waterfalls flowing into each other. The day was breathtaking and amazing—one of the most memorable of my life.

> *"The highest reward of man's toil is not what he gets for it, but what he becomes by it."*
>
> –JOHN RUSKIN

Then we rolled into Hana to find...nothing but a tiny little village. There's absolutely nothing to do in Hana itself. I was disappointed at first because I thought the whole point was to get to Hana.

I've found this to be an accurate metaphor for life. We get so focused on and consumed with the destination itself. We think our destinations, or our accomplishments and achievements, define us.

But this journey of Limitless really is about the journey itself. You have to learn to be fulfilled while moving in the direction of your dreams and allowing the laws of creation to manifest your desire in the appropriate time and space. Less important than your accomplishments is who you become on the journey.

Without this critical mind shift, the pursuit of Limitless becomes a frantic, anxious quest that can actually undermine us. It can deepen, rather than alleviate, our sense of inadequacy that got us to start the journey in the first place. Without the right mindset, when we don't achieve our goals on our timeline, we feel like failures. Most importantly, we simply don't appreciate the process of growth on the journey.

Here's how to embrace and enjoy the journey:

Focus on Presence

It's good to learn from the past and plan for the future. But all too often we harbor regret from the past and obsess with the future, thus robbing us of our happiness in the present moment.

Both the past and the future are only in your mind. All you have is right here, right now, this moment. Yes, by all means dream of the things you want to accomplish and experience. Make and execute plans to achieve your goals. But truly live in this moment.

"To live is the rarest thing in the world. Most people just exist, that is all."

–OSCAR WILDE

Take a moment right now to pause and drink in the present moment. Look around you. What do you see? Feel your body, your hands, your feet. Breathe deeply. Empty your mind of all thoughts and simply *be*. Now make that a regular habit and watch how your anxiety and stress decrease and your happiness increases.

Reconcile the past by doing your belief breakthrough work to bring you back into the present. Use the laws of manifesting to bring the future into the present. Equipped with both belief breakthrough and the Laws of Conscious Creation, you possess the tools to be fully present.

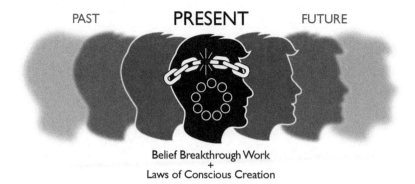

PAST   PRESENT   FUTURE

Belief Breakthrough Work
+
Laws of Conscious Creation

Practice Conscious Gratitude

Pausing to count our blessings is a powerful way to stop negative emotions in their tracks. Robert Emmons, psychologist and author of *Thanks! How the New Science of Gratitude Can Make You Happier,* says that people who cultivate and practice gratitude are 25 percent happier than those who do not.

In a study performed by Emmons and a colleague, they divided several hundred people into three groups. All of them agreed to write in diaries. The first group was asked to write about good things or bad things; it didn't matter. The second group was asked to write only about bad things, and the third group was asked only to write about good things they were thankful for.

The participants who wrote about the things they were grateful for in their lives daily ended up, in follow-up assessments, being more alert, more enthusiastic and optimistic, and more energetic than the other participants in the other two groups. They had less stress and less feelings of depression. They found time to exercise during the duration of the study period, as opposed to those in the other groups. They also said they were able to make progress towards personal goals.

Neuroscientist Alex Korb, PhD, calls this effect "the upward spiral," in his book, *The Upward Spiral: Using Neuroscience to Reverse the Course of Depression, One Small Change at a Time.* According to his research, gratitude has the same biological effect as well-known and widely used antidepressant drugs, such as Wellbutrin, which boost the neurotransmitter dopamine. He writes, "The benefits of gratitude start with the dopamine system, because feeling grateful activates the brain stem region that produces dopamine. Additionally, gratitude toward others increases activity in social dopamine circuits, which makes social interactions more enjoyable."

Additionally, when we think of things for which we're grateful, our brain is forced to focus on the positive aspects of our life, which increases serotonin production in the anterior cingulate cortex—in the same way that Prozac does. Korb explains,

> It's not finding gratitude that matters most; it's remembering to look in the first place. Remembering to be grateful is a form of emotional intelligence. One study found that it actually affected neuron density in both the ventromedial and lateral prefrontal cortex. These density changes suggest that as emotional intelligence increases, the neurons in these areas become more efficient. With higher emotional intelligence, it simply takes less effort to be grateful.

In 2016 my family and I, along with twenty Limitless tribe members, went on a humanitarian trip to Kenya. We repaired local school buildings, built an orphanage, helped establish two new women's empowerment centers, did a clean water project, gave livestock, and provided a number of other relief efforts. This was my first time visiting rural Africa. I was amazed by how little the people had, but far more amazed by how present, peaceful and grateful they were. My whole perspective shifted witnessing these beautiful people live from a space of gratitude.

Be present and grateful as you do your breakthrough work.

Celebrate Little Victories

Make it a point to celebrate your progress, however small and insignificant it seems. Celebrate every pound lost, even if the goal is to lose fifty. Celebrate every dollar earned, even if the goal is to make

$10,000. Celebrate every choice to be happy when working on improving a relationship.

In truth, *no* progress is insignificant! It all matters. We all love to be encouraged and recognized by others. Why not do it for yourself? You'll travel much faster and enjoy the journey much more when you give yourself encouragement rather than criticism.

> *"We learn wisdom from failure much more than from success; we often discover what will do, by finding out what will not do; and he who never made a mistake never made a discovery."*
>
> –SAMUEL SMILES

You may not be where you want to be right now. But think of where you were five years ago, or ten years ago. What improvements do you see? How are you better? What have you accomplished?

Part of this is seeing all the evidence that your efforts are working. More precisely, it's interpreting all evidence through that lens—even the evidence that appears to contradict. Ultimately, it's all just an interpretation anyway, right? So why not interpret evidence as everything is going your way—even your mistakes and challenges?

Speaking of which…

Embrace Challenges and Mistakes

You're going to encounter obstacles. You're going to make mistakes. That's just part of the journey. In fact, that's the whole reason for the journey—to learn and grow.

Learn to reframe your obstacles as challenges, and your mistakes as learning. Reframe risks as experiments—you're not being crazy, you're just testing to see what works and what doesn't. Instead of being an emotional mess when things don't go as expected, be a scientist and learn from the experiment. Make wisdom the new object of your obsession. Value the lessons more than the results and your desires will manifest as natural byproducts. Belief breakthrough is the process of learning the lessons that health, wealth and happiness are made of.

> *"Everything that is past is either a learning experience to grow on, a beautiful memory to reflect on, or a motivating factor to act upon."*
>
> –DENIS WAITLEY

Remember that "problems" are merely perceptions in the mind. Learn to view your problems as opportunities to grow and develop. It is so empowering to laugh in the face of disappointment, choose bliss when you fall short, and feel peace when your world appears to be falling apart.

Don't forget to have fun with this process! You're learning and growing. You're becoming who you were born to become. You're fulfilling your potential.

Reconnect with What Limitless is Really About

Remember my definitions of what it means to be limitless in each of the four domains of life?

- **Limitless Power:** Being our highest and best self in every moment.
- **Limitless Wealth:** Having access to any resources necessary to fulfill every moment in its highest and best way.
- **Limitless Health:** Having the physical health, energy, and ability to fulfill every moment in its highest and best way.
- **Limitless Connection:** Having unconditional love for ourselves and others to fulfill every moment in its highest and best way.

"When we are motivated by goals that have deep meaning, by dreams that need completion, by pure love that needs expressing, then we truly live life."

–GREG ANDERSON

I remind you of these because I really want you to understand what this Limitless journey is really about. It's not about accumulating material things so we can show off how successful we are. It's not about living the high life and stroking our ego. It's about becoming the best version of ourselves and using our gifts, light, and power to make a difference for others.

I once visited King Tut's tomb in the Valley of Kings in Egypt. It's an enormous monument to a man who tried to bring his possessions and power into the next life. The ancient pharaohs believed they could take things into the next life with them. They illustrate this with hieroglyphic images of the boat that transports them from this life to the next. They always show so much more on the ship traveling into the next life than they started with.

But no one—not even pharaohs—have the power to take earthly possessions to the next life. So what are we really collecting in our journey of life? In a limitless life, we are collecting fulfillment—the intangible but unmistakable feeling we get when we spend a moment in the most inspiring way possible as our highest and best self.

"Our most valuable possessions are those which when shared multiply; our least valuable possessions are those which when shared diminish."

–WILLIAM DANFORTH

Whatever you achieve in life may be better than the village of Hana, but I guarantee it won't be more valuable than the road you take to get there. For it's on the road that you become who you were born to be.

CHAPTER 27

ONE LIFE TO LIVE

It happened when I was eighteen years old. My family was vacationing at Cannon Beach, Oregon, a beautiful little town on the coast. We went there every summer. This was going to be my last time taking that family trip before I left home.

My younger sister, Laurie, and I were wading in the ocean and riding the waves. On this beach, the ocean slopes out very gradually, so you have to go way out to be even waist deep, where you can hardly see people on the shore. It was a windy day, which made for great waves. The swells were eight to ten feet tall.

I caught a massive wave. When the wave passed, I could barely touch my toe to the ground. Suddenly, I felt a strong rip current. I immediately backed up toward the shore until I was on solid ground and out of the rip tide.

I looked for my sister and noticed with alarm that she was being pulled out into the ocean. I yelled at her, "Laurie, swim back in!" She was getting further and further away and I could tell she was tired. She wasn't a strong swimmer. I knew she was in trouble, and my blood ran chill. I kept jumping up and down and shouting at her.

I looked back at the shore and saw that my father had seen us and was running for help. But I knew he'd never make it back in time to save her.

I had a choice in that moment: jump in and take a huge risk to save my sister or watch her drown and regret it for the rest of my life. There was no way I was going to live with that. I jumped in and swam toward her as fast as I could.

When I got to her, she was so tired that she was starting to go under. I used my Boy Scouts training to grab a hold of her properly and start carrying her back towards shore. But I wasn't strong enough to do anything other than keep our heads above water, and even that was an extreme struggle. We were both exhausted.

I was struck with the terrifying realization, "This is it. We're both going to die." I felt so helpless. I was overcome with regret for all the things I hadn't done, experienced, and accomplished. I had not lived my purpose for being born.

I started screaming prayers to God, as if they could rise above the noise of the ocean. I desperately wanted to be heard.

To this day I know with all my heart that it was a miracle: A huge wave came right in that moment and swept us toward the shore until we could stand up. My sister was so tired that I had to carry her out of the water. My mom was bawling and cried, "You saved your sister's life!"

I responded, "I didn't save anyone's life. We were saved."

In that moment I vowed I would never take my life for granted. I vowed to live my life to the fullest. That experience has given me the strength to face some of my most painful limiting beliefs. It has given me the courage to push through the darkness of my worst trials. It has propelled me to do everything I can to live a fulfilling life and to make the greatest difference I can in the short time I have.

> *"Our obligation is to give meaning to life and in doing so to overcome the passive, indifferent life."*
>
> –ELIE WIESEL

I love my life. I LOVE my life! I have been so blessed. I want with all my heart for you to feel the same about your life.

I don't believe it's an accident that you're reading this book. In some vast, incomprehensible scheme, for some great and unfathomable purpose, you and I have been drawn together. We have been searching for each other, and now we have been found. We have shared a lot of time together as you have read this book.

I'm so honored to play a role in your life, as you have in mine. You have one life to live. You've got one shot to make it as breathtaking and awe-inspiring as possible. I ask you in the words of the poet Mary Oliver, "Tell me, what is it you plan to do with your one wild and precious life?"

My burning hope is that you will choose to cast off the shackles of limiting beliefs and unleash your infinite potential in service to the world. This is about much more than your personal happiness—the world needs you. The world needs your gifts and your light. The world needs you to become your best self.

You've spent valuable time reading about my life and many others who are applying the principles of Limitless to break through their limitations and create their ideal life.

Now it's *your* turn.

I don't want you sitting on the sidelines watching other people's lives change. I want you to jump into the trenches, do the work for yourself, and begin experiencing your own breakthroughs.

It's your turn to crush your limitations.

It's your turn to discover your genius, light, and purpose.

It's your turn to heal.

It's your turn to shine.

It's your turn to claim the limitless power, wealth, health, and connection that are your birthright.

The only thing stopping you is your own beliefs. Everything you need to transform your life is inside you. You have the power. Will you claim it?

"Twenty years from now you will be more disappointed by the things you didn't do than by the ones you did do. So throw off the bowlines. Sail away from the safe harbor. Catch the trade winds in your sails. Explore. Dream. Discover."

–H. JACKSON BROWN, JR.

···

···

···

···

···

···

···

···

···

···

···

···

···

···

···

···

···

···

···

···

BELIEF BREAKTHROUGH SCRIPT

STEP 1	**GROUND**
	Use deep breathing with your eyes closed to get into a meditative state. The purpose of grounding is to separate from your thoughts and connect to intuition. Clear your mind of all thoughts and prepare to receive answers.
STEP 2	**IDENTIFY A LIMITING BELIEF**
	Ask yourself, "What is the number one limiting belief coming up for me?" Listen for the intuitive answer. Trust that whatever comes up is exactly what you need to work on in this moment, especially if it doesn't seem to make sensee.
STEP 3	**EXPLORE YOUR MEMORIES**
	Ask yourself, "What is the first memory that comes up when I think this thought?" Trust that whatever memory arises is the perfect place to focus your breakthrough work.
STEP 4	**IDENTIFY THE DEEPER LIMITING BELIEF**
	Ask yourself, "What did I decide about myself when I experienced this?" What comes from this is the deeper belief than you found in Step 2 and is the one you really need to work with.

	EXAMINE THE COST OF THE LIMITING BELIEF
STEP 5	Ask yourself, "What is the cost of believing this thought?" Examine how this belief is showing up in your life. How has it affected your results in the past and present? How will it affect you in the future if you don't change it? Consider how it impacts other aspects of your life, including finances, physical health, relationships, and personal power.
	GIVE YOURSELF PERMISSION TO SHIFT
STEP 6	Consciously choose to shift your beliefs and make a change.
	CREATE A NEW BELIEF
STEP 7	Make the choice to change your old limiting belief to a new, empowering belief that will serve you better. State the new belief in first person and in the present tense.
	REWRITE YOUR STORY
STEP 8	Go back to this memory from which you created your false belief. Imagine reinterpreting the experience in a way that serves you better and that is more aligned with the truth of the new belief.
	CLAIM YOUR NEW BELIEF
STEP 9	Shift the energy and emotion anchored to the memory to a strong positive emotion. State your new belief out loud with confidence, conviction, and power. Say it repeatedly. Declare it in a way that feels most authentic to you. Commit to living this new belief, and find evidence to support it.

THE 5 STEPS OF MANIFESTING BREAKTHROUGH RESULTS

	CLEARLY DEFINE WHAT YOU WANT
STEP 1	Get crystal clear on exactly what you want to gain and achieve. What are you trying to make happen? How will you measure success? Can you see it in your mind's eye? Can you feel it? Once you've defined what you want, you must write it down. The goal must also be believable to you. If you don't believe to your bones that the goal is possible, you'll never achieve it. Choose goals that stretch your mind without breaking it.
	TAKE BOLD ACTION TOWARD YOUR GOAL
STEP 2	Set your intention, and then give everything you have to make it a reality. It's not enough to set a goal—you must also create a plan. Map out exactly what needs to happen in order for your goal to manifest. Detail precisely what you plan on doing to achieve your goal. Set benchmarks to track your progress. Plans must be adaptable. You have to be persistent, buoyant, and flexible. Learn from your mistakes and failures. Use the Law of Intuition to make decisions along the way. Trust and follow your intuition—even and especially when it seems crazy.

STEP 3	**BELIEVE AND ACT AS IF YOUR GOAL WERE ALREADY REALITY**
	Live as if your breakthrough is a reality, as if it were already happening. Feel it as if it were real. Use your imagination. If your breakthrough goal were to manifest right now, how would it feel? Conjure those emotions and bask in them. Your emotion is based on your "why." When your why is big enough and you want something bad enough, those emotions drive your behavior, not your logic. You can spend as much time with your manifestation in your mind as you would in reality. Either way is real to your mind.

STEP 4	**MASTER BELIEF BREAKTHROUGH**
	Go on a search-and-destroy mission to uncover and change every false belief that arises. Your goal is less dependent on hard work than it is on purifying your beliefs. Install a Limitless filter in your mind. Let every thought and spoken word represent an investment into what you want. Never invest in what you don't want. Enough breakthroughs equal transformation. Enough transformation equals a life-changing breakthrough.

STEP 5	**DO YOUR PART AND TRUST GOD TO DO HIS**
	Your part is to know the why and what. God's part is to do the when and how. Have faith that God is manifesting the how, whether it looks like it or not. You don't know how your goal will be manifest—and you don't need to know. You simply need to live the laws and take action toward your goal.

NEW BELIEFS REFERENCE GUIDE

1,000+ NEW BELIEFS TO TRANSFORM YOUR LIFE

This guide is a definitive list of the most common limiting beliefs I've encountered in working with thousands of people. With each limiting belief, you'll find examples of new beliefs to replace it with. The purpose of this guide is to 1) help you identify your limiting beliefs, and 2) to give you ideas of new beliefs. Visit and revisit this guide in your daily belief breakthrough work. It is particularly helpful if you struggle with creating new beliefs with which to replace your limiting beliefs.

I also invite you to study this guide to build a powerful "belief manifesto" from the new beliefs that resonate with you most. Read your belief manifesto out loud daily to inspirational music. You could even record yourself reading your manifesto, set the recording to music, and listen to it daily.

Remember that new beliefs should be present, positive, and powerful. Furthermore, they should originate from within you and not be contingent on the choices of others. For example, if you say, "I am loved by others," then you create a believe that requires the love of others for you to flourish. On the other hand, if you say, "I love me," then the belief comes from within.

TABLE OF CONTENTS

PERSONAL POWER BELIEFS

WEALTH BELIEFS

HEALTH BELIEFS

CONNECTION BELIEFS

PERSONAL POWER BELIEFS

Personal Power Beliefs Related to Myself

Limiting Belief:
- There's something wrong with me.

New Beliefs:
- I accept me in this moment.
- I am exactly as I should be.
- I am whole.
- Every experience helps me grow.

Limiting Belief:
- I am a loser.

New Beliefs:
- I am precious and priceless, like every other soul.
- I love and accept myself.
- I learn my lessons and move forward with my life.
- I take all the proper steps to correct my mistakes.
- I forgive myself.

Limiting Belief:
- I am damaged goods. My past controls me.

New Beliefs:
- I am whole.
- I am complete.
- I learn my lessons and move forward.
- I live in the present and release the past.
- I think, speak, and live in the present.
- I take ownership of my past and move forward boldly with the valuable lessons I have learned.

Limiting Belief:
- I am disgusting/filthy/wicked/evil.

New Beliefs:
- I forgive myself.
- I am clean and pure.
- I am magnificent and beautiful.
- I am good.
- I embody divine goodness.
- I choose righteousness.
- I make good choices.

Limiting Belief:
- I am too [insert characteristic, e.g. young, old, small, weak, etc.].

New Beliefs:
- I am the perfect [insert characteristic] for my next steps.
- I use my age to my advantage.

- I love and accept my current state.
- I am the perfect age to take my next steps.
- I am powerful.
- I am bigger than any circumstance or situation.

Limiting Belief:
- I am expendable and replaceable.

New Beliefs:
- I belong here.
- I am indispensable.
- I am needed.
- I live my purpose.
- I use my unique gifts to serve others.

Limiting Belief:
- I am afraid of what others will think about my decisions. I make decisions to keep the peace or to please others.

New Beliefs:
- I honor myself by making good choices.
- I am confident my choices are the best for me.
- I am open and excited to see the result of every decision.
- My decisions support my inner peace.

Limiting Belief:
- I am fake/a liar/a fraud.

New Beliefs:
- I accept, love, and embrace who I am.
- I am authentic.
- I am honest and truthful.
- I live, breathe, and defend truth.

Limiting Belief:
- I am not allowed to express myself (be happy, be sad, play, etc.).

New Beliefs:
- I love expressing my true authentic self.
- I own my voice.
- I allow myself to feel.
- I give myself permission to play.

Limiting Belief:
- I am not fun/likable.

New Beliefs:
- I am fun.
- I like me.
- I accept myself.

Limiting Belief:
- I am not loveable/special.

New Beliefs:
- I am loveable.
- I am special.
- I am valuable.

Limiting Belief:
- I am not okay with who I am/my personality.

New Beliefs:
- I love and accept myself.
- I am excited to be me.
- I love my life/my personality.

Limiting Belief:
- I am shy.

New Beliefs:
- I am outgoing.
- I am bold.
- I am fearless.
- I love people.

Limiting Belief:
- I am not ready.

New Beliefs:
- I am ready now.
- I stand ready at all times.
- I am an action taker.

Limiting Belief:
- I am procrastinator. I am always late or running out of time.

New Beliefs:
- I manage my time wisely.
- I start on time and end on time.
- I take action at the perfect time to create results and fulfillment.
- I spend my time on important things.
- I leverage my time to my advantage.
- There is always enough time for what is important to me.
- There is always enough time for the right choices.
- I always complete the right tasks at the right time.
- I choose what things I get done.

Limiting Belief:
- I am selfish if I have what I want.

New Beliefs:
- Doing what I want benefits the world.
- I am an example of creating the life I want.
- Fulfilling my purpose, blesses others.

Limiting Belief:
- I am stubborn.

New Beliefs:
- I embrace change.
- I am flexible.
- I am teachable.
- I love changing to step into my potential.

Limiting Belief:
- I am ugly/I am careless about how I look.

New Beliefs:
- I am beautiful/handsome.
- I have unconditional love for me and others.
- I am well dressed and well groomed.
- I take pride in my hygiene and appearance.
- I wear clothes that reflect my highest and best self.
- I dress authentically.

Limiting Belief:
- I am ungrateful/unkind.

New Beliefs:
- I am grateful.
- I express gratitude daily.
- I am kind to all people and in all situations.
- I see the best in everyone I meet.

Limiting Belief:
- I create drama. My life is a mess.

New Beliefs:
- I create peace.
- I find lessons, gifts, and purpose in my experiences.
- Learning from my past brings forth greater value for me and the world.
- I learn from my experiences and create greater order, beauty, and results.

Limiting Belief:
- I'm not creative.

New Beliefs:
- I am creative.
- I am a creator.
- I am resourceful.

Limiting Belief:
- I'm too busy/overwhelmed/stressed.

New Beliefs:
- My life is balanced.
- I focus on thoughts that serve me.
- I embrace my life path.
- I accomplish all that is needful.
- I delegate when needed.
- I know when to delegate and when to accomplish things myself.
- I experience peace in every obligation and responsibility.
- There is always enough time for every choice I make.

Limiting Belief:
- I am out of balance.

New Beliefs:
- I create balance in my life.
- I am in alignment in all areas of my life.
- I live my perfect balance of work, rest, purpose and play while being deeply connected to everyone around me
- I am in perfect sync and alignment.

Limiting Belief:
- I've reached my plateau.

New Beliefs:
- My potential is infinite.
- I continue to grow.
- All learning brings growth.
- I am always the student.
- I love taking action on what I am learning.
- I am progressing.
- I step powerfully into the next level of my life.
- I trust my next step.

Limiting Belief:
- When I speak the truth, bad things happen.

New Beliefs:
- I am honest regardless of the consequences.
- Honesty brings me peace.
- The truth sets me free.

Limiting Belief:
- I don't know what I want.

New Beliefs:
- I know exactly what I want and what brings me joy.
- I prioritize my time to create clarity for what I want.

Personal Power Beliefs Related to My Value

Limiting Belief:
- I am not good enough.

New Beliefs:
- I am good enough.
- I accept me.
- I love and accept myself unconditionally.
- I rejoice at the thought of me.
- I love myself unconditionally.
- I forgive myself.
- I love myself.
- I am an amazing individual.

Limiting Belief:
- I am worthless/unworthy/unimportant.

New Beliefs:
- I am worthy.
- I have infinite worth.
- I am important.
- I am divine.
- I am precious.
- I am a priceless gift.
- I make a difference.
- I am a powerful leader.
- I am valuable.
- I am invaluable.
- I am loved and wanted.

Limiting Belief:
- I can't invest in myself.

New Beliefs:
- I invest in myself through books, training, and mentoring.
- I create what I want wherever I am.
- I easily manifest the mentors I need.

Limiting Belief:
- I am afraid to live my purpose.

New Beliefs:
- I am confident in my purpose.
- I stand boldly in my purpose.
- I live my purpose.

Limiting Belief:
- Living my purpose is hard.

New Beliefs:
- Living my purpose is joyful and easy.
- I naturally and easily accomplish my purpose.

Limiting Belief:
- God doesn't approve of me living my purpose.

New Beliefs:
- I live the purpose that God calls me to.
- I fulfill my purpose as I align with what God wants me to do.
- People are brought to God as I live my purpose.

Limiting Belief:
- I can't be helped.

New Beliefs:
- I help myself.
- There is always help when I need it.
- I am resourceful.
- I have all the support I need.
- I am empowered by my abilities.
- I am powerful.
- I am divine.
- I humbly accept my greatness within and choose to share it.

Limiting Belief:
- I don't deserve help/service.

New Beliefs:
- I am worthy of the service and gifts I receive.

Limiting Belief:
- I don't get anything that I want.

New Beliefs:
- I manifest with faith.
- I receive all I ask for in the moment I need it most.
- I easily manifest exactly what I want.
- I always receive the perfect outcome at the perfect time.

- The outcome of my decision is perfect for what I need now.
- I embrace the unexpected.

Limiting Belief:
- I don't deserve it (joy, happiness, success, acknowledgement, etc.).

New Beliefs:
- I embrace my birthright of choice to be happy, abundant, connected, and powerful.
- My life is a miraculous life.
- I am joyful.
- I choose my happiness now.
- Happiness is available to me.
- Happiness comes from inside me.

Limiting Belief:
- It's unsafe to be vulnerable.

New Beliefs:
- My vulnerability creates safety, connection, and strength.
- I am vulnerable in ways that honor me.
- My vulnerability blesses those around me.

Limiting Belief:
- There are no miracles in my life.

New Beliefs:
- I witness miracles all around me.
- My life is a miracle.

Limiting Belief:
- I don't inspire me or anyone else. I don't have a powerful message.

New Beliefs:
- I am inspiring.
- I am inspirational to me.
- I attract people who are inspired by me.
- I have a powerful message.
- I am powerful and confident as I deliver my message.
- I think, speak, and communicate with absolute clarity.
- I am confident in my communication abilities.
- I am an influential person.
- My influence grows every day.
- My choices expand my influence every day.
- My influence leaves a legacy that changes the world.

Limiting Belief:
- I don't know why I am here. I don't know how to find my message. I don't have a purpose.

New Beliefs:
- My life has meaning and purpose.
- I know my message.
- I spend time refining my purpose.
- I live on purpose, with purpose.
- I live in perfect alignment with my purpose.

Limiting Belief:
- I'll never be free of my junk/limiting beliefs.

New Beliefs:
- I am limitless as I break through my limits every day.
- I keep things that bring me joy and happily release everything else.
- I learn from my past and move forward.
- My life is full of things that bring me joy.
- Limiting beliefs are limited; my opportunity for growth is limitless.

Limiting Belief:
- My audience is limited. Someone's already doing it, or they are more successful.

New Beliefs:
- I bless the world in ways that are unique to me.
- My audience grows exponentially.
- I am a movement leader.
- I bring a unique perspective and influence that the world is looking for.
- I have a unique message and a unique way of delivering it.
- I am my own success.
- My success is unique to me.
- I celebrate the success of others and I celebrate my success.

Limiting Belief:
- My choices are meaningless and don't matter.

New Beliefs:
- My decisions are important.
- My decisions have value.
- My choices matter.
- My decisions honor me, and I honor my decisions.

Limiting Belief:
- My employers don't value me. My contribution is not recognized or appreciated.

New Beliefs:
- I value me.
- I recognize me.
- I validate me.
- I appreciate my contribution.
- I value my employers and my employment.

Limiting Belief:
- My ideas are dumb. I don't have any ideas.

New Beliefs:
- Ideas flow to me constantly.
- I am innovative.
- My ideas are creative and powerful.
- I know there is a way and I find it.
- My ideas are meaningful to me.
- My ideas lead to big results.
- I am open-minded.

Limiting Belief:
- My thoughts and my feelings don't matter. I need to suppress my emotions.

New Beliefs:
- My thoughts and feelings are important.
- I feel my emotions and learn from them.
- I acknowledge my emotions.
- I embrace my emotions.
- I live a life of free expression.
- I honor the emotion I feel in the present moment.

Personal Power Beliefs Related to My Capabilities

Limiting Belief:
- I can't do it.

New Beliefs:
- I can do it.
- I am strong enough.
- I can do anything, I can do everything, I am amazing.
- I am worthy of and equal to my task.

Limiting Belief:
- I don't have enough faith. I don't believe in myself.

New Beliefs:
- I am a man/woman of faith.
- I have faith to move my universe.
- I live by faith.
- I believe in me.
- I have faith in others.

Limiting Belief:
- I am scared to fail/change. I afraid of the unknown.

New Beliefs:
- I embrace and appreciate all that I have.
- I am resilient.
- Every experience carries an opportunity and valuable life lesson.
- I live in the present.
- I am wealthy beyond measure.
- I am confident, bold, fearless, and courageous.
- I acknowledge my emotions and I move forward.

Limiting Belief:
- I don't have enough strength for this.

New Beliefs:
- I am strong.
- I have enough strength/energy for everything I face.
- I am able to do the things I choose to do.

Limiting Belief:
- I don't know what's best for me. I don't trust my intuition.

New Beliefs:
- I know what's best for me.
- I ground, ask, listen, trust, and act on my intuition.
- I study my options and trust my intuition to make the best choices.
- I know me best; others know what is best for them.
- I follow my intuition with faith even when the choice doesn't make sense.
- I trust my intuition.
- I trust myself.
- I receive intuition when I ask for it.

Limiting Belief:
- No matter what I do, I don't succeed. I can't do anything right.

New Beliefs:
- I am successful.
- I learn the lessons of success.
- I am doing all the right things, and that is success.
- I always give my best and my best is good enough.
- I see evidence all around me of my success.
- I celebrate each time I succeed.
- I easily accomplish my goals and dreams.
- Everything happens in its perfect timing.

Limiting Belief:
- I have no idea what I am doing. I'm not capable of creating what I want.

New Beliefs:
- I listen, receive, and follow inspired guidance.
- I am supported.
- I know my next steps.
- I access all the knowledge I need through study and intuition.
- I am supported by God, mentors, and experts who provide guidance for me. I have access to the knowledge I need.
- I am guided by intuition.
- I know how to find out my next step.
- I find solutions.

Limiting Belief:
- I sabotage myself. I can't progress because I can't see where I lack.

New Beliefs:
- I step forward boldly and confidently.
- I make daily progress.
- I seize every moment to live and grow.
- My world is centered on joy.
- My life comes together perfectly, and I am extremely happy.

Limiting Belief:
- I'm just going to make mistakes and fail. I won't succeed. Nothing ever changes.

New Beliefs:
- I learn from my experiences.
- I continue learning and growing.
- I create solutions and opportunities.
- I accept all my choices and their consequences.
- I have all the tools to succeed.
- I am a success.
- My faith and actions produce a successful outcome.
- Every step I make is useful.
- I make progress.
- Things always work out for my highest and best good.
- I am learning every step of the way.
- Success is stepping into my highest and best self.
- I determine the definition of success.
- I see every experience as opportunity for success.
- I make the necessary shifts for my success.
- My path is one of constant improvement and growth.

Limiting Belief:
- I'm not smart enough.
New Beliefs:
- I am focused.
- I listen to intuition.
- I trust myself.
- I am a learner.
- Learning comes easily and naturally to me.
- I seek out mentors who help me learn and grow at the speed of my potential.
- The information I need comes precisely at the perfect time.
- I comprehend everything I need to know.

Limiting Belief:
- My brain doesn't work right. It takes me too long to process. I can't focus.
New Beliefs:
- I am brilliant.
- My brain functions properly.
- My mind and intellect are clear.
- I easily memorize the information I need to remember.
- I focus on what is important.
- I travel perfectly at the speed of my potential.

Limiting Belief:
- It's too much work. Success is hard.
New Beliefs:
- Success is easy.
- Success is a state of being I choose into in every moment.
- I embrace the work needed to change.
- I take immediate and appropriate action.
- I happily choose what I do.
- I quickly complete necessary tasks with joy.
- I am supported in my efforts.

- I am committed to doing what is required to be successful.
- I am committed to staying the course through to completion.

Limiting Belief:
- It's never been done before.
New Beliefs:
- I have innovative ideas.
- I am a pioneer.

Limiting Belief:
- Change is too hard and/or risky.
New Beliefs:
- Change is easy.
- I embrace change.
- I love change.
- I easily step into my power.
- I easily find solutions.
- I easily accomplish my goals and dreams.
- Everything goes my way.
- I follow my intuition.
- I love the energizing feeling of attempting something new.
- I experience love, progress, and fulfillment every day.

Limiting Belief:
- I am afraid of taking the stage/I'm not worthy to speak.
New Beliefs:
- I courageously share my message with the world.
- I am courageous.
- I am open to inspiration when I speak.
- I am worthy to share my message.
- My words are important.
- I easily and effortlessly facilitate education, learning, and transformation.

Limiting Belief:
- I am not a leader.
New Beliefs:
- I am an amazing leader.
- I am a life-changing leader.
- I am a worthy leader.
- I am a powerful leader.
- I lead those I feel called to.

Limiting Belief:
- I am not good at making decisions. I am afraid I'll make the wrong decision.
New Beliefs:
- I choose wisely and I choose well.
- I decide quickly and confidently.
- I am confident in my decision-making ability.
- I trust my intuition.
- I am an excellent decision maker.
- I know what's best for me.
- My choices are powerful.

- I make good decisions.
- Each decision has a specific lifespan.
- I can make a new decision in any moment.

Limiting Belief:
- I am not in charge of my life.

New Beliefs:
- I am in charge of me.
- I am the chairman of the board.
- I am the master of my fate.
- My choices set me free.
- I am in control of my happiness.
- My happiness is in my hands.

Limiting Belief:
- I am not qualified. I don't have enough credibility.

New Beliefs:
- I am credible.
- I am good enough for me and good enough to help others.
- I stand in my power with my personality, gifts, talents, and abilities.
- I claim my talents.
- There are people whom I feel called to speak to, teach, and mentor.
- My experience makes me credible.

Limiting Belief:
- I betray my own dreams. I can't manifest.

New Beliefs:
- I honor and work towards my dreams.
- I am manifesting every day.
- I manifest my dreams.
- I create my results.

Limiting Belief:
- I can't control my thoughts.

New Beliefs:
- I choose positive, inspiring, and purposeful thoughts.
- I consciously choose my thoughts.

Limiting Belief:
- I can't decide on everything all at once. Having too many decisions overwhelms me.

New Beliefs:
- I take my decisions one at a time.
- I am calm when faced with decisions.
- I give myself the appropriate time to make wise decisions.

Limiting Belief:
- I can't handle criticism.

New Beliefs:
- I find, embrace, and create positivity everywhere.
- I seek and embrace feedback.
- I am open and adaptable.
- Feedback helps me to grow.

Limiting Belief:
- I can't invite people.

New Beliefs:
- I make powerful invitations.
- I express myself with passion.
- I am a master influencer.

Limiting Belief:
- I can't control my reaction/emotions.

New Beliefs:
- I consciously choose my reactions.
- I act in a way that serves me.
- I act after clearly seeing all the information.
- I am the master of my emotions.
- I have incredible emotional awareness.
- Every emotion has a message for me.
- I am willing to shift my energy for my greatest benefit.
- I am an emotion genius.
- I am a great observer of emotions.
- I maintain my peace in all circumstances.
- I embrace my emotions.
- I select my emotions purposefully.
- Emotions are a gift.

Limiting Belief:
- I can't monetize my gifts and talents.

New Beliefs:
- My gifts are valuable.
- My gifts are profitable.
- My gifts produce value and meaning.
- My greatest wealth is achieved through serving others with my gifts.

Limiting Belief:
- I don't have time for [play, family, myself, responsibilities].

New Beliefs:
- I create time for the right things.
- There is always enough time for the right choices.
- I choose how I spend my time.
- Time is an abundant resource.

Limiting Belief:
- I don't know when to give in or stand my ground. I don't have a voice.

New Beliefs:
- I know when to be flexible and when to be firm.
- I intuitively know when to take a stand or let things pass.
- I have a voice and I use it.
- I am a powerful mentor and the right people hear my message.

Limiting Belief:
- I don't finish things. I can't accomplish goals.

New Beliefs:
- I always finish whatever I desire.

- I am a finisher.
- I am the leader who starts the ball rolling.
- I complete what honors me.

Limiting Belief:
- I don't have a choice. Fate chooses for me.

New Beliefs:
- I consciously choose everything about my reality.
- I am always at choice.
- I control my own destiny.
- I am in control.
- I honor myself.
- I control my thoughts and actions.
- My choices are limitless.
- There is always a choice that is right for me.

Limiting Belief:
- I don't trust God. I resist inspiration.

New Beliefs:
- God knows what is best for me, I trust Him completely.
- God is always available when I reach out to Him.
- I embrace inspiration.
- I embrace my intuition.

Limiting Belief:
- I have bad timing.

New Beliefs:
- I have good timing.
- Timing is one of my greatest strengths.
- Everything happens in its perfect time.

Limiting Belief:
- I have no integrity. I don't keep my commitments. No one can trust me.

New Beliefs:
- I honor my commitments.
- I have integrity and do what I say.
- I am trustworthy.
- I am reliable.
- I am honest and ethical.

Limiting Belief:
- Asking for help shows weakness.

New Beliefs:
- I take action and ask for help when I need it.
- I honor myself when I ask for help.
- I am grateful help is available when I need it.
- Asking for help shows my strength.
- I allow others to serve me.

Limiting Belief:
- It's too late to fix things.

New Beliefs:
- I create solutions now.
- Now is the perfect time for me to fix things.
- I am forgiving. I forgive me.

Limiting Belief:
- It's too late for me. I missed my chance.

New Beliefs:
- My chance is now.
- I live without regrets.
- The timing of my journey is perfect.

Limiting Belief:
- I'm not in control of my time.

New Beliefs:
- I invest my time in alignment with my highest and best choices.
- I am a steward of my time.
- I choose how I spend each moment.
- I choose how I share time with others.

Limiting Belief:
- My results are too small. It'll take too long.

New Beliefs:
- I acknowledge all my results.
- I celebrate each result.
- My results constantly grow and improve.

Limiting Belief:
- I am not tech-savvy.

New Beliefs:
- I am a tech genius.
- I am a fast learner.
- I embrace technology that helps me move faster toward my goals.

Personal Power Beliefs Related to Relationships

Limiting Belief:
- Nobody listens to me.

New Beliefs:
- I listen to me.
- I hear and understand me.
- I see me.

Limiting Belief:
- I get left out/I am not wanted/I don't belong/I am an outsider.

New Beliefs:
- I am included.
- I choose in to others' activities as it honors me.
- I belong by virtue of my choice.
- I am heard and understood.
- I belong.
- I am always in the right place at the right time.

Limiting Belief:
- I go unnoticed. I am invisible.

New Beliefs:
- I am seen.
- I see me and recognize my efforts.
- I am my biggest supporter.

Limiting Belief:
- I'll be judged/mocked for following my heart.

New Beliefs:
- I am blessed by following my inspiration.
- I trust my intuition and take action on it.
- I allow others their perceptions.

Limiting Belief:
- I am afraid I will mess up and hurt someone.

New Beliefs:
- I control my actions and words.
- I am good at figuring things out.
- My motives are pure and loving.
- I succeed and learn with every experience.
- There is value in every experience.

Limiting Belief:
- I am always blamed. It's always my fault.

New Beliefs:
- I take responsibility for my part and release everything else.
- I see the positive in what I learn.

Limiting Belief:
- I'm surrounded by the wrong people.

New Beliefs:
- I surround myself with people whom I want to be more like.
- I seek out and follow good people.

Limiting Belief:
- I don't know whom to trust.

New Beliefs:
- I trust myself.
- I trust my judgment.
- I follow my intuition.
- It serves me to trust people for my own growth and benefit.
- I am trustworthy.

Limiting Belief:
- I have to change me to be accepted. I am rejected when I speak my truth.

New Beliefs:
- I accept and love me as I am, and I continually progress forward.
- I embrace me for the truth I speak.
- I speak the truth and allow the audience to choose their reaction.
- I stand for my truth with confidence and let others do the same.
- I show up in my truth and freely allow others to do the same.
- I embrace and accept the greatness in me.
- As I show up in truth, I am able to serve with greater capacity.
- I celebrate each time I authentically show up as my highest and best self.

Limiting Belief:
- I have to do it all alone. I'm not supported.

New Beliefs:
- I am surrounded by loving support.
- I surround myself with those who help and support me.
- I am strong.
- I support me.
- I ask for help when I need it and I receive help with gratitude.
- I contribute wholly and completely.
- I honor myself in the choices I make.
- Fulfilling my responsibilities feels light.
- Seeking help in my responsibilities makes them light.
- God supports me in every step I take.
- I show up for others in ways that honor me.

Limiting Belief:
- I need permission to be successful/do the things I love.

New Beliefs:
- I honor myself by doing what I love.
- I live my life to the fullest.
- I claim success as my natural mode of operation.

Limiting Belief:
- I am an annoying/loud/toxic person.

New Beliefs:
- I am pleasant/agreeable/kind.
- I enjoy being around me.
- I embrace the way I express myself.
- I invite light and love into people's lives.
- I forgive myself.
- I am forgiving.
- I take responsibility for my part in life.
- I have a lot to offer.
- I accept myself and love being me.

Limiting Belief:
- I have to ask permission to feel emotions.

New Beliefs:
- I have permission to feel emotions.
- Emotions are a gift available to everyone.
- I choose how I feel.
- I choose [insert emotion] because that serves me.

Limiting Belief:
- I have to meet others' expectations. I am a people-pleaser.

New Beliefs:
- I live up to and surpass my own expectations.
- I accept how I show up.
- I create my own beautiful reality.
- I let others' perceptions remain their business.
- I am authentic.
- I am pleased with my choices.
- I honor my personal beliefs and values.

Limiting Belief:
- I have to take responsibility/blame/be the bigger person.

New Beliefs:
- I stand for what's right in all circumstances.

Limiting Belief:
- My success puts others below me.

New Beliefs:
- Standing in my greatness invites others to do the same.
- As I stand in my greatness, I elevate others.
- I invite others to stand in their greatness.

Limiting Belief:
- People steal my ideas. I never get the credit.

New Beliefs:
- I am surrounded by like-minded people who have great ideas.
- I have great ideas that others get behind.
- I have many people who are on board with my ideas.
- I have a gift of generating useful ideas.
- It's easy to enroll people in my ideas.
- I share my ideas freely in order to bless the world.
- I create tremendous value and I receive value in exchange.
- I am richly blessed for the service I give.

WEALTH BELIEFS

Wealth Beliefs Related to Money

Limiting Belief:
- Money is the root of all evil.

New Beliefs:
- Money is a useful resource, which I leverage to do good.
- Money creates possibilities for good.
- Money is my ally and my asset.

Limiting Belief:
- I don't have enough money.

New Beliefs:
- I have more than enough money for my needs and wants.
- More than enough money shows up for me exactly when I need it.
- There is money everywhere around me.
- I am an expert at creating value and generating money.
- I am grateful for the money I have.

Limiting Belief:
- I can't afford it.

New Beliefs:
- I create the resources for everything I choose.
- I always have enough money for the choices I make.
- I wisely choose how I allocate my resources.

Limiting Belief:
- I can't do what I want because of money.

New Beliefs:
- I am free to do what I want with my money.
- I choose my path and attitude at all times.
- I am free to live my purpose.

Limiting Belief:
- Money can't buy happiness.

New Beliefs:
- I choose to be happy with any amount of money.
- I am happy, content and peaceful with the resources in my life.

Limiting Belief:
- Making money isn't fun.

New Beliefs:
- Making money is fun.
- I love getting paid to produce value for other people.
- I love what I do, and my work is fun.

Limiting Belief:
- More money creates more problems.

New Beliefs:
- More money, more solutions.
- Things are easy when money is involved.
- Financial abundance means freedom.

Limiting Belief:
- Money doesn't matter.

New Beliefs:
- Money is a useful resource.
- Money provides me with more possibilities.
- I matter.

Limiting Belief:
- There's not enough money for everyone.

New Beliefs:
- There is always enough abundance for everyone and to spare.

Limiting Belief:
- Debt is bad.

New Beliefs:
- Debt is a tool of leverage.
- I leverage debt wisely and make wise investments to grow my wealth and improve my life.

Limiting Belief:
- The economy is down; my environment makes me poor.

New Beliefs:
- The economy easily supports my work and business.
- I produce great income in every economy/ environment.
- My personal economy/environment improves every day.
- I choose my environment.

Wealth Beliefs Related to Personal Value

Limiting Belief:
- I don't deserve to be wealthy.

New Beliefs:
- I am worthy and grateful for the abundance that is all around me.
- Abundance is my birthright.
- I deserve all good things.
- I am wealthy in all areas of my life.
- I choose to be wealthy.
- I gratefully receive money.

Limiting Belief:
- I am not worthy of the money I am asking.

New Beliefs:
- I am worth the investment.
- The information I have is worth the investment clients make.
- I continually develop my skills to increase my value.

Limiting Belief:
- People don't see my value.

New Beliefs:
- I see my value in myself and others.
- I see me.
- I see the incredible value I offer the world with my gifts, abilities, and purpose.
- I express gratitude for the value I give and receive.

Limiting Belief:
- I don't have enough credibility to make more money.

New Beliefs:
- I am credible to me.
- I let others see the credibility I feel for myself.
- I am influential and affluent.
- I have integrity.
- I honor the trust others place in me.

Limiting Belief:
- Rich people are greedy, selfish, and corrupt.

New Beliefs:
- I am good and I choose to do good with money.
- People are free to choose how they spend their money.
- Money magnifies my desire to take care of my family and do incredible good in the world.
- Rich people are focused and committed to increasing their stewardships.

Limiting Belief:
- It's bad to be rich; money poisons and corrupts people.

New Beliefs:
- I am wealthy, grounded, and good.
- I use money for good.
- I become wealthy easily and ethically.
- My success magnifies my goodness.
- I am righteous and blessed.
- The world is filled with many wealthy people who do so much good.

Limiting Belief:
- Poverty is noble and keeps me humble.

New Beliefs:
- Wealth is my birthright.

- I humbly attract and access the resources I need.
- I am humble and blessed beyond my needs.
- I bless others with my abundance.
- I am humble and express gratitude for the rich blessings in my life

---

Limiting Belief:
- I don't have enough to give to charity.

New Beliefs:
- I am charitable.
- I always manifest a surplus to help others.
- Abundance begins with giving.
- I give freely.

Limiting Belief:
- I hate that I am in debt.

New Beliefs:
- I am accountable for my choices and enjoy paying for them.
- I commit a portion of my income every month for the privilege of living free.

Limiting Belief:
- I can't accept/don't deserve gifts.

New Beliefs:
- I am worthy of receiving gifts.
- I gratefully receive gifts.
- I give and receive.

Limiting Belief:
- If I spend money on me, I am wasting it.

New Beliefs:
- I am worthy of investing in myself.
- I spend the right amount of money on my wants and needs.
- I am worth every investment of time, energy, and money.
- I have value.
- I honor my needs.

Wealth Beliefs Related to Personal Capabilities

Limiting Belief:
- Making money is hard for me.

New Beliefs:
- Making money is easy for me.
- I am a master at making money.
- I am an expert producer.
- I create value in the world and I am compensated for my abilities.
- I invest in my ability to make money.
- I am committed to the tasks that bring me money.
- I appreciate the avenues of income I currently have.

Limiting Belief:
- I don't handle money well.

New Beliefs:
- I am trustworthy and responsible with money.
- I am disciplined and wise with my money.
- I easily track where my money is and how much is accessible to me.
- I gain more wisdom on the flow of money every day.
- I easily set aside money for the things I need and want.
- I am a money expert.

Limiting Belief:
- I am/will always be poor.

New Beliefs:
- I have all the money I want and more.
- Wealth and abundance are my birthright.
- I choose wealth and prosperity.
- I live in complete abundance.
- I feel deep gratitude for all my blessings.
- I am an expert at producing a surplus of what I need.

Limiting Belief:
- I don't make enough money consistently.

New Beliefs:
- Prosperity and abundance are attracted to me.
- I have more than enough money to fulfill my obligations, needs, and wants.
- My needs are always met.
- The money I need is always available.
- I love my stable income.

Limiting Belief:
- Finances are stressful.

New Beliefs:
- I am at peace with my finances.
- I choose positive emotions about money.
- I am peaceful and relaxed as I effortlessly take care of my responsibilities.
- I am grateful for all of my obligations.
- It is satisfying for me to pay my obligations.

Limiting Belief:
- I can't make money by following my passion and living my purpose.

New Beliefs:
- I am prosperous as I serve others with my passion and purpose.
- I give value in a way that returns value to me.
- I am rewarded well for sharing my gifts.
- I love learning new ways to monetize my passion and purpose.
- My passions have value.
- I develop new passions that create value.
- I am passionate about giving value.

Limiting Belief:
- I can't find the resources I need.

New Beliefs:
- I recognize the abundance around me.
- There is always more than enough.
- I attract the resources and tools that support my path.
- My life is filled with opportunities that produce greater abundance for me.
- I am grateful for the abundance in my life.

Limiting Belief:
- I am not manifesting money fast enough.

New Beliefs:
- My finances progress at the perfect pace.
- Money is showing up perfectly for me.
- There is a perfect timeline as my purpose unfolds.
- I live in gratitude knowing all my needs are met.
- I trust the Law of Gestation.

Limiting Belief:
- I can't trust money to show up for me when I need it.

New Beliefs:
- I trust money to show up for me.
- I ask and seek for the money I need.
- Money always finds me.
- I trust myself to show up and produce the results I need.

Limiting Belief:
- I'll never figure this abundance thing out.

New Beliefs:
- I live in abundance.
- Abundance and prosperity are my birthright.
- I attract all the resources I need.
- I have all the resources I need to be abundant.

Limiting Belief:
- I need money to make money.

New Beliefs:
- I make money by creating value.
- I attract all the resources I need to fulfill my purpose and achieve my dreams.
- All the resources I need are available now.
- Money attracts more money.

Limiting Belief:
- Work is hard.

New Beliefs:
- Work is rewarding, fun, and easy.
- I am grateful to be able to work.
- Parts of my work are simple and quick.
- I love working through a challenge.
- I choose work that is fun.

Limiting Belief:
- I need handouts.

New Beliefs:
- I am independent.

- I am a good receiver.
- I love learning how to create the results in my life.
- I am an expert at manifesting.

Limiting Belief:
- My business will fail.

New Beliefs:
- My business succeeds.
- I make wise business decisions.
- I learn lessons from everything that happens in my business.
- I am wiser with each business experience.

Limiting Belief:
- I am not good at/I don't like sales.

New Beliefs:
- I am an expert at presenting myself and the opportunities I believe in.
- I love selling my value by solving problems.
- I excel at sales.
- I am a salesperson.
- I am a closer.

Limiting Belief:
- I am bad at/I don't like at following up.

New Beliefs:
- I follow through.
- I follow up with amazing commitment.
- I am disciplined to do what's necessary.
- I am an expert finisher.
- I love following up with people on a regular basis.

Limiting Belief:
- I don't know how to prioritize my time.

New Beliefs:
- I manage my time efficiently.
- I have an abundance of time.
- I have all the time I need for every inspired choice I make.
- There is always enough time for the right choices.
- I create clarity every day on my next steps and then do them.

Wealth Beliefs
Related to Relationships

Limiting Belief:
- People will treat me differently if I am wealthy.

New Beliefs:
- I am the same person with any amount of wealth.
- I treat all people with love and respect.
- I choose to be the highest and best me in every situation.

Limiting Belief:
- You can't have good relationships and money.

New Beliefs:
- I grow my wealth and meaningful relationships.
- Easy access to money gives me the resources to make choices that enhance my relationships.
- Peace and serenity about money allows me to show up at peace in my relationships.
- I am blessed with an abundance of wealth and amazing relationships.

Limiting Belief:
- Money changes people.

New Beliefs:
- Money amplifies the good I do in the world.
- Money is a magnifier; people choose how they show up.
- Money allows me to show up with more resources and opportunities.

Limiting Belief:
- I have to take advantage of people to get money.

New Beliefs:
- I receive money through serving others.
- I am a powerful servant.
- I create value for other people.
- I love, honor and respect people as I create value for them.
- People are free to choose whether to work with me or not.
- I work with those I feel inspired to serve.
- I honor the agency of others to make their highest and best choices.

Limiting Belief:
- I can't take care of my family.

New Beliefs:
- I more than adequately provide for my family's needs and wants.
- I am an incredible provider.
- I care for my family.
- I am committed to providing for my family.

Limiting Belief:
- My spouse and I fight about money.

New Beliefs:
- I am calm as I discuss money.
- I create a safe space to discuss money.
- I communicate my values about money freely and I allow my spouse to do the same.
- My spouse and I work as a team to allocate the resources appropriately for our family.

Limiting Belief:
- My spouse doesn't trust my financial decisions.

New Beliefs:
- I make good financial decisions.

- I trust my financial decisions.
- I trust my spouse's financial decisions.

Limiting Belief:
- My family expects me to make more money.

New Beliefs:
- I successfully provide all the resources my family wants and needs.
- I focus on my goals and values.
- I am grateful for my ability to make money.
- I share my thoughts and feelings about money openly with my family.

Limiting Belief:
- People don't want to do business with me.

New Beliefs:
- People love doing business with me.
- I am always attracting more and more of the right clients.
- I am committed to creating powerful win-win situations.

Limiting Belief:
- I don't know the right people I need to succeed.

New Beliefs:
- I attract the people and resources that support my success.
- I am connected to all the people I need to grow and succeed.
- I am committed to helping others achieve success.

Limiting Belief:
- No one in my family or close circle of friends makes money.

New Beliefs:
- I am the first to make money.
- I lead the way in doing good things.
- I surround myself with successful people.
- I embrace all people, regardless of their financial status.
- I am richly blessed with friends of all circumstances.

Limiting Belief:
- Other people don't believe I can make money.

New Beliefs:
- I believe in my ability to make money.
- I am an amazing producer.
- I live my dreams.
- I approve of myself and my choices.

Limiting Belief:
- Other people think I am selfish with my money.

New Beliefs:
- My abundance blesses other people.
- I am a wise steward over money.
- I am generous with my money.
- I honor myself with the financial choices I make.

Health Beliefs Related to Body

Limiting Belief:
- My body doesn't respond to exercise.

New Beliefs:
- My body responds well to exercise.
- My body loves to exercise.
- I love exercising.
- I celebrate every noticeable improvement in my body.
- I know my body is improving every time I exercise.

Limiting Belief:
- My body doesn't show results fast enough/ I can't see my progress.

New Beliefs:
- My body progresses perfectly.
- Everything I do for my body counts.
- I love and graciously accept the progress of my body.
- I visualize my progress daily.
- I celebrate every step of progress.
- I am successful at caring for my body.

Limiting Belief:
- My genes/hormones make me fat/unhealthy and there's nothing I can do about it.

New Beliefs:
- My genes/hormones support my most healthy and fit body.
- Health is my birthright.
- My current health choices create a new future for me and my family.
- My good choices produce my healthy, fit body.
- I do what is required to create the body I choose.
- I am whole.

Limiting Belief:
- I am too _____ [insert characteristic, e.g. fat, thin, short, tall, etc.].

New Beliefs:
- I love my body's size.
- I am the perfect size in this moment.
- I embrace my body's stature.
- I am the perfect height.
- I love every step of developing and caring for my body.
- I am lean fit, strong, capable and healthy.
- I get healthier every day.

Limiting Belief:
- I don't like my [insert body part].

New Beliefs:
- I love and accept my beautiful [insert body part].
- My [body part] is uniquely mine.
- I am an individual who is recognizable by my quirks.
- I am tender and gentle with myself.
- I love my incredible body.
- I embrace the incredible gift of my body.
- My body improves.

Limiting Belief:
- I'm too tired/don't have the energy to take care of my body.

New Beliefs:
- I am energized as I care for my body.
- I choose vitality.
- I honor my body and its needs.
- I have all the energy I need.
- I get all the rest/sleep I need.

Limiting Belief:
- My body is broken/fails me.

New Beliefs:
- I am healthy and whole.
- My body serves me.
- I love and accept my body.
- I am committed to my health.
- My body supports me in my purpose and daily actions.
- I love how my body shows up perfectly for me.

Limiting Belief:
- I'm getting old/I am not what I used to be.

New Beliefs:
- I look and feel amazing.
- I am my most fit and healthy self.
- I am rewarded with health, energy and ability with every good choice I make.
- I am grateful for my body's continuous health.
- I accept my body with gratitude.
- I accept every chapter of my life with gratitude.
- I am better than I used to be.

Limiting Belief:
- I will always be in pain.

New Beliefs:
- I learn what I need to know in order to heal.
- I feel healthy.
- My body feels good.
- I am whole.
- I choose a peaceful, healthy body.

Health Beliefs
Related to Personal Value

Limiting Belief:
- I don't deserve to be healthy/beautiful.

New Beliefs:
- Health and beauty are my birthright.
- I was born beautiful and worthy.
- I am beautiful and loved as I am.
- I accept myself.

Limiting Belief:
- I don't respect my body.

New Beliefs:
- I honor my body with my choices.
- I listen to my body's needs and take good care of it.
- I honor my body and how it serves me.
- I am an incredible steward over my body.
- I love, adore, and care for my body.

Limiting Belief:
- I can't be happy unless I am thin.

New Beliefs:
- I love my body unconditionally.
- I choose happiness in all circumstances.
- I am happy with my body whether it is overweight, underweight, or anywhere in between.

Limiting Belief:
- I don't have time to exercise/my health is not a priority.

New Beliefs:
- I love taking time to take care of me.
- I give my time to the things that are important to me.
- I can move my body anytime, anywhere.
- Taking care of my body is one of my top priorities.
- My health choices are top priority.

Limiting Belief:
- I need food as a reward.

New Beliefs:
- I reward myself with improving and increasing health.
- I reward myself by validating myself for my efforts and progress.
- I reward my body for all it does for me with the nutrition that increases its ability to perform optimally.

Limiting Belief:
- Healthy food is expensive.

New Beliefs:
- It is fun and exciting to invest in my health with good food.
- I love investing in my health.

- Healthy food is the simplest and easiest to prepare.
- I save time when I prepare healthy food.
- My body and health is worth the investment.

Limiting Belief:
- I'm too busy to make healthy choices.

New Beliefs:
- There is a perfect amount of time for all the choices I make.
- I love taking time to take care of me.
- I give my time to the things that are important to me.
- I honor my body by giving it the rest and healing it needs.

Limiting Belief:
- My body is the only thing of value.

New Beliefs:
- I value my mind, my body, and my spirit.
- My body is a part of my highest, best, and most sacred self, which is precious, priceless and limitless.
- I value my body and all its parts.
- I am grateful for my body.

Health Beliefs
Related to Capabilities

Limiting Belief:
- The spirit is willing but the flesh is weak. I don't have control over my body.

New Beliefs:
- I am the master of my body and mind.
- My body and spirit support each other.
- I connect with my mind, heart, and body.
- My body obeys me.

Limiting Belief:
- I don't know how to take care of my body.

New Beliefs:
- I know how to take care of my body.
- I listen to my body and respond accordingly.
- I know my body best.
- I hire experts to help me care for my body.

Limiting Belief:
- Being healthy is hard.

New Beliefs:
- It's easy to live a healthy lifestyle.
- I love taking care of my body by making good food and exercise choices.
- I am committed to me.
- I take steps towards a healthier lifestyle every day.
- I make my health a priority every day.

Limiting Belief:
- I can't control my cravings or portions.

New Beliefs:
- I chose foods and portions that honor my body.
- I listen to my body and stop eating when it is satisfied.
- I choose the cleanest, most natural foods available.

Limiting Belief:
- Losing weight is hard.

New Beliefs:
- I easily release excess weight.
- I step courageously into my healthy body.
- I am the perfect weight for the choices I have made.
- I easily and quickly return to my optimal weight.
- My body knows precisely the perfect weight to be.
- I love doing the work to witness my body shift into its potential.

Limiting Belief:
- Working out is hard. I don't like exercise.

New Beliefs:
- Working out is easy.
- I get fit doing what I love.
- I love the feeling of working out my body.
- I work out consistently.
- I am always finding fun new ways to exercise.
- I enjoy taking care of myself.

Limiting Belief:
- I struggle to stay healthy/consistent.

New Beliefs:
- Health is my natural state of being.
- I consistently make choices to stay healthy.
- I am healthy.
- I am consistent in my exercise routine.
- Every action I take moves me towards improved health.
- I am committed to my health journey.

Limiting Belief:
- My body is weak.

New Beliefs:
- My body is strong.
- I am strong.
- My body is extremely capable of its tasks.
- My body moves perfectly.
- I am amazed at what my body can do.
- I take my body to new heights and bring it to new and amazing capabilities.

Limiting Belief:
- My body isn't perfect/I'm not beautiful I don't look perfect.

New Beliefs:
- I am beautiful.

- I love my body.
- I love every part of my body.
- I am happy with my body.
- My body is a gift.
- My body is a beautiful creation.
- I love where I am at in my journey and I look forward to continued progress.

Limiting Belief:
- I can't [insert characteristic, e.g. breathe, move freely, keep up, etc.].

New Beliefs:
- My body functions perfectly.
- I am able to push further with each passing day.
- I possess incredible flexibility.
- My body moves with ease and comfort.
- I have all the oxygen I need.
- I celebrate everything my body can do.
- I take joy in every bit of progress my body makes.

Limiting Belief:
- I can't/don't like working out [insert time, e.g. in the morning, evening, weekends, etc.].

New Beliefs:
- My body feels especially good in the mornings.
- I find the perfect time to move my body.
- I create the optimal time for exercise.
- I choose my priorities and my schedule.
- I prioritize my workout time every day.

Limiting Belief:
- I am not [insert characteristic, e.g. fast, strong, a dancer, a runner, a swimmer, an athlete, etc.].

New Beliefs:
- I am [insert characteristic].
- I am strong, fast, and powerful.
- I love how I move and progress at my pace.
- I am exactly where I need to be.
- I move my body with freedom and joy.
- I learn athletic skills.
- I build new strength every day.

Limiting Belief:
- I can't work out due to injury.

New Beliefs:
- I love finding ways to exercise my body.
- I access experts who expand my exercising possibilities.

Limiting Belief:
- I have [insert diseased body part].

New Beliefs:
- I am whole.
- My [diseased body part] grows stronger and stronger every day.
- My [diseased body part] is perfectly at ease.
- My [diseased body part] is whole.

Limiting Belief:
- I need medication. Doctors don't know what is wrong with me.

New Beliefs:
- I have the power to heal my body.
- I know exactly what my body needs.
- I know how to nurture and care for my body.
- I choose to be well.
- I use medication responsibly.
- My body functions perfectly.

Limiting Belief:
- I am dying.

New Beliefs:
- I choose to live.
- I choose life.
- I am alive.

Health Beliefs
Related to Relationships

Limiting Belief:
- I can't eat healthy at family events.

New Beliefs:
- I choose health in all situations.
- I easily select the healthy food options when presented with any choice of food.
- I am a great food planner.
- I honor the agency of others while honoring my needs.
- I create valuable traditions with people as the main focus.
- I create true connection with people.
- I create new traditions with healthy food choices.
- I connect with my family in various ways.

Limiting Belief:
- I have to be sick to get love and attention.

New Beliefs:
- I hear me, love me, and I give myself the attention I need.
- I love myself and attend to my needs.
- I am supported and cared for.
- I love me enough to be well.
- I am seen and valued. I value me.

Limiting Belief:
- If I lose weight, I won't be safe anymore.

New Beliefs:
- I am healthy, fit, and safe.
- My logic and intuition help me make good choices, which keep me safe.
- I choose an adventurous life.
- Body confidence provides all the security and safety I need.
- Being healthier makes me safer.

Limiting Belief:
- If I am thin/beautiful, I'll only been wanted/noticed for my looks.

New Beliefs:
- My worth is defined by how I see myself.
- I am noticed for all my amazing characteristics.
- My body/looks is just one way of expressing who I am.

Limiting Belief:
- My lack of health is a barrier between me and those I love.

New Beliefs:
- I create deep connections.
- I embrace my body and create meaningful connection now.
- I find ways to connect.

Limiting Belief:
- It's harder to be healthy after kids.

New Beliefs:
- I am healthy for my children.
- I maintain my health because my kids are so active.
- I take care of me and can take care of my kids.

Limiting Belief:
- I'm uncomfortable because my family thinks my health practices are weird.

New Beliefs:
- I am confident in my health choices.
- I respect the choices of others while honoring my needs.
- I surround myself with loving support.
- I seek comfort in connection with people and God.
- Food feeds my body. I use it to nourish my body.

CONNECTION BELIEFS

Connection Beliefs Related to Myself

Limiting Belief:
- I am not [insert adjective, e.g. smart, beautiful, teachable, loving, strong, etc.].

New Beliefs:
- I am [insert adjective].
- I am constantly learning and growing.
- I love me.

Limiting Belief:
- I annoy others; people can't handle me.

New Beliefs:
- I am enjoyable to be with.
- I surround myself with people who love and support me.
- I enjoy spending time with me.
- The right people stay with me.
- I love how people come and go in my life.

Limiting Belief:
- People use me and take advantage of me.

New Beliefs:
- I am responsible for my choices and interactions.
- I make space to be and do what I love.
- I respect myself.

Limiting Belief:
- I don't even know who I am. I have to follow the crowd.

New Beliefs:
- I know who I am.
- I know everything I need to know about me in this moment.
- I make the best decisions for me.
- I spend time discovering my talents, preferences, and gifts.
- I am a leader.

Limiting Belief:
- I can't control my passions. I am impure, defiled, filthy.

New Beliefs:
- I harness my passions.
- I am pure.
- I practice purity and virtue.
- I focus on pure thoughts.
- I am a treasure.
- I am passionate and I love expressing myself in a way that uplifts others.

Limiting Belief:
- I don't like any part of myself/I hate myself.

New Beliefs:
- I love all of me.
- I enjoy learning new ways to love me.
- I am grateful to be me.
- I love my [insert specific quality].
- I am loveable.
- I can find many qualities about me that I like.

Limiting Belief:
- All I see are my mistakes.

New Beliefs:
- I see the best in myself and others.
- Every experience allows me to grow.
- I am grateful to be me.

Limiting Belief:
- I am dysfunctional.

New Beliefs:
- I am conscious, powerful, and at peace with my life.
- I accept myself.
- I am my highest and best self.
- I embrace my structured life of purpose.

Limiting Belief:
- I have no ambition.

New Beliefs:
- I am ambitious. I dream big.
- I motivate myself and live my dreams.
- I am committed to my choices.
- I am energetic and enthusiastic.

Limiting Belief:
- I have no imagination/I can't dream.

New Beliefs:
- I am imaginative/a dreamer.
- I am infinitely creative.
- My imagination is fun and I allow it to flow.
- I channel my ideas appropriately.
- I am connected to my imaginative my inner child.

Limiting Belief:
- I don't have any more love to give.

New Beliefs:
- I am filled with love to give.
- I have an endless supply of love.
- An infinite supply of love energy flows around me at all times.
- My love is replenished as I share it.

Limiting Belief:
- I'm afraid of commitment.

New Beliefs:
- I am committed to every choice I make.
- I am committed to what is important to me.
- I love committing to the right people and causes.
- I am committed to my happiness.
- I am passionate about commitment.

Limiting Belief:
- I am selfish.

New Beliefs:
- I am selfless, humble, and a powerful force for good.
- I love serving myself and others.
- I take good care of me.

Limiting Belief:
- I am an embarrassment.

New Beliefs:
- I am an asset.
- I am gifted.
- I belong.
- I am comfortable and outgoing.

Limiting Belief:
- The world needs to revolve around me.

New Beliefs:
- I recognize my value and place in the universe and recognize those around me for their value and place in the world.
- I take care of my world and the world of others.
- I make the world a better place.
- I am a key player in my world.

Limiting Belief:
- I use people.

New Beliefs:
- I access my relationships for pure and positive purposes.
- All people are important.
- I see people in their greatness.

Limiting Belief:
- I am arrogant.

New Beliefs:
- I am humble and wise.
- I see my worth and value.
- I am a wise steward of the knowledge and experience I have been given.

Limiting Belief:
- I get annoyed with people/children.

New Beliefs:
- I love people.
- I embrace others' personalities.
- I am patient.
- I am tolerant and kind.
- I see and enjoy the unique qualities of children.

- I see diversity and differences as strengths.
- I love others unconditionally.
- I choose my emotional response to other people's behavior.

Connection Beliefs
Related to Personal Value

Limiting Belief:
- I can't accept love. I don't deserve love.

New Beliefs:
- I am worthy of love.
- I love me.
- I receive love from others.
- I am ready for love to come my way.
- I attract love effortlessly.
- I always have love in my life.
- I am grateful for the love that is around me.

Limiting Belief:
- I am not wanted/needed/accepted/liked/ desirable.

New Beliefs:
- I am wanted/needed/accepted/liked/ desirable.
- I love and accept myself.
- I choose me.
- I play a crucial role in this universe.
- I attract the right people to me at all times.
- I am sought after by wonderful people.

Limiting Belief:
- I'm not worthy of being loved.

New Beliefs:
- I am worthy of love.
- I am lovable.
- My worth is infinite.
- I receive all the love I choose.

Limiting Belief:
- No one respects/listens to me.

New Beliefs:
- I respect myself.
- I honor myself.
- I value myself.
- I respect others.

Limiting Belief:
- I can't be vulnerable/show emotion in front of people.

New Beliefs:
- I embrace my emotions.
- I choose how I feel and others get to choose how they feel.
- I honor my true self in every moment.
- I accept my authentic self.

- I embrace my strengths and weaknesses.
- When I am real/vulnerable, other people connect with me.

Limiting Belief:
- I have nothing to offer.

New Beliefs:
- My talents are worth contributing.
- I have value to share.
- I am the only me that will ever live.
- I admire myself and others.

Limiting Belief:
- No one values what I have to offer.

New Beliefs:
- I value what I have to offer.
- My light is a gift to other people.
- There is someone I can help today.

Limiting Belief:
- I am not worthy of a good relationship.

New Beliefs:
- I am worthy and deserving of a loving relationship.
- I create amazing relationships.
- I am a contributor to a good relationship.
- I see the worth of others and myself.

Limiting Belief:
- People don't have time for me.

New Beliefs:
- I make plenty of time for myself.
- Others benefit from the time they spend with me.

Limiting Belief:
- My dreams /life/purpose don't matter.

New Beliefs:
- My dreams are important.
- My dreams are unique and powerful.
- I influence and impact others by living my purpose.

Limiting Belief:
- No one will love me if they know who I really am.

New Beliefs:
- I attract love by being myself.
- I am loved as I am.
- I embrace my authentic self.
- I love and accept me.
- I choose relationships where I can be me.
- I am best when I am me.

Limiting Belief:
- God doesn't care about me.

New Beliefs:
- God loves me.
- God is always aware of me.
- I care about God.

Limiting Belief:
- I am the only one who loves me.

New Beliefs:
- I am surrounded by love.
- Countless people show love to me regularly.

Limiting Belief:
- I have a hard time accepting compliments from people.

New Beliefs:
- I gratefully acknowledge my greatness.
- I see my worth.
- I am a good receiver.
- I am grateful that others take the time to see me.
- I see the greatness in others.

Limiting Belief:
- I need to be better than others.

New Beliefs:
- I see the contributions of others.
- I am constantly developing my skills and talents.
- Others have gifts in areas that are different than mine.
- I learn from everyone.
- Everyone has value.

Connection Beliefs Related to Capabilities

Limiting Belief:
- I don't know how to talk to or connect with people.

New Beliefs:
- I am an expert at communicating with others.
- I stand in my power in social situations.
- My ability to connect is especially meaningful to some people.
- I connect easily with people in the best ways.

Limiting Belief:
- I can't connect with anyone/let people in.

New Beliefs:
- I am connected to myself.
- I connect with people in ways that honor me
- I open myself up for others.
- I am open to new relationships.
- The perfect people come into my life.

Limiting Belief:
- I can't stick up for myself/express myself/ask questions.

New Beliefs:
- I stand in my power.
- I always have the ability to choose.
- I make my own choices.

- I allow others to make their own choices.
- Asking questions provides clarity.
- I say yes to what serves me.

Limiting Belief:
- I don't know where to find the people who love me/I don't know the right people.

New Beliefs:
- I know where to find the people who love me, and I feel them surrounding me.
- I am surrounded by people who love and support me.
- The right people flow into my life at the perfect time.

Limiting Belief:
- I don't understand people.

New Beliefs:
- I have a gift for understanding people.
- I see the greatness in everyone I meet.
- My mind and heart are open to seeing others as they are.

Limiting Belief:
- Being around people is overwhelming.

New Beliefs:
- I establish healthy boundaries.
- I confidently interact with others.
- I am responsible for my emotions.

Limiting Belief:
- I offend people. I'm unaware of others emotions/feelings.

New Beliefs:
- I speak my truth and I respect how people choose to feel.
- I am respectful of others' emotions and hold space for them.
- Others get to choose how they see me.
- I am aware and considerate of people.
- I see others in their greatness.

Limiting Belief:
- I commit to the wrong things. I shouldn't be doing this.

New Beliefs:
- I commit to what is in alignment with my highest and best good.
- I honor myself by making choices in alignment with my highest and best self.
- I make good choices.
- I give my attention to the at hand.

Limiting Belief:
- I am afraid of other's responses. I have to walk on egg shells.

New Beliefs:
- I respond to others with compassion.

- Others are free to like or dislike me, and I love myself either way.
- I walk with purpose and confidence.
- I honor myself with my words and choices regardless of how others perceive them.
- I embrace the people around me.
- I am confident in social settings.

Limiting Belief:
- Other people are lucky/have it better than me. I resent the success of others.

New Beliefs:
- I love seeing other people's blessings.
- I seek mentoring from those who are where I want to be.
- I celebrate others' successes.
- I am blessed.
- I am dedicated to creating my own success.
- I love where I am at in my life right now.

Limiting Belief:
- I already know everything.

New Beliefs:
- I progress every day.
- Each day is a learning opportunity.
- Change is natural and constant.

Limiting Belief:
- I don't need help.

New Beliefs:
- I willing receive and give help.
- I am gifted.
- I see the gifts of others.

Connection Beliefs Related to Relationships

Limiting Belief:
- No one loves me or cares about me.

New Beliefs:
- I have dear friends and people who love and support me.
- I love me. I care about me.
- I am worthy of love.
- My life is a beautiful gift.

Limiting Belief:
- I run away from love. I push people away.

New Beliefs:
- I embrace the love of others.
- I receive love.
- My vulnerability and availability are my strengths.
- I effortlessly attract people into my life who love and support me and bring out the best in me.
- I am open to experiencing love in my life.

Limiting Belief:
- I let other people down. I can't handle disappointing others.

New Beliefs:
- I follow through on all my commitments.
- I am an uplifting influence in the lives of others.
- I hold space for others.
- Other people are responsible for their own reactions.

Limiting Belief:
- No one understands me. I am alone.

New Beliefs:
- I understand me.
- I communicate clearly.
- I am supported.
- I am at peace with others and with myself.

Limiting Belief:
- People leave me.

New Beliefs:
- I hold space for people to come and go in my life.
- I invite the people I want in my life.
- I celebrate when God creates room for new relationships in my life.
- I am grateful for the relationships I have and have had.

Limiting Belief:
- I don't have good/any friends.

New Beliefs:
- I am a great friend.
- I have great friends.
- I attract the kind of friends I want in my life.
- I learn positive things from the people in my life.
- I easily create lasting and fulfilling relationships.
- I am surrounded by loving and supportive people.

Limiting Belief:
- People might hurt me/people reject me.

New Beliefs:
- I see the blessing people are to me.
- I choose to feel gratitude and learn in every moment.
- I embrace and respect others.
- People are free to choose how they feel about me and I love them either way.
- I choose how I respond to others.
- I choose to love and trust people.
- I show love and acceptance to those around me.
- I represent a life I love and allow others to show up in whatever way they choose.

Limiting Belief:
- Relationships are all painful. Love hurts.

New Beliefs:
- Love heals.
- I am grateful for my ability to feel love.
- I choose to experience all aspects of love.
- My life is filled with love.
- I experience perfect bliss in my relationships.
- Relationships bring joy.
- I trust myself and my intuition.
- I use my intuition to make good choices.

Limiting Belief:
- I don't need people/I don't like being around people.

New Beliefs:
- I find joy in being with people.
- I have a strong connection with others and create space to give and receive.
- I choose to allow people in my life.
- I embrace the people around me.
- I am energized by the people around me.
- I am confident in social settings.

Limiting Belief:
- I don't fit in. I am a loner.

New Beliefs:
- I am invited and included.
- I join with those who resonate with me and my purpose.
- I am part of a community.
- I choose to surround myself with like-minded people.
- I am sought after by wonderful people.

Limiting Belief:
- I attract dysfunctional/toxic relationships.

New Beliefs:
- I attract enriching and fulfilling relationships.
- All my relationships have been perfect for me.
- My relationships of the past have provided perfect experiences and training for the present.
- Everyone comes into my life for a beautiful purpose.
- I attract the right people in my life.
- I bring love and unity to all my relationships.

Limiting Belief:
- My [insert family member, e.g. mom, dad, sibling, etc.] didn't love me.

New Beliefs:
- I love me.
- I am supported by people who love me.
- I love my [insert person] unconditionally.
- I surround myself with people who love me.

Limiting Belief:
- If only [insert family member] were perfect, then [insert outcome, e.g. happy, able to connect, successful, etc.].

New Beliefs:
- I see the best in myself and others.
- I am good at looking deeper into the heart of people.
- I easily recognize people's strengths and talents.
- I attract people who support me and my purpose.
- I choose what I believe about myself.

Limiting Belief:
- People are stupid/selfish/fake.

New Beliefs:
- I see goodness and intelligence in everyone.
- There are so many kind, loving people in the world.
- People are doing their best with what they have.
- I see the authentic greatness in others.

Limiting Belief:
- God doesn't give me clear answers.

New Beliefs:
- I hear and understand God's answers.
- God answers my prayers.
- I listen, receive, recognize, and follow inspired guidance.

Limiting Belief:
- Others are out to get me.

New Beliefs:
- People and angels conspire for my good.
- People are free to like or dislike me, and I love them either way.
- I am greater than any circumstance.
- I am confident in who I am.

Limiting Belief:
- Men/women are [insert stereotype/characteristic].

New Beliefs:
- I am surrounded by people who are amazing, kind, loving, and caring.
- I treat myself the way I love to be treated.
- I honor men/women however they show up.
- I invite appropriate treatment from men/women.
- I see men/women for who they are in their divine greatness.
- I honor and respect men/women.

Limiting Belief:
- If I am successful, my loved one will suffer/be jealous.

New Beliefs:
- As I succeed, my love ones are uplifted.
- Honoring me honors my marriage/spouse/family.
- My brilliance attracts greatness.

Limiting Belief:
- I have to bend over backwards/sacrifice myself for others.

New Beliefs:
- I choose when I serve others and do so willingly.
- I serve in a capacity that honors me.
- When I serve me, I serve others.
- My genuine charity and service is a gift to the receiver and me.

Limiting Belief:
- I have to do everything myself. No one will help me.

New Beliefs:
- I attract the right people to assist me when and where I need them.
- I take ownership of the things that really matter to me.
- I take on only those tasks that serve and fulfill me.
- I love working on my own and with others.

Limiting Belief:
- I am not a good enough spouse/parent/lover/friend.

New Beliefs:
- I am an excellent spouse/parent/lover/friend.
- I am the perfect nurturer for my children.
- I create space for my loved ones.
- I honor the needs of others and myself.

Limiting Belief:
- Sexual intimacy is bad/sinful.

New Beliefs:
- Intimacy is God-given.
- Love and intimacy are here for me to experience.
- I enjoy physical intimacy with my partner.
- Wanting sexual intimacy is natural and good.
- I want sexual intimacy to express my deep love for my spouse/partner and for the gift it is to me.

Limiting Belief:
- I am not good enough for my spouse/significant other.

New Beliefs:
- I am good and worthy of love.
- I choose unconditional love for me and my loved ones.
- I invite my partner into physical intimacy without any expectations.
- I am a confident lover.

NOTES

Chapter 9

[1] http://www.rickhanson.net/stephen-colbert-we-dont-need-to-keep-fear-alive/

[2] Pascual-Leone, A., Nguyet, D., Cohen, LG, Brasil-Neto, JP, Cammarota, A., and Hallett, M. Modulation of muscle responses evoked by transcranial magnetic stimulation during the acquisition of new fine motor skills. *Journal of Neurophysiology*. 1995 Sep;74(3):1037-45.

[3] Berger C, Ehrsson H. Mental imagery changes multisensory perception. Current Biology. 2013 Jul;23(14):1367-72.

[4] Bergland, Christopher. "Imagination Can Change Perceptions of Reality." *Psychology Today* online. June 28, 2013. https://www.psychologytoday.com/blog/the-athletes-way/201306/imagination-can-change-perceptions-reality

[5] Wikipedia. "Cognitive Dissonance." https://en.wikipedia.org/wiki/Cognitive_dissonance

Chapter 24

[1] https://www.micromentor.org/learn-more/impact

[2] "How Becoming a Mentor Can Boost Your Career" by Lisa Quast. Forbes online, October 31, 2011.

CLAIM YOUR FREE GIFT:
Two Tickets to Attend the Next Limitless Live Seminar ($998 Value)

Limitless three-day live seminars are the fastest, most powerful way to breakthrough to your limitless life. Join us to:

1. Identify the limiting beliefs that have been holding you back.
2. Unwind and release your false beliefs.
3. Reprogram your mind with new empowering beliefs to create your ideal life.

This transformational event will give you the vital knowledge and principles you need to unleash:

- **Limitless Wealth:** Claim your birthright of prosperity and abundance.
- **Limitless Health:** Unlock the vast power of your mind and body.
- **Limitless Connection:** Experience unconditional bliss and fulfillment with your spouse, family, and loved ones.
- **Limitless Power:** Discover and live your Sacred Purpose to leave your mark on the world.

For upcoming dates and locations, visit www.LimitlessSeminar.com. To claim your free tickets and register for the event, send an email to tickets@LimitlessMentor.com and include your name, phone number, and promo code FREEBOOKTICKETS.